P9-DHA-451

Getting the
Word Out

The **Art Calendar** Guides

Getting Exposure: The Artist's Guide to Exhibiting the Work
Getting the Word Out: The Artist's Guide to Self-Promotion
Making A Living as an Artist

Getting the Word Out

THE ARTIST'S GUIDE TO SELF-PROMOTION

The Editors of *Art Calendar*

THE LYONS PRESS
Guilford, Connecticut
An imprint of The Globe Pequot Press

Copyright © 1995, 1998 by Barbara L. Dougherty Inc./TA Art Calendar
Copyright © 2002 by Barbara L. Dougherty/Art & Info
Edited by Carolyn Blakeslee, Drew Steis, and Barb Dougherty

ALL RIGHTS RESERVED. No part of this book may be reproduced or transmitted in any form by any means, electronic or mechanical, including photocopying and recording, or by any information storage and retrieval system, except as may be expressly permitted by the 1976 Copyright Act or in writing from the publisher. Requests for permission should be addressed to The Globe Pequot Press, PO Box 480, Guilford, CT 06437.

The Lyons Press is an imprint of The Globe Pequot Press

Printed in the United States of America

10 9 8 7 6 5 4 3 2 1

ISBN: 1-58574-609-6

Library of Congress Cataloging-in-Publication data is available on file.

Dedicated to artists and writers everywhere.
Special thanks to the folks who contributed
to this book.

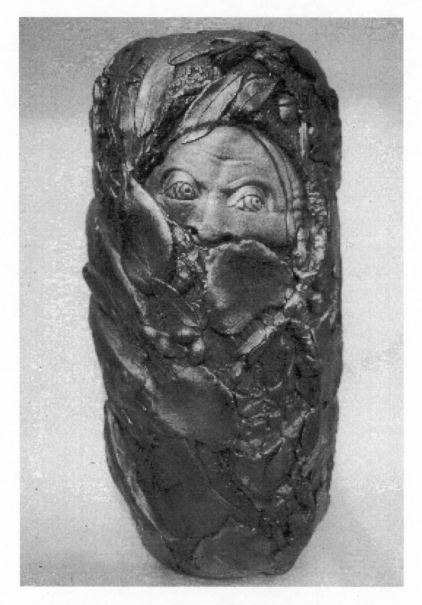

And She Dreams of Her Demon Lover, 1993, raku glaze on clay, 21"x11"x11", Doris H. Miller, San Antonio, Texas

Table of Contents

The Finishing Touch, 1991, oil on panel, 30"x24", Peter T. Quidley,
Chatham, Massachusetts

foreword

In a political campaign for elective office, the candidate knows that only 50 percent of what she or he does is effective with the electorate. But no one knows which 50 percent is effective. So candidates continue to do 100 percent if they want to get elected. So should artists do 100 percent of the things described in *Getting the Word Out* if they want to be successful in promoting their art. From the portfolio, résumé, and artist statement to documentation of completed art and using the media to sell art, *Getting the Word Out* is a blueprint for successful art promotion.

Artists learn to translate what they see or imagine into two- or three-dimensional images called art. That learning experience can either be formal training at an art school or on-the-job experience while actually creating art. The one thing artists are not taught is how to turn their art into a livelihood. One of the most-often overlooked areas of an artist's career is getting the word out; an artist is the best person to explain his or her art to the buying public. But an artist is the least likely to want to actively try to sell the art that he or she has created. After being repeatedly asked at *Art Calendar* how best to promote art, we put together the most-often-asked questions and researched the best answers. The result is *Getting the Word Out*.

As art is not static, neither is art promotion. We at *Art Calendar* are confident that this updated edition will be valuable to all artists who sincerely want to make a living from their art.

—Barb Dougherty
Publisher, *Art Calendar*

PART 1

Your Portfolio and Documentation

Bright March Day, 1997, oil on paper, 18" x 24", Elvi Jo Dougherty, Upper Fairmount, Maryland

CHAPTER 1

Your Complete Presentation Portfolio

Components of Your Portfolio

Carolyn Blakeslee

You have chosen to communicate with people, and to make a living, by producing visual art. Written and other materials produced to supplement and complement visual art can serve several purposes: They can enrich the viewer's understanding of the work, deepen the viewer's appreciation of the artist, enhance the artist's understanding of his own work and the direction it is taking, generate publicity, and facilitate sales.

Materials designed to supplement your artwork come in the following forms: business card, resumé, bio, artist's statement, slide information sheet, audiotapes, videotapes, articles and reviews by others, and articles and other writing by you.

Business Card

If you're like most artists, you don't take your portfolios with you wherever you go. But some of the most successful artists don't leave home without it. At the very least, have a business card made which presents, in color, one of your artworks on the front, and your name and contact information on the back.

When you meet someone you would like to follow-up with, exchange cards—within the next few days, call to set up an appointment to show your portfolio.

Resumé

Your resumé is the next-most basic of your presentation tools.

A resumé is a business document that tells, in a brief space and a relatively dry format, what you have done with the last several years of your life. It gives the viewer an idea of how educated you are, how experienced you are, where you have shown, and how you have been recognized. If your resumé and other materials are well-crafted and attractive, it also gives him a positive impression of your creativity and your competence in other areas of your life.

It serves a social function as well: It makes the viewer of your portfolio more comfortable. Besides introducing him to your background, it gives him a place to put his hands other than into pockets, it gives him a focal point when it is time to break eye contact, and it makes him feel more secure about investing time and money in you and your work.

Bio

A bio is a shortened prose version of your resumé. Your resumé has, at the top, your name and address, then a chronological list of solo shows, selected group exhibitions, selected collections, and so on. Your bio abandons the list format and consists of a paragraph to a page, written in the third person, highlighting the events of which you are most proud. These may include shows, awards, commissions, major collections, and personal information about your home, studio, family, travel—facets of your life that have made an impression on you and your work.

Bios are especially useful for those writing about you: reporters, catalogers, gallery directors, publicists. Although writers enjoy writing, they find it helpful, especially when on deadline, to have information already in capsule form, rather than having to winnow their own prose from your resumé. So feel free to juice it up a bit; the challenge will be to make it readable and catchy while still conveying strong information in a reporterly fashion. Avoid self-accolade; your press clippings should communicate to people that you are The Greatest Show on Earth, not your bio. However, you may annotate, in a neutral way, your major accomplishments and landmarks here.

Artist's Statement

How many times have you worked something out by writing—in your journal, on a scratchpad, in your sketchbook? Writing your artist's statement can be an "Aha" as well as a joyful experience, and it can end up being a component of your business plan.

But self-knowledge is a fringe benefit of the artist's statement. The purpose of writing one is to let the viewer in—to increase his understanding and appreciation of what you are doing and why.

Imagine yourself back in your art history class. It is 8 A.M., and you would rather be in bed. Slides are being shown and discussed. The artwork is beautiful, though, and you start to wake up. As the lecturer explains the intricacies of light and shadow, thematic material, cultural factors of the time, the difficulties of the technique used, you hear little murmurs of "Oh!" and "Hmm," and you ask questions.

Your artist's statement is your opportunity to conduct a mini-art-history class about yourself and your work. Your statement is a way to catch the reader's interest and attention.

A statement might include information about your technique, your approach to working, your philosophy as it is expressed in your art, and major life experiences that have influenced your art.

Avoid criticspeak. Straightforward, honest writing is always refreshing, especially to someone whose business involves having to read criticspeak every day. Also avoid a patronizing tone, or, on the other hand, overfamiliarity. Do not succumb to self-accolade; you are explaining what you do, why, where, when, how. Although it may involve some mighty personal and heartfelt information, it is nevertheless real information from the horse's mouth—not opinion—about why you work the way you do. Finally, avoid self-deprecation. For example, a common line in statements is, "I am attempting to . . . " Never say you are trying to do something, say you are doing it.

Probably the most successful approach is to write your statement like a combination of a good letter and a short story, written to a person whom you do not yet know but feel that you would like to be friends with. You will be exposing your soul and mind to him to some extent, but you will be doing so in an organized fashion with your most accomplished and polished face showing.

Slide Information Sheet

Sure, everyone has a slide sheet. You just number your slides, and make a sheet numbered to correspond to the slides, giving the title, medium, size, completion date, etc.

But there is much more you can do with a slide information sheet. Beneath the caption information, you can write a sentence or a paragraph about how the work came about. In effect, you can use your slide information sheet to be a series of mini-artist statements about each piece.

Audiotape

Perhaps you are gifted in music, and one of your pipe dreams is to have your music played while your artwork is on display. Maybe you were interviewed on the radio. If you are reasonably happy with the results of your particular audio output, include a cassette tape in your portfolio.

Videotape

I would not be surprised to see videotapes become a standard part of the artist's portfolio. During just a few minutes, a video can give the viewer a tour of your studio and your environment, offer a moving-picture idea of who you are and what you are like, and present a bunch of your artworks too—both in your studio and installed elsewhere. That's not even taking into consideration the creative possibilities of your video presentation.

Your video can do double duty, too: many local cable TV stations are looking for fillers, arts pieces, and human/community interest pieces, and your video could fill any of these slots if it is well produced.

Articles and Reviews by Others

Press clippings about you are where opinions get to show. Even ads and one-line gallery listings are fine. The purpose of this component of your presentation package is to let the viewer know that you are quite capable of getting publicity, and that your name is already in fact becoming known.

Articles and Other Writing by You

If writing is a part of your output, feature some of your writing in your portfolio in whatever way strikes you as being right. For example, if you are a poet, allow your poems to have a presence in your portfolio. Or, if you have published articles, tuck tearsheets into your portfolio.

Making a Portable Portfolio Book

Now that you are in a mindset of producing or organizing your presentation materials, think about making a portable portfolio you can take with you everywhere. Here are some uses of a portable portfolio book:

- You will be able to do spur-of-the-moment presentations when caught away from home. People feel free to give photo presentations of their children, so why shouldn't you feel free also to show your artwork? Your portfolio book can be placed in your pocketbook or briefcase and brought out when necessary.
- You can take your portable book with you when traveling much more easily than you can take original artwork.
- Many dealers do not like to visit artists' studios—there is too much pressure on everyone. The portable portfolio book will enable you to present much of your work at an appointment with a gallery director.
- When you have a show, you might wish to place your portfolio book on the reception desk or on a sculpture pedestal. The book can deepen the gallery visitor's understanding and interest in you and your work, and it can help the dealer sell it.

Your portable portfolio will contain the following items: resumé and/or bio; artist's statement; slides, 4"x5" transparencies, B/W photos, and/or color photos; slide and transparency information sheet; price list (retail prices); tearsheets of articles and reviews; and show invitations or catalogs. You might also wish to include other materials, such as a photograph or two of yourself and your studio.

Most artists find that a three-ring binder is quite practical for holding their portfolio materials. Others prefer to get a fancier version thereof, such as a binder which can be zipped all the way around. The latter product will protect your stuff better. Of course, it never hurts to take a different approach—as an artist, you could do almost anything with it, such as create a piece of "book art" which happens to have your resumé and what not in it. You could work with a different notebook size or format, even making a miniature. The smaller Day-Timer notebooks can be adapted. Or you could make a special box and place everything into it—you get the idea. But for this article I will assume you are working with a standard-sized notebook.

You will need several holders and dividers for your materials:

- Clear protector pages, with a sheet of black paper, should be used in your opaque sections. Protector pages will keep your resumé, bio, statement, price list, and slide information sheet clean. The advantage to using black paper in your opaque sections is that you can put printed sheets or photographic prints into the protector page on both sides, and it looks neater—the backs of the other pages or photos won't be seen peeking around the edges of the one being viewed. These pages are also nice for presenting your color 5"x7" or 8"x10" photographic prints; black backgrounds tend to make the colors pop more than white backgrounds do.

- Clear plastic protector pages without black paper may be used to protect your 4"x5" transparencies. Also, hinged black window mats are available for both slides and transparencies, and they make a dramatic and crisp presentation.
- Clear slide sheets, generally sporting twenty slots, house one's slides.
- If you don't feel like putting your reviews and other tearsheets into clear protector pages, you might consider pocket pages for holding them. Many such materials can be placed into the pockets inside the covers of notebooks, too, although I prefer to put my business cards and brochures into those.
- Dividers. Dividers can serve to call attention to some major facet of your resumé; for example, if you have several photographs of artworks that were installed as a result of commissions, you should feature those in a separate section, called "Commissioned Artworks" or something like that. The photo will be of the artwork in its site, and the location may be given as the specific address or just the city. Dividers can be as simple as tabbed notebook dividers, or as elaborate as something you make yourself. Rub-on letters, in a variety of wonderful typefaces and styles, are available at graphic arts supply stores—that kind of detail can give your dividers a typeset quality. You can also use calligraphy.

Most portfolio books I have seen open with the resumé, which is followed by the bio, statement, then just about any mixture of the visual presentation materials, and finally the reviews and catalogs. But with this project, as with any other, you should do anything you want. Perhaps you will start off with a photo of one of your works, perhaps you will use photo pages as dividers—no matter how you organize it, have fun.

When you are done, get some feedback. Go first to loved ones and to professionals in the field, and then make your appointments with the people you want to carry your work. And don't leave home without it.

Your presentation tools can help present your artwork in the best light. Like selecting the proper frame or pedestal, your presentation package gives the viewer a context in which to see your work, or new facets of it. Thus, your presentation tools can truly assist you in generating sales, publicity, and understanding. And putting together a smashing portfolio can be just as rewarding as completing an artwork—approached in a creative, dynamic way, it becomes an art form, an artist's book if you will, of its own.

CHAPTER 2

The Résumé

A Résumé That Works for You

Peggy Hadden

Revamping my resumé falls into the same category as cleaning my oven. It is one of my least favorite things to do. However, a polished resumé can be of enormous help to the artist.

A good resumé will present one's artistic strengths in the best light and help ensure access for an artist wherever he sends it. It can function as an unpaid round-the-clock employee, going into places where the artist seeks access, saying wonderful things that one rarely has the chance or the nerve to say about oneself.

First, get out your resumé and examine it closely. Is it current? Does it organize the information about you in a coherent and interesting way? Will it impress the people it should impress?

Artists tend to be loners; we rarely share information and hence end up reinventing the wheel every time we want to learn something. I am a secret resumé junkie. I always read other artists' resumés when visiting galleries and take one away with me when they're available. I always learn something from them, and I heartily recommend this practice.

Study other artists' resumés. Are they balanced on the page, or lopsidedly hugging one margin? What about spelling errors or inconsistent punctuation? Are the print size and typestyle easy to read with comfortable margins and ample spaces between each section enabling the reader's eyes to rest?

Don't read other artists' resumés to be impressed—read them for the hidden information available in them. And don't become distressed by what others seem to have accomplished. Cast an objective eye over the material. What have they done that you've also done—only they made it sound more impressive? Start a file of resumés that have made a good impression on you and look at them the next time you're taking a break from your creative work.

Now look at your resumé again. Is the best stuff hidden?

I remember receiving a resumé from an artist I didn't know well. She was from another city, so much of the information about where she had exhibited was unfamiliar to me and therefore not all that impressive. However, at the bottom of the second page, I found this: "Art in Embassies Program, U.S. Dept. of State. Artworks in the American embassies of Sweden, Kenya, and Taiwan." I had to dig through almost two pages to get to the most impressive credit on her resumé!

Sometimes the things that don't impress us at all will greatly impress someone else. For this reason, I recommend that you ask someone whose opinion you trust to look at where you've put what on your resumé. Be sure that your biggest accomplishments are easily found—put them right up front where they will get you the attention you deserve. As my greatest successes are in the corporate collections area, I've placed that category right at the top, under my name and phone number. Never mind that most artists seem to put this section at the bottom of the resumé. The point is, lead with your strongest suit; let your accomplishments work for you.

For clarity, each section of your resumé should begin with your most recent achievements and list your achievements chronologically backwards, ending with things that were the longest ago. The titles for each section should be in bold type or otherwise clearly offset so that they strongly stand out. In sections in which you have lots of items, such as "Group Exhibitions," you might want to delete less important shows and call this subheading "Selected Group Exhibitions." If you're faced with drastically cutting your resumé so that it fits onto one page—some competitions will not accept a resumé longer than one page—you could call this category "Exhibition Highlights."

If you have access to a word processor, you can set up a master resumé and subtract or highlight things to tailor it to the particular project for which you wish to be considered.

One-page resumés used to be the standard, but I am now seeing artists' resumés that run to five or six pages. This seems a little obsessive and I doubt that anyone reads them. It also suggests to me that the artist's insecurity is showing, and I'm sure that's the last thing he wants to convey.

What the reader needs to know are the highlights and the variety of your background. Don't worry if you're short of exhibition experience. If you've studied with a well-known artist/teacher, put that in under the education heading—and perhaps begin with it. The same applies if you've worked as a well-known artist's studio assistant. List any art colonies you've attended. In fact, the more names of recognized people and places you are associated with, the better.

Many artists list their art colony experiences under the heading "Fellowships and Grants." While the fellowship one receives at a colony is usually a combination of honor, room, and board rather than money, these experiences—though certainly impressive in and of themselves—might look even more impressive under a "Fellowships" or "Grants" heading.

I saw one artist's resumé wherein he said under "Education" that he was educated privately. What does that mean? Maybe his family was wealthy and had him tutored at home, privately. Maybe he went to the library and read up on art history—that's private, too.

The point of the above two examples is that there is no one right way to construct your resumé. There are, however, some nuts and bolts rules about producing and presenting your resumé. First, always print it on good-quality paper. Second, proofread and proofread—names, dates, and addresses are especially prone to spelling errors. After reading through several times to be sure the information is correct, the easiest way to proofread—is to read each line backwards, so that the content becomes unimportant and you can focus on each word. Finally, keep your old resumés and look at them from time to time. You can learn from things you've done and then discarded. You might even decide to revamp a current resumé into a style you have previously devised. Be your own best teacher.

Back to categories. Don't forget to include the location where you were born. It may seem mundane to you, but to the reader it might seem exotic, or it might turn out to be his hometown, in which case you and he now have something in common.

Include your jurying experiences. People are impressed if you have judged art competitions.

Here are some other categories you might not have thought of for listing your accomplishments. These have all come from resumés I have seen:

- One-Person, or Solo, Shows
- Two-Person Shows
- Touring Exhibitions
- Museum Shows
- Permanent Public Collections
- Private Collections

- Corporate Collections
- Commissions
- Site-Specific Public Art
- Bibliography (books and other publications in which you were quoted or are listed)
- Publications (magazines that printed articles or other items you wrote)
- Reviews (articles or other items written about you)
- Catalogs
- Artist-in-Residence Fellowships
- Scholarships
- Lectures
- Workshops Conducted
- Studio Visits (groups who came to see you)
- Featured Artist
- Awards (include medals and honorable mentions)
- Consultant (someone asked your opinion)
- Finalist (your almost-accomplishments)
- Broadcasts
- Citations
- Board of Directors
- Professional Memberships
- Related Experience

Finally, you can even capitalize on your future. List upcoming events such as your "Upcoming Museum Exhibition" or "Upcoming Residential Fellowship."

CHAPTER 3

The Artist's Statement

Make a Statement!

Peggy Hadden

A thoughtfully worded statement can be a wonderful accompanying narrator for your artwork, but creating that statement may take almost as long as creating the work it describes. I think an artist's statement is especially hard to get down on paper because one's ego is involved. Also, because artists tend not to be very verbal, it's hard to find the right words.

Why, you ask, can't my work just stand on its own? Certainly, this has been the rationale for lots of artists who have opted not to "gild the lily." But, think again. A statement is of value for several reasons:

- It helps gallery directors, art consultants, and others understand, explain, and sell your work—even your well-meaning supporters, who somehow always say the wrong thing.
- It helps critics, biographers, and catalog essayists to prepare articles and reviews about you. Sometimes people are a bit lazy, which is why I've found my own words in the middle of a review written about my work by some supposedly "astute" reviewer.
- It can be used again by you, in shorter formats, for grant applications and project proposals.

Let's say you're sending a slide packet a long distance away, and a cover letter really isn't the place to get into explaining and describing your work. This is where an artist's statement may be helpful. And if writing about things that are close to you makes you uncomfortable, try writing it in the third person ("he says, she asserts . . . ").

Statements can cover the technical side of creating, the materials and methods used ("the artist uses over twenty coats of painstakingly applied lacquer to achieve . . . "), and the actual type of work ("monumental site-specific sculpture"), as well as the purpose or philosophy of the work.

Let's say you don't know exactly why your art looks the way it does. I have a statement that was given out at a prestigious museum show, in which the artist writes, "I feel that the work cannot be interpreted in terms of its subject matter." It's fine to say you don't know; many very bright people do things for reasons that aren't immediately clear to them. Don't be pompous, though, or employ grandiose expressions. The reader will spot insincerity instantly, and then you've damaged the integrity of your work.

Avoid phrases like "I am attempting" because it sounds like maybe you aren't succeeding, just attempting.

Also avoid getting too technical. You made the art, and it is mysterious or gorgeous or whatever, but there is a little bit of alchemy about the artist—and that is enticing. If they knew you made those wonderful feathered sculptures by dismantling feather-dusters from the local dime store, it would take away from the mystery they evoked in the first place.

Watch out for jargon and clichés. Nothing will date you or your artwork faster. And things you've written have a way of following you around.

OK, enough of what not to do. How does the artist go about creating a statement that can add to his overall professional profile?

A good way to begin might be to take writing an artist's statement in small steps. This is not something to begin the night before it needs to be used. Start out with three to five words that describe your work. One of these should be the medium in which you work. Another might place you in the context of a style or medium that is your specialty—sculptor, watercolorist, realist, etc. Put each word on an index card and leave them out on a table where you'll see them for a week. It's OK to change something if you feel that another word is more appropriate.

Next, develop these words into two or three sentences. Over the next week, show these sentences to friends who know your work. Get some feedback about the accuracy of what you've written. Could it be clearer? Then try to read it as an outsider who is unfamiliar with your work.

If personal anecdotes or memories from your past have shaped your work, and you feel comfortable sharing them, then by all means, do. A good statement might explain, for example, that because the artist emigrated to the U.S. during wartime, passing through many national borders where passport stamps were so important, he later utilized them in his artwork (Saul Steinberg). This information adds another level of understanding for the viewer.

Don't forget the value of shared experience. Common threads such as feelings—loneliness, fear, satisfaction, or wonder—are part of everyone's experience. They are, however, rarely discussed or brought out. The artist, through the artwork, admits to some of these feelings. Using a statement wisely, you can enhance your work and induce the viewer to relate more to you and your work.

Artists' statements usually appear on a single sheet of paper with just the artist's name in larger type at the top. A statement does not have a byline unless it was written by someone else, but you should include the copyright sign (©), the year you wrote the statement, and your name. This will protect your statement from being used without your permission.

At an exhibition, the place to look for a statement would be at the entrance, along with the price list and guest register. You can make multiple copies, as they will walk out with forgetful viewers, or you may want to cover the statement with a clear plastic cover, as some galleries do. This seems to inspire viewers to return them before they leave.

A statement is always a work in progress. While you won't need to start from scratch every time you revise it, you will probably need to shorten or lengthen it from time to time. Once you've started out, you'll find yourself on the way toward an objective, yet personal, description of your art. Enjoy the journey.

Rewrite Your Statement?

Alan Bamberger

Recently an artist wrote to me to ask my advice. He said, "I provide a resumé, several photographs, and an artist's statement to anyone who inquires about my work. Several people have commented that my statement is a little hard to understand and that maybe I should think about redoing it. However, it fairly represents what I do and, although I never say this, the people who comment this way don't generally know that much about art. Any suggestions?"

This artist should probably redo the statement.

People who inquire about your art are obviously interested in it—whenever that happens, you should do everything in your power to make their experiences positive. If you are receiving this "negative" comment quite regularly, it probably means that a lot more readers have the same reaction to your statement than you realize. After all, most people keep contradictory opinions to themselves.

Look at those who comment as people who are trying to help you, not as people who are speaking from positions of ignorance. Many artists spend so much time around other artists and art people that they often lose sight of the general public and what their average level of understanding is. Artist statements that are peppered with art jargon or "artspeak" may make perfect sense to insiders, but mean little or nothing to everyone else.

Don't fall into that trap. If you're like the great majority of artists, you want to communicate through your art, sell your art, and be successful. Let your art do the talking and let it mean whatever it means to whoever sees it. When someone approaches you with a desire to have a serious deep discussion about your art, then get technical. The rest of the time, relate in a way viewers can understand and feel comfortable with.

As for redoing your statement, when someone comments on how confusing it is, ask what they don't understand and allow them to ask questions and make suggestions. You don't have to implement every single thing you hear, but with repeated feedback the types of revisions that would better suit the general public will surely become clear. Sometimes those who appear to know the least are really the wisest. Never ignore the few who are brave enough to step forward and share their feelings with you.

CHAPTER 4

References

Asking for Recommendations

Peggy Hadden

A written recommendation is a document that vouches for your character or ability. As artists, we need them for various facets of our professional lives. You may be applying for a grant where references are required—a Guggenheim fellowship, for instance. Or you may want to go to an art colony to work; on a residency fellowship application, recommendations probably have more to do with your character (will you set fire to the sleeping quarters?) than with your talent. Or perhaps you are seeking a prestigious teaching post; a good recommendation will go a long way toward helping you to get the position.

We all use and live with recommendations, formal and informal, as a part of daily life. But it was recently brought to my attention that being asked to give a recommendation was not always a position in which one wants to find oneself.

This prompted me to learn more about the process from artists who are often asked for recommendations because of their affiliations. I talked with three artists: a teacher of art at a college, the director of a nonprofit artists' organization, and the director of a seminar program for artists at a local museum. On many points they vehemently disagreed; however, these conversations changed the way I view recommendations and may change the way you view them, too.

Putting together a recommendation letter takes time and creativity—on your behalf. Many artists think it is an honor to be asked for a recommendation. However, as one of my authorities put it, "It's not an honor after you've received fifty requests."

If possible, select a recommendation writer who knows something about the position or award for which you are applying. Otherwise, if you give more information on the kind of applicant being sought to the person writing your recommendation, then he can address these qualities directly in your letter of recommendation. For example, if past winners of this award have been "rugged individualists" but you are described as "a real team player," the reference might not serve you well.

Often, a person named as a reference will not need to write a letter right away; you will only be asked to supply your reference's name and contact information. However, be sure that he (a) won't be surprised to get a phone call on your behalf, and (b) will write said letter when it becomes necessary. Never use names for references you haven't checked with first and gotten a positive answer from.

Be sure to allow enough time for the recommendation to be written. I was amazed to learn that it takes about four hours to write a good letter of recommendation. So, calling someone to request a letter when it's due the same week can, at best, compromise what kind of letter it will be. You also run the risk that the letter will not be mailed in time, or at all.

On the other hand, if you request your recommendation letter too far in advance, there is the possibility that the recommendor might forget. A reminder phone call is probably a good idea. You can say, "I know I had mentioned applying for this and asked for your help, but I just wanted to let you know that I am definitely applying and the application deadline is [x]."

Know in advance how the person feels about your work. This isn't always possible, but it will help you to be more confident you'll get the quality of recommendation you want. Certainly, the bigger the "name" your reference has, the more attention his letter will get. However, if his reaction to your work is weak, a solid endorsement from someone lesser known may end up serving you better. If you have been out of touch for a while, be sure to update your acquaintance by sending slides of new work. Among the artists I asked, there was some disagreement on giving a recommendation to someone who has been out of touch for a year or more. While the college-connected artist felt that it was fine to recommend a former student after years of not being in contact, the arts organization director—from another perspective—felt differently. In terms of the applicant's professional involvement with his arts community, for someone from the community to be able to speak for that person it would be necessary that he and his work be seen recently.

I asked my authorities about shortening the length of time it took to write a recommendation letter by concocting a form letter which, with modifications, could be used over and over. My advisors were largely against it. The college teacher was most vehement: "A form letter means nothing. It's a non-recommenda-tion . . . and institutions keep those letters on file. If they go back to see what I've said about someone else and it's the same letter, or very similar, then they'll discount it and me." The arts organization person agrees. "It's not worth anything. A good recommenda-tion is tailored, like a jacket. If you received a recommendation for someone which was obviously a form letter, you'd assume that the person who sent it didn't want to give a recommendation."

The museum-affiliated artist saw it a little differently. "Museum curators sometimes have a generic letter, just because they receive so many requests. I don't see a problem with that. The name of the institution with that recommendor's credentials is what is most important. If you need two or three recommendations, use different kinds—perhaps the generic one from an institution-connected person, then one from a person who may be lesser known but gives you a warmer, more personal letter."

Endorsing an individual who was not qualified, my advisors felt, would put their own names and reputations at risk. "It's difficult—if you have a colleague, someone you've known for years, but you don't feel is a good artist, you can write a letter stress-ing things that the artist does do well, but you also need to gauge the letter so that the writer retains a good appearance and the letter is not filled with fallacies. I could hurt someone in the future if this letter turned out to be filled with untruths," said one of my experts.

"That's true, and not only that, if I endorse the work of an artist who's technically not very good, I compromise the reputations of all the other artists who are part of our group," said another. They all felt that an artist should have some connection to the person writing the recommendation. For many artists who give recommendations, it's as important to get it right for themselves as for the artist they're endorsing.

All three of the artists I interviewed for this article are in the position of wearing two hats. They need recommendations too, and must ask for them as well as give them. As one said, "This is not a one-way street." For this reason, if you are asked to recom-mend someone, it is not something to treat lightly or refuse because you fear it will take too much time. It's a wise career decision for you to sacrifice the time it takes. If your letter helped someone get a prestigious award, then now maybe he is in a better posi-tion to help you.

Always thank the person recommending you—consider sending them some flowers or a bottle of wine, but certainly at least send a thank-you note. My advisors told me that many times they've written several recommendations over time for the same artists. Keep your relationship with your recommendor on good terms, so that if it becomes necessary you can ask them to recommend you again later.

CHAPTER 5

Photographic Documentation: Slides

Taking Pictures of Pictures: Slide Photography

Steve Meltzer

A few weeks ago, in what felt like a scene from *Star Trek*, I "beamed" a color slide around the world. In a state of panic, a photo agency in Bombay called my U.S. photo agency asking for a certain image of mine for a slide show.

Rather than send them the original slide, an agency staffer loaded my slide into a laser scanner that "read" the image, converting colors and tones into millions of bytes of information. The data was entered into a computer that was connected by modem to a telephone line and sent around the world via a fixed-orbit satellite.

The signal was received in India by a large dish antenna and sent down another phone line to another modem and computer. This computer used the data to command another device to project a laser beam onto a piece of photographic film, exposing the film and creating an exact duplicate of my original slide.

This is the state of the art of photographic imaging.

At about the same time, I was a juror for a Percent-for-Art visual arts competition. Nearly seventy artists competed for a $7,500 purchase. But before I got to see a single entry, almost a third of the entrants were disqualified because of the poor quality of their color slides.

This is the state of the art of photographic imaging for too many artists, and it is a shame.

I'm a working photographer and I've been shooting art and craftwork for nearly 20 years. Through my writing and teaching I've tried to convince artists and craftspeople that they need to take the photography of their work seriously, that they need to consider photography—and particularly the 35mm color slide—to be as important to their artistic careers as paints and charcoal, canvas and clay. But the photos submitted to the Percent-for-Art competition are a reminder that while the world is rapidly changing, not everyone is changing with it.

When I began photographing art, the use of 35mm color slides was an oddity. Most art was photographed with large format cameras that produced 4"x5" transparencies. This format was used because most magazines and other publishers needed big color transparencies for reproduction and it was difficult in those days for most printers to get decent color separations from slides.

Slides are now the standard format for image scanning.

The use of 35mm slides has become widespread in response to the growing demands of grant programs, the birth of the show and fair movement, the establishment of artist registries, and the flourishing of galleries.

Yet even with all this growth, it has been the digital revolution of the 1990s that has finally given the 35mm color slide preeminence. It has become, at least for now, the standard format for digital scanning and, once digitized, produces stunningly sharp images for magazines and books. The digital images can be transmitted over great distances, used in publications, printed for display, and cut, shaped, and manipulated for other uses.

So the slide, no longer just a medium for art documentation, is rapidly becoming the "gateway" tool connecting artists with other media and with all sorts of communications technology.

Like fine cooking, photographic documentation of visual art pieces appears simple at first but requires practice to get just right. You make mistakes along the way but eventually you learn what to do.

With this in mind, here's the basic recipe—that is, technique—for photographing 2-D work. Compare it to the way you're working and see if it doesn't improve your photographs.

For documentation work you need the following equipment, at a minimum:
1. Paper and pencil.
2. A 35mm single lens reflex (SLR) camera with a lens between 50mm and 105mm in focal length.
3. A tripod. A tripod. A tripod. (Need I say it again?)
4. A tape measure.

5. Film: your choice of color slide film, color print film, or black and white print film.

If you are shooting outdoors, it's best to shoot on a bright but overcast day. On a sunny day there's too much glare and shadowing to get top-notch results. Putting the work on the shadow side of a building doesn't help, either; the light in shadow is reflected off the blue part of the sky and will turn your work blue.

Therefore, it is far easier to work in a studio space. For that you'll need:

6. Two matched lights with stands.

Working indoors is wise because it allows you lots of control. If you are shooting slides with 500-watt tungsten floodlights, remember to use a matching film like Fujichrome 64T or Kodak Ektachrome 64T. Shooting outdoors with electronic flashes, try a slide film like Fujichrome Provira or Sensia 100. For color prints, color correction is added in the printing process, although I prefer to use the blue lamps with color print film.

I'm 6'1" and my comfortable working eye level is at a height of 66" (5'6"). When I shoot any 2-D work—woven pieces, batiks, etc.—I take out my trusty tape measure and hang the work so its center is exactly 66" high. Then I attach the camera to the tripod and crank it up so the middle of the lens sits at a height of exactly 66". Shooting in the studio, I set the light stands so the center of each light is at—you guessed it—66".

To find your own working height, before shooting any images, measure the distance from the bridge of your nose to the ground. Whatever it is will be your working height.

Now move the camera so that the whole piece can be seen in the viewfinder frame with a little space around its edges. For this example, let's say that distance is about 10' from a work that measures 5'x3'.

It is essential that you use a single lens reflex camera in documentation. It is critical to "square up" work in the frame. The sides of the work must be parallel to the viewfinder frame edges. This is impossible to do with a point-and-shoot camera.

Next set the lights about 8' apart, one on each side of the camera. Cover the windows, turn on the photo lights, and turn off the room lights. Point the lights toward the work but not at its center. Aim them so that the circles of light blend smoothly and cover the whole work uniformly.

To check the lighting, walk up to the work and, reaching out with the pencil, gently touch the center of the work. The two shadows cast by the pencil should be of equal intensity and blend to produce a straight line parallel to the floor. If they do not, move the lights until these shadows look right.

Another hint here. If you are photographing a textured work, move the light on the right back a few feet. The shadows will now be unequal, emphasizing the texture.

Back to the camera—now for exposure time. Most cameras have built-in meters that sort of tell you correct exposure. When you begin to shoot your work, make notes of the settings for each exposure you take. This will help you learn what is the truly "correct" exposure.

The first thing you need to do to determine the correct exposure is to set the camera to the film's speed rating, indicated on the film cartridge and incorporated in the film's name, i.e. Fujichrome 100.

Then set the lens to an aperture of f/8 or f/11 and find the shutter speed that produces the correct exposure indicated by the camera meter. Make an exposure at this setting, then a second at the next fastest shutter speed, and another at the next slowest speed. Repeat this process for each piece you photograph, and keep detailed notes.

When you get the film back, check the photos against your notes and see which settings produced the best pictures.

With luck, by your second roll of film you will be producing credible photographs of your work that you can send to museum registries and galleries and that open the doors to the entire world of computer imaging.

Slide Labeling:
Proposed Industry Standards

Kay McCrohan

I used to think the greatest act of faith was to plant bulbs in the fall in hopes they would bloom in the spring. I now realize that this act is dwarfed by my autumn ritual of applying for the variety of shows and opportunities listed in *Art Calendar*. After all, the planting of a bulb only requires digging a hole, lining it with fertilizer, and dropping the bulb in. The only pitfall I can see is the possibility of putting it in upside down, but even that isn't necessarily a problem—Mother Nature often seems to be able to figure out which end is up.

On the other hand, the faith ritual of show applications is thwarted by the myriad rites of entry. Each show has its own sequence of required information, all of which culminates in the sacrosanct icon of The Slide.

The Slide, the artifact, the ultimate representation of your work, must pay obeisance to the varying demands of each show. The most mysterious of all the markings, however, is the Red Dot. Placed in the wrong location, your slide will appear any way except right-side-up. Unaided by Mother Nature, it will stay that way.

I use my computer to print out slide labels. If the slide has been used for a previous show entry, it must be relabeled. This results in either a damaged slide from removing the old label, or label buildup. Either way, it's a time-consuming process. I have come to the conclusion that it's time to rebel: it's time to demand a universal show application and slide labeling format.

Actually, there is a universal format for slide cataloging—this I learned during my discussion with Carol Pulin, director of the American Print Alliance. The information should appear in this order on a slide: the artist's last name first name, title of work, date, dimensions, and medium/technique. This format is used by the Library of Congress as well as by college and university libraries. It is an appropriate format for slide registries. The logic of putting the artist's last name first allows the viewer to locate the artist, not the obscure reference of "The Daffodil" filed under "T." Only an art historian has a memory for that.

Most important, the Red Dot goes in the lower left corner. Here's why. Slides are put in the carousel upside down. Thus, once in the carousel, the slide's Red Dot will appear on the slide's upper right corner, the most visible edge. The projectionist can see at a glance if all the slides are correctly oriented. The artist's name, while the slide is in the carousel, is upside down—on the bottom or the side, and out of sight—thus no jurist could be influenced by seeing the artist's name on a slide.

By creating a universal format the show organizers would not only encourage more show applications, they might also get responses more quickly. It would allow the artist to label multiple copies of slides at one time, thus having them ready for opportunities as they are presented.

With all that added time on my hands I could even find time to plant more bulbs or create more great art.

Presentation: Your Slide Packet Says a Lot About You

Peggy Hadden

Last year, I curated an exhibition of collages featuring the work of 19 artists. To select them I went to several local slide registries, where I looked at slides from more than 300 artists who specialized in collage.

What I learned from this experience was that many artists do a terrible job of labeling their slides. Some slides barely had the artist's name on them. Further, there was an appalling lack of the information necessary for me to make decisions about including an artist's work in the show I was organizing. Without an indication of the top of the work, the media used, or a title, I was on my own. At least two artists whose art I liked could not be reached because the slides had no addresses or telephone numbers and there was no resumé in their file. Since all work looks the same size on a 2"x2" slide, if the artist had not included dimensions, how could I tell if their work would fit into the gallery space I had in mind—or if the scale of their work would mesh with other art I was selecting? By temporarily setting aside my "artist hat" and putting on a "curator's hat," I learned several things about why artworks sometimes get eliminated.

There is another reason why complete labels benefit the artist. Often a work's title helps the viewer understand what his eyes are seeing. I know, I know, they should love it at first sight but, in fact, we all try to make sense out of what we see. In particular, when submitting work for a theme show, the title may prompt a closer inspection of the work. While artists often cite not wanting to limit the viewer with the specificity of a title, there are times when having a title works for rather than against you. If your work is abstract, a title may hold the viewer's gaze for a longer period of time, allowing for associations to be made or subtleties to be appreciated.

Following is the minimum information that should be included on a slide: artist's name, title of work, medium, dimensions, date. Note that in the dimensions, height always precedes width; depth is last.

Now, we all agree that labeling slides is no fun. True, but let's face it, when you send out a slide package, you probably aren't going along with it to explain what the viewer is seeing. And if it is difficult to read the information on the slide, assuming it is there, the reader is less inclined to make the effort. Unless you write in a beautiful calligraphic script, hand-labeled slides can make a truly messy appearance. Now picture a whole sheet of twenty slides, their ballpoint scrawls going in every direction.

If you are presenting your art in a professional way, the work itself gets more attention. Isn't it worth it? Here are some solutions to the drudgery of labeling slides.

Rubber Stamps

This is the method I use. I had the following rubber stamps made:

- An arrow to indicate the top of the slide
- A name and address stamp that just fits the wide margin
- A stamp with the copyright symbol (©), the current year, and my name, information that together indicates my ownership of the copyright (i.e., ©1992 Peggy Hadden)
- A stamp for the media I use most (acrylic/pastel on paper)

This only leaves two bits of information to be written in—the title and dimensions. Rubber stamps require a small investment and most of them can be used for years.

You can pick up speed in stamping by laying out all of the slides right-side-up before you start.

Pressure-Sensitive Labels

During research for this article I met someone who had worked for a well-known artist, labeling his slides. She told me that in every gallery in SoHo, the job most disliked by the folks employed by the galleries is labeling slides. She said she kept trying to figure out ways to shorten the process, to stop "reinventing the wheel" with every slide. She's now self-employed running a business that makes pressure-sensitive labels for artists to peel off and put on the slides themselves. She uses a 15-pitch typewriter system that can put four lines of data onto the slide mount. I have seen other systems like this that can hold six lines of information. The desktop publishing systems enable the user to set type as small as 4 point.

The Avery company manufactures small pressure-sensitive labels that will fit on the wide part of a slide carrier. The labels are $\frac{1}{2}$"x1$\frac{3}{4}$", Avery product #5267. If you cannot find them at your local office supply store, call the Quill company (708-634-

4800), or write to Avery Commercial Products Division, Azusa, CA 91702; Edison, NJ 08902; Elmhurst, IL 60126; or Gainesville, GA 30503.

Direct-Imprint Labeling

The most finished look of all: direct-imprint labeling right on the slide mount. This service is now available through many slide duplicating services around the country. Up to eight lines per slide with twenty-two characters per line allows you to give more information about your artwork such as the gallery or museum where the work may be viewed, the name of the collector who owns it, a photo credit, etc. More information about the work (e.g. handmade paper) can also be included. There are small minimums (four dupes with imprinting) and you place the order at the same place and time that you order your dupes. This process costs more than rubber stamps or pressure-sensitive labels, but the look is top drawer. Maybe for a special project for which you are submitting work you'll want to splurge.

Happy labeling.

CHAPTER 6

Photographic Documentation: Videos

Making a Video: Art, Documentation, Collaboration, Life

Barbara Dougherty

One of my favorite movies of all time is *The Loneliness of the Long Distance Runner.* Until recently, I imagined my life as an artist to be very much like a long run all alone, spending innumerable hours alone in thought, contemplation, and creation.

How can this fit with the new excitement in our community over networking, collaboration, and interactive art? Could this new excitement be the very energy we need to change the "Lone Ranger" image of the artist? Could this new excitement help us transcend the additional chains of the "make it and market it" attitude in today's art world?

When I was in New York at the College Art Association conference, I met an artist who was risking everything she knew to discover the meaning of collaboration. Linda Freeman had been a professional oil painter for more than 15 years, making 8'x9' canvases that were expressions of texture and poetry. About five years ago she gave this up and began to produce and direct documentary videos about artists.

Freeman was introduced to this medium at the New School for Social Research in New York. Next, she worked for a cable TV company where she produced and directed a half-hour documentary on homeless teenagers. After that production she decided to do multicultural work.

She visited popular museums and learned the names of prominent African-American artists. To date she has produced five videos in this area, all independent productions done on low budgets. Most of the funding came from grants obtained with the help of grantwriters. Freeman says she just doesn't have the skill to write good grant proposals, and she has learned to get help from others.

I think this attitude—learning to get help from others and acknowledging her own lack of expertise—is the basis of her success. It says a lot about her skills and fondness for collaboration.

I viewed four of her videos, *Robert Colescott: The One Two Punch, Betye and Alison Saar, Jacob Lawrence: The Glory of Expression,* and *Faith Ringgold: The Last Story Quilt.* Freeman's experience in obtaining funding for these productions was that—contrary to popular opinion about the grant-giving community—her subject matter (minority artists, multicultural focus) did not necessarily make it easier to get grants. Freeman found that many grant-making institutions have a bias against film and video projects. However, Freeman is a spirited woman who does not redirect her intentions because of the bias or desires of others. She kept working at the inspiration that gave her energy.

She worked with three-person crews on her films. She likes working with others because "the ideas get bigger . . . when you work with other people they too have ideas and thoughts, and it all just gets bigger." She downright looks forward to experiencing different points of view.

Collaboration can have its drawbacks, though. She spoke of a camera person who just would not work from her directions; ultimately she had to find someone else. Overall, though, she speaks of the experience of video production as one of sharing, dialog, and interaction.

When I asked Freeman if she misses painting, she replied "Yes" in a very longing and nostalgic way. However, she said it was really just another medium—for her, it is all expression and idea. She said that when she painted it was difficult to get feedback. On the other hand, with video, people give responses that lack the inhibitions associated with comments on paintings. She said that people don't know how to criticize a painting, but they find and mention all the glitches in a video. Thus, the art of video involves a vision and having a visual dialogue that is, for her, not in a vacuum, as her painting was.

Freeman's videos have a definite style. Many of her techniques can be powerful tools applied to the creation of a video to introduce yourself as an artist. For instance, she gave a very intimate view of each artist in his own environment. Though the artist was working and talking through most of each video, while you watched art-in-progress you also saw finished work. An alternative style would be to show the artwork as though you were showing a series of slides. Linda Freeman's method of filmmaking made it easy to look at the work carefully and gave a sense that the work was dynamic.

She also uses film clips in the public domain, available at film and video libraries like the Works Progress Administration (WPA) film library. These clips added a powerful dimension to the artists' stories. As one artist spoke, for instance, about the civil rights days in the South, the viewer saw old film clips of the March to Selma. This was like being immersed in the artist's memory. Freeman said it is not difficult to obtain these clips, nor is it hard to transfer these to the video format.

Another dimension to Linda Freeman's videomaking style is to film the artist involved in a creative activity other than art-making. For instance, Robert Colescott was playing the drums in the final moments of his video. Faith Ringgold did a rap piece. The depth and texture of each video was enhanced by adding such personal, rich details about each artist's life.

She also used, in all four films, some short clips of children crayoning. These worked like invitations to paint. The sense it conveyed was that the instinct to make art is natural, childlike, and pure.

There are a host of considerations confronting artists nowadays. Is video a good medium for sharing art? Is it a good way of presentation? Can the creative experience be enhanced by mutuality and collaboration? If we delve into these new technologies, can we apply creative style to the effort, or will we just get wrapped up into mechanical production and technology? Is it difficult to get into?

Certainly Linda Freeman's attitude, energy, and productions are good answers to many of these questions.

If you would like to experiment with the techniques of video production, there are many ways of going about it. Linda says her productions cost her $20,000 each. Of course, productions can cost much more, but it doesn't have to cost that much.

I, too, have produced four videos, which have been shown on public television, and a host of commercials. The first production I did was the most difficult learning experience: I didn't know enough about the medium to avoid being talked into spending money unnecessarily. This production cost me $7,000. However, the last three productions cost me less than $1,000 each, including 100 copies of each tape dubbed in VHS format.

A great way to learn to do video without a large investment is to sign up for classes at a local public or cable TV station. The best way to locate one in your community is to call your local cable provider since they usually help fund public stations. The presence of public stations is mandated to protect our First Amendment rights—that is, instead of having only programs that big advertisers will finance, the public stations have any production anyone wants to show so long as they qualify to use the equipment and do not violate other statutes.

To qualify to use the equipment, one simply participates in low-cost classes that certify the user. I'm not the only one I know of who has made use of these kinds of programs—a friend of mine started taking classes at a public station in Santa Barbara, and only four months later he was producing his first program, a piece on endangered wetlands.

If you don't have access to a public TV station, you can still do a lot with home video equipment. If you cannot afford to buy a camera, equipment can be rented or even borrowed—check with friends, libraries, colleges, and high schools and other educational institutions.

Whenever possible, use a tripod to avoid disconcerting camera movement.

It is a good idea to do the project collaboratively—involve some creative friends. You should have two or three cameras shooting a scene simultaneously so you can edit together the different views; this may help your piece look professional rather than home-produced. If other cameras are not available, try shooting a scene over a few times so that you provide alternative points of view. You can also use old photos, or some of the new public domain visual image clips available on CD-ROM. You can even use some of the relatively new Macintosh or IBM computer software and edit slides, photos, audio recordings, and video together on your desktop, then export your completed video back into the video format.

This brings me full circle to a thought that has been on my mind for a few months now. What is really the project of the visual artist? Is it to produce and present? Or is it possible that we should spend more time interpreting the world and the different means of expressions? being less concerned with who is going to buy our art? being more concerned with our creative urges? being more concerned with the cultural imperative to enhance our lives beyond practical realities into the emotional, spiritual, and creative realm?

The time of multimedia is upon us! Enjoy.

Linda Freeman can be reached at L&S Video, Inc., 45 Stronowaye, Chappaqua, NY 10514, 914-238-9366.

CHAPTER 7

Written Documentation of Your Artwork

Maximize the Value of Your Art

Alan Bamberger

Artists, like everyone else, have to plan ahead for their financial futures. No matter who you are, you're going to grow old, you're going to slow down, you're going to retire. And unless you're independently wealthy, you'll need to provide yourself with some sort of a livable income. Stocks, bonds, KEOGHs, IRAs, pension plans, and other traditional investments are ways of helping to guarantee that income.

But you, as an artist, have one additional investment that absolutely should not be overlooked: your art. What you do for your art now can significantly increase its value for all time.

Even if your art does not sell well now and, when it does, it doesn't sell for much, you still must consider the big picture. You've got to look decades ahead. You are steadily building a body of work that will one day, assuming you continue producing, become quite large and reflective of the way you have spent your artistic career.

Regardless of your current situation, you can bet that at some point in the future someone will express interest in either collecting or marketing your art. This might not happen until you're well into your fifties or sixties, but rest assured that it will. You'll certainly have the inventory by that time, or maybe you have that inventory now.

But it's what you have in addition to that inventory that's the key to maximizing its value and collectibility.

Imagine, for example, two antique paintings that are physically identical in every respect. One is signed by the artist and that's it. The other is signed, dated, titled, and accompanied by a variety of relevant information and documentation about the artist as well as the painting itself. Which painting would you rather own? If you were an art dealer, which one would you rather sell? Which one do you think is more valuable? If you chose the second, you're correct on all counts.

Right now, galleries that show your art might not seem all that interested in keeping incidental data on file. They're in business to sell art, they do it however they can, and if that means keeping you in the background, then that's what they do. But eventually, it's the artists—not the dealers—who capture the imaginations of the collectors. Eventually, people will want to know all about you and your career. And the more information they get, the more they'll value your art not only in terms of collectibility, but also in terms of dollars and cents.

You, the artist, are the one best qualified to record this information. Be as brief or as thorough and detailed as you wish. Make it public or keep it private. But do it. The following suggestions might sound silly or unnecessary at this moment, but if you doubt their value, pick up any book or catalog that's ever been written about any artist, and see how the details enhance your understanding and appreciation of what that artist's life and work were all about.

Document every significant work of art you produce.

Keep records of when each piece is started, finished, how long you take to complete it, what processes you use, and so on. Depending on how far you want to go, keep photographic records of works in progress as well as of completed pieces. Someone might want to publish a book or catalog of your work someday, and "in progress" documentation would be invaluable.

Save sketches, studies, and minor works that relate to major ones.

Retain them in files, folders, drawers, or storage areas labeled according to the paintings or sculptures that they were made for.

Sign, date, and title all of your art, including minor works and preliminary sketches.

If you don't want writing to be visible to viewers, put it on the backs or bases of the art. Placing this information somewhere on the art itself is usually the best procedure, although you can also provide it separately. You may even want to sign, date, or briefly annotate pieces that you have little or no intention of finishing, but still intend to keep.

Many artists pass away leaving dozens and sometimes even hundreds of unsigned, undated, untitled pieces of work. Dealers and descendants either have to sell them as such, or stamp them with estate stamps, print certificates of authenticity, fabricate titles, and so on. None of these procedures are worth anything near what original signatures, dates, and titles are, in terms of dollar value as well as collectibility.

Keep track of where everything is.

Record every sale you make, the date of the sale, the name and address of the buyer, the selling or barter price, and any other noteworthy details of the transaction. This data comes in mighty handy in case any books, catalogs or retrospectives are in your future and you need to locate any art.

Even mistakes are important.

Not every little error you ever make needs to be remembered, but at least pay attention to significant mistakes, abandoned ideas, failed attempts that mark turning points in your career, and so on. Describe how far you got, why you started in the first place, what went wrong, and why you stopped. This will help others better understand the progression and evolution of your career.

Save art related correspondence.

Save correspondence with friends, relatives, artists, dealers, collectors, museums, publishers, and so on. Keep in mind that good, cohesive correspondence can make great books, catalogs, or feature articles in and of themselves.

One way or another, keep those records.

You probably occasionally hear an artist say that his or her only mission is to produce art and not to be encumbered with accounting activities. If you share this opinion, find someone to do it for you. Or if it's writing that gets to you, record your data and thoughts on audiotape, make periodic videotapes of yourself at work or talking about your work, and so on. And never make the mistake of believing that record keeping is unnecessary because you can remember everything—you can't.

Keep on producing.

Never get discouraged, no matter how little attention is paid to your art. One of the key factors in a market eventually developing for an artist's work is whether enough exists for a dealer or gallery to promote and profit from on a continuing basis. If an artist has only twenty salable pieces after 20 years of producing, for instance, then few if any dealers would be willing to put a major effort into selling it because the total possible financial return is minimal.

The future of your art lies, to a remarkable extent, with you. Count on it and prepare for it.

Providing Care Instructions
for Your Clients

Carolyn Blakeslee

I recommend including "Care and Feeding" instructions with materials you give to a client along with the artwork he has bought from you. These instructions should include basic care such as everyday precautions, routine cleaning, recommendations for proper storage, whom to contact in the event of damage, etc.

If your work can't take much exposure to direct sunlight, say so. If your work requiring electricity should be unplugged during an electrical storm, give a warning. If the work can't tolerate excessive heat or cold or static electricity, spell it out.

Routine cleaning is another issue. For example, if your wearable piece shouldn't be dry-cleaned because the gold resist will come out or the fabric will disintegrate, say so. You should caution owners of framed artworks not to use full-strength glass cleaner, not to spray it, and not to go all the way to the edge of the frame where it meets the glass, because the glass cleaner could escape onto the mat or the artwork and cause damage. Oil paintings should never be routinely cleaned with chemicals, nor should bronzes—if a slightly damp soft cloth used sparingly is all that's needed, make it clear.

It doesn't hurt to include instructions for dealing with emergencies, either. For instance, if a framed painting is dropped and the protective glass cracks or breaks, all kinds of damage can be done to the underlying artwork even if it looks like nothing bad has happened to it.

If the art has parts which will wear out and need replacing, instructions for obtaining and installing replacement parts should be offered.

A client should also know how best to store the piece. If he moves, for example, and needs to put the art away for a while, or if he has a rotating collection, you should specify ideal storage conditions. Environmental conditions such as light, temperature, humidity, protection from insects and vermin, and fluctuations in those conditions are some of the factors which might be addressed.

I also document, on a separate sheet, exactly what materials I used in each oil painting: the name of the material, its manufacturer, and in some instances where I got the materials. I detail where I got the canvas and what kind it is, the brand of gesso and how many coats were applied, the pigments used on the underpainting, the pigments used on the upper layer(s), and what kind of varnish I used.

The paintings are going to be around a lot longer than I am, and by the time they need cleaning or restoring I won't be around to be able to tell anyone anything about the painting. This way a permanent record hopefully will go with my paintings—as long as people remember to photocopy the records onto new paper as the paper gets old!

Finally, you should ask your clients to let you know when they move so you can keep them informed of your shows and other career developments, apprise them of new findings which might affect the care or value of the art they bought from you, and be able to find them in case you need to borrow the piece back for a show, catalog, etc.

This sort of "care and feeding" of your clients is good for them and good for you. Professional behavior lets people know you value your work and demonstrates to your clients that you value their patronage enough to tell them how to protect their investment to the best of your ability. It is not a whole lot different from courtesy, really.

If you are not sure how your work should be handled, cleaned, and otherwise cared for, call a licensed restoration expert for advice. I have found that the professionals in the conservation department at the Smithsonian and the National Gallery of Art have been open and helpful when I have had questions about certain procedures. They consider themselves to be public servants, and they seem to get a kick out of hearing from an artist who cares enough about her work to make sure it will be around for awhile.

CHAPTER 8

The Approach: Cover Letters

Developing Artist's Statements and Cover Letters

Caroll Michels

Most people are intimidated by visual art, including many people who buy and sell art. Thanks to a lousy educational system, the fear of visual art is perpetuated throughout our schooling as we are bombarded with conflicting messages regarding the importance and relevance of visual art in our culture. Visual art is either presented as a "filler" subject—not in the same league, for example, as science, mathematics, or history—or as a discipline that can only be appreciated and understood by those possessing a high I.Q., a talent, or a substantial background in art history.

Lacking genius intelligence or a Ph.D. in art history, most people are at a loss to respond to visual art, fearing that their perceptions might not be right and they will appear stupid. Consequently, presentation materials, such as resumés, artist statements, and cover letters are important props because they serve as tools to help people determine that it is OK to like your work.

An artist's statement can be used in several ways: as a tool to help dealers, art consultants and advisors sell your work, and as background information in helping writers, critics, and curators prepare articles, reviews, and exhibition catalogs. In addition, an artist's statement can be incorporated into a cover letter and into grant applications.

Following are guidelines for preparing presentation materials and suggestions for maximizing their effectiveness.

Artist's Statements

A certain naiveté exists on the part of many artists in assuming that everyone is automatically going to "get" or comprehend their work on the exact level on which it was intended to be perceived. Although an artist's statement can be an effective tool in helping insecure people better understand your work, one does not have to be insecure about visual art to appreciate the aid of an artist's statement.

But translating your vision from a visual vocabulary into prose is an exercise that often meets with much resistance. For several years I have conducted workshops on a variety of career-related subjects including "Developing Artist's Statements." Many workshop participants view the task of preparing an artist's statement to be as pleasant as a tooth extraction. And I often find the task of getting artists to describe their work in a meaningful and interesting way to be not unlike that of pulling teeth!

As a warm-up exercise, participants are asked to describe the work of an artist they admire. For the most part, passionate adjectives and poetic phrases flow with unrestrained ease. But after the warm-up, when artists are asked to describe their own work, dry abstractions and art jargon clichés fill the page.

Although on one hand, artists vehemently criticize the overintellectualized style of writing used in art magazines, many believe that their work will not be taken seriously unless they imitate what they despise.

An artist statement can focus on one or more topics, such as symbols and metaphors, materials and techniques, themes or issues underlying or influencing your work.

Avoid using weak phrases that reflect insecurities, confusion, or unsuccessful feelings, such as "I am attempting," "I hope," or "I am trying." The statement should be coherent, to the point, and retain reader interest. For example:

Art in all of its many forms makes me feel connected to something more grand. Exuberant movement and rotating images imply energy and space beyond the obvious boundaries of the canvas. Shadows of transparent color and heavily textured surfaces speak of nature without evoking landscape. — *Anne Raymond, New York*

Color, texture and shape are the core of my relief paintings. Inspired by the rugged untamed beauty of Malta, my native country, I translate these explosive and mythical images of time and nature with mixed media of paper, wood, and pigments. The surfaces of my paintings are worked to reflect these images. —*David Camilleri, New York*

My forms have memory. They remind me of things I used to examine as a child. For example, my father's Zippo cigarette lighter was my first experience with sculpture as an enigma: its weight, perfect form, and mysterious inscription on the bottom were sources of fascination. Greek warriors, knives, tongues, industrial air vents, and farm tools were objects that at one time I must have examined closely. Now they appear as abstracted shapes in my work. These images remind me of something deep down in my memory. They are psychological symbols, like the Virgin Mary. But they have no church to give them structural coherence. This process is a form of visual amnesia on the verge of memory. —*Ann Lowe, San Lorenzo, New Mexico*

Cover Letters

A cover letter is not only a courtesy, it can also provide a context to help people view your work. Some people need the context of art world validation, such as the information provided in a resumé. Some people are not concerned with glitz but want to know what your work is all about. Others need a combination of glitz and meat.

An effective letter can cover all grounds. It should include the following:

- An introductory paragraph, stating who you are and the purpose of the letter. For example: "I am a sculptor and am writing to acquaint you with my work."
- A brag paragraph that plucks from your resumé a few credentials. For example: "I have had one-person exhibitions at the Wallace Gallery, and have been included in group exhibitions at the Contemporary Art Museum and Ridgefield Museum. In addition, my work is in public and corporate collections." Or, "I have exhibited at museums and galleries, including the Alternative Space Museum, New York City; the Hogan Gallery, Detroit; and the Covington Gallery, Houston. In addition, my work is in various public and corporate collections, including the Whitehurst Museum and the Marsh and Webster Corporation."
- A short artist's statement. See the examples given above.
- A concluding paragraph. For example: "Enclosed are [slides, photographs, or brochure] featuring recent examples of my work. If you find my work of interest I would be pleased to send additional material." Or "enclosed are [slides, photographs, or a brochure] featuring recent examples of my work. If you find

my work of interest I would be pleased to arrange a studio visit in the near future."

If applicable, a cover letter can point out that you are including copies of press reviews or essays by curators. For example: "I am enclosing copies of reviews written by Mary Smith, art critic of *Daily Times* and John Jones, contributing editor of *Art Monthly.*" Or "I am enclosing a reprint of the introduction to the catalog of the traveling exhibition 'Northwest Artists' written by curator Helen Holmes."

And, if applicable, include a paragraph listing the reasons you are contacting this particular gallery or curator. For example: "I have visited your gallery on several occasions and believe my work shares an affinity with the artists featured." Or "I attended the exhibition 'Modern Dreams' and based on the selection of artists featured in the show, I thought that you would be interested in my work."

Depending on your career stage, it might not be possible to include a brag paragraph, reviews, or essays. But an artist's statement can be integrated into the letter regardless of whether you have been working as an artist for 10 months or 10 years.

Writing a cover letter and including any or all of the elements outlined above is no guarantee that you will get what you want. However, with a well-written cover letter you have a better chance of making an impression and setting yourself apart from the hundreds of artists who send packages to dealers, curators, collectors, and exhibition sponsors with "form" letters, insipid letters, or no cover letters at all.

Cover Letters

Peggy Hadden

When I first began presenting work to the art world, I sent slides out one set at a time, tentatively, without a cover letter. Looking back now, it seems like I was trying to edge into a gallery unnoticed—when, in fact, just the opposite was true. I wanted very much to be noticed. Sad to report, the slides would usually come back in the same condition, with no acknowledgment letter—an event particularly disappointing for an artist. I failed to grasp that if I wanted to receive a letter, it would help if I sent one.

In fact, the responses and what I learned from them improved dramatically when I began writing a few words to the person to whom the packet was addressed. Thus evolved a series of ideas for writing art-related cover letters more effectively.

- Have a plan. From the first sentence, get their attention—state why you are writing to this person. Briefly introduce your work and give reasons why you think this person will be interested in seeing it. Motivate prompt, easy-to-take action.

- Use a tone that emphasizes the reader. Avoid an "I, me, my" attitude. From the reader's point of view, why are you writing to him? Why should he be interested?

- Be concise. The art world is one place where monotonous, overblown writing has become the style. But you are not writing reviews, and you are writing to busy people. They will only become annoyed by wordy, verbose messages and probably not spend time reading them, either. Evaluate your sentences and weigh every word. Is it relevant? Necessary? Shorter words are more forceful. Stress words of one syllable to get your point across. Also, vary the length of your sentences.

- Decide what you want and ask for it. Be as specific as possible. Make your request persuasively. Do this early in the letter, with reasons following for why you should receive a "yes." Don't put the reasons first and then make your request—building up to a grand conclusion in a letter is an art form that disappeared with the advent of junk mail. Shortened attention spans now give you less opportunity and make brevity essential.

- Paint a picture. You can achieve strength for your idea/artwork by portraying a clear image in the reader's mind of how it might be utilized for his circumstances—gallery, park, atrium, museum, boardroom, etc.

Also, relate your reader to your work. Here's what I mean. My work has been collected by several financial institutions. By mentioning this when I approach a similar business, I wordlessly convey that my work has been bought by and "fits" with similar groups. This kind of reassurance strengthens your case with any reader to whom you are appealing. They will respond positively to the mention of those in your past whom they consider their colleagues.

- Avoid weak words and negative phrasing. I once worked for a woman who taught short-story writing. Whenever I used the word "very" she would stop me and say, "'Very' is a very weak word." She would ask me to go back and replace "very" with a more concrete or descriptive term. I now consciously avoid using "very" because it fails to enhance. Be sure your words do the job you send them out to do.

Words like "sorry," "cannot," and "no" are disagreeable, negative, and unpleasant. Goodwill is an intangible quality that is extremely important for the artist. To receive the goodwill of others, one must offer goodwill to them. Positive language stresses the light rather than the dark. It emphasizes what can be done rather than what cannot. Your art world reader will be drawn to an optimistic attitude. There are always several ways to say the same thing.

For example, this is weak: "I hope you like my work." A better way: "I thought you might have a project for which my new work would be just right."

Avoid any suggestion that what you are asking for is not possible, that your request or idea could not succeed, or that the person you are addressing is too busy to be reading your letter.

- Motivate action. Offer to present your work in person. State where your studio is and that you would be delighted to show your work there or at another more convenient location.

Suggest that if there is interest you will send larger photos or transparencies that portray your work in a better format than the slides you're now sending. Stress your availability to discuss your work or particular idea further. If you have proposed a project or event, offer references who will vouch for your experience or expertise. Supply your reader with the necessary information to make a positive decision.

- The first and last sentences of your letter should be the most forceful. Make sure that your first sentence connects with your reader and has his point of view in mind. The last sentence should emphasize the desired action and hint at a timetable. Don't say "soon," say "this season."
- Do not thank them in advance for what you are requesting. This usurps their right to decide. If you want to thank them, then thank them for their attention to your letter.
- Use a short P.S. This allows for a brief summing up in case your entire letter wasn't read. It can convey optimism in shorthand, leaving your reader with a good feeling.
- Get the name of the addressee right. Always address materials to the gallery director or museum curator by name. A friend of mine has recently been on the

receiving end of slide submissions, and her pet peeve is to receive mail addressed to "Dear Gallery Owner." She says it is impersonal and seems as if the artist doesn't care enough about his slides to find out who he was sending them to.

It's easy to get the correct name by looking up the space in a national gallery listings guide, such as the art magazines' annual issues, usually summer editions. Many libraries have directories of art personnel in their reference departments. Or call the space and be sure you have the person's correct name, spelling, and title before you send anything to them.

One good reason for sending your stuff to the director is that you're starting at the top; your work might be passed on to be viewed by someone else, but don't help it get deferred or lost by addressing it to the "viewing staff."

Now let's consider the responses you might get and how you can use them. The optimum response is, of course, initial interest generated by the quality of your work and the goodwill of your cover message. But even when the response is negative and the acknowledgment is obviously a form letter, I often get a few sentences written in a P.S. by hand from the person to whom I've addressed my materials. Sometimes surprisingly encouraging things are said. Sometimes the response I received had nothing to do with my work (e.g., an illness is forcing the gallery to close, or the dealer may feel that my work is too similar to an artist whom he already shows) and suggests another move; they will refer me to another gallery and say to use them as a reference. Those "footnotes" can contain information that is useful later—in a chance meeting with them or in my next submission to their gallery.

Sometimes, over months and years of cover letters and responses, a relationship between you and your reader develops. I have communicated for several years with a gallery owner who is still unable to include my work in her gallery roster but who writes that she enjoys seeing my periodic submissions, that she follows the progress of my work with interest—she often cites examples and her memory really surprises me—and that she hopes I'll stay in touch. This is one of those every-six-months exchanges I'm willing to invest in—they help me stay connected with various parts of the art world and may pay off one of these days.

To sum up, your letter can help your work be well received, whether immediately or in the long run. Give yourself every chance to succeed.

Writing Effective Business Letters

Constance Hallinan Lagan

Whether you are contacting galleries in an effort to obtain representation, asking past customers to purchase again, introducing yourself to potential buyers, asking for supplier information, submitting a proposal to an interior designer, writing to an art magazine, or applying for a grant, your business letter speaks for you. When your business letter is poorly planned and awkwardly constructed, the harm it does is often permanent.

If you have doubts regarding your own ability to write well, you are not alone. In a national survey conducted by a communications consulting firm, 79 percent of responding business executives listed the ability to write as the single most neglected skill in business; 53 percent rated their own writing ability as poor; and 59 percent rated the correspondence they received as poor or only fair.

During my business-writing seminars, I stress to my students that there are three steps to writing a good business letter. Each step is equally crucial: planning, writing, and editing.

The Planning Step

First, think about the purpose of your letter: to advertise, introduce, approve, request, confirm, resolve, congratulate, accept, thank, persuade, compliment, complain. Have in mind who your audience is—write for your reader, not for yourself. Be clear on what you want to achieve with your letter: a decision, resignation, donation, vote, appointment, contract, payment, phone call, order, referral, etc.

Next, pre-write your letter using one of the following three techniques: brainstorming, mindmapping, or freewriting. Brainstorming stresses quantity—not quality—of ideas, encourages "piggyback" and add-on ideas, and prohibits editing and evaluating. Mindmapping is a graphic technique whereby you draw a circle in the center of a piece of paper with the subject of the letter written in the circle; you then draw branches from the circle to designate main topics or concerns of the letter (who, what, when, where, why, how); finally, you draw secondary branches off the main ones to indicate smaller but related topics. Freewriting requires you to write without stopping, with no concern for spelling, punctuation, editing, or criticizing.

Finally, organize your material using one of the following three approaches: chronological, problem-solving (cause and effect), or the decreasing order of importance approach (inverted pyramid).

The Writing Step

Begin writing by preparing an outline consisting of three parts: the opening (grab the reader's attention, get directly to the point, and set a professional and courteous tone), the middle (the body of the letter), and the closing (motivate the reader to act).

Next, write the letter, using your pre-writing notes and outline.

The Editing Step

First, consider the written words. Eliminate unnecessary words. Relax stuffy language. Simplify every phrase. Shorten sentences. Define your purpose early in the letter. Make your request directly. Give the reader a specific deadline. Write in the active voice. Use positive sentences. Keep the tone consistent. Close on a strong note. Test the letter's content against your message: Did you say what you meant to say?

Next, study the visual impact of your letter. Leave white space—one-inch margins on all sides. Incorporate lists and headings into your piece to create additional white space. Break up long paragraphs to add a positive visual impact. Highlight your key thoughts.

The benefits of effective written communication are threefold: Good business letters save time and money, provide a written record, and allow both senders and receivers to communicate when it is convenient.

Are Your Letters Effective?

There are three and only three possible outcomes to writing and sending business letters: no response, an aggressive response, or a cooperative response. Effective letters do not lead to misunderstandings, do not make readers feel threatened or defensive, do not leave questions unaddressed, do not go unanswered. Effective letters do elicit cooperative responses.

Business letters do more than convey information and request responses. They also reveal much about you. Through your letters, you project your personality—by your choice of words, your degree of neatness, your ability to spell well, and your ability to set a pleasant tone. If your written communication is the first form of contact you have with someone, it can make or break a future business relationship.

If you need assistance in developing your business-letter-writing skills, hire a consultant to teach you the ins and outs of business-letter writing or engage the services of a copywriter to prepare your written communications from start to finish.

Yes, effective business letter writing skills are that important to your success.

Showstopper Cover Letters?

Alan Bamberger

In a letter to me, an artist wrote, "I occasionally read articles that refer to showstopper resumés or introductory letters guaranteed to have buyers or gallery owners begging for more. Have you seen any of these?"

You might be placing a little too much emphasis on these documents. The ability to be clever, cute, or able to stop the show, as you put it, is not the key to selling art. Your question implies that writing effectively about yourself and your art is a shortcut to success. The fact is, no shortcuts exist.

In the great scheme of things, introductory letters count for very little. Resumés count more, but only in the sense that they relate career accomplishments and convince readers of your ability to deliver on your promises. What counts most is your ability to identify and reach those gallery owners and other potential buyers who are best suited for your art.

Instead of concentrating on letter and resumé development, concentrate on that. Look back on your career and figure out what characteristics your biggest fans share, particularly the ones who spend money on your work. Identify that segment of the art community in order to target your marketing effectively, and don't waste a lot of time contacting those who don't fit your buyer profile.

The main point to keep in mind regarding any initial contact, whether in person or in writing, is to keep it brief. Get your introductory message across in two to three sentences at the most. You see politicians doing this on television all the time. Viewers clearly comprehend the message; they decide whether they want to hear more, and if so they ask for it.

The last thing you want potential buyers to do is to get bogged down in a sea of words and be so exhausted when the time comes to see your slides that they couldn't care less. Many artists mistakenly believe that relating their life stories is an essential ingredient to understanding their art; this is not necessarily true. Allow potential buyers to enjoy your art at their own pace, let it speak to them without your speaking for it, keep conversations focused on your business goals, and provide background and interpretation to those who request it.

PART 2

Printed Materials

Petrobook, 1994, neon, carved acrylic, limestone, and paint, 12" x 15" x 6",
Vincent Koloski, San Francisco, California

CHAPTER 9

Reproductions You Can Sell and Use for Advertising

Some Thoughts on Selling Reproductions of Your Art

Carolyn Blakeslee

Last year, a friend of mine approached me with a dilemma. He had already had two paintings printed into limited edition—two hundred each—photo-offset reproductions. The "prints" were generating a lot of interest from dealers—but no one would handle them unless he signed and numbered them. He didn't feel right about signing and numbering them because they weren't hand-pulled prints; he believed that although the print run was limited, they would more accurately be called posters or reproductions.

The issue is his sense of integrity vs. the need for recouping his investment.

My feeling is, integrity is all we really have—or give—in life. And I'm with him; I object to the industry's purveying photo-offset work as "prints" when those works should be called posters, photo-offset reproductions, anything other than prints. As printmakers will tell you at any opportunity, artists' hand-pulled original prints are the only artworks that can accurately be called "prints." True prints' images have never existed in another medium.

For better or worse, the industry standard supports the practice of signing and numbering photo-offset reproductions and selling them as prints. Lots of artists, publishers, and dealers get wealthy that way. Lots of people love buying those works, enjoy owning them, and the value of some of these works actually does appreciate over the years. So let me be clear: I'm not arguing against selling photo-offset work, for I do think there's a time, place, and market for them. But I am saying it's misleading to offer them as "prints." Many states and several congressmen agree: consumer laws relating to limited edition prints are in place in several states already and pending in several other state legislatures as well as the U.S. Congress.

One problem my friend has is that he has already invested a substantial amount of money in this project. As to the dealers' interest, if they're talking consignment they haven't got anything to lose—if they're willing to buy outright, then that's real interest.

So the question becomes, "Do you need the money?" If you do, but you can't bring yourself to go along with signing and numbering your photo-offset prints, here are a few alternative ways to recoup your investment.

Compromise

Go ahead and sell the prints. Sign them—no harm done. You can provide documentation with each print including a certificate of authenticity guaranteeing that only 200 reproductions were produced in [year] and no more will ever be printed. For more information on documentation, refer to Alan Bamberger's article "Maximize the Value of Your Art."

Be an Activist—Work to Change the Industry

This is a variation of the above suggestion. Instead of, or with, a certificate of authenticity, with your reproduction include a "tip sheet" or disclosure statement. This could include topics like an explanation of how offset reproductions are made; how to tell the difference between photo-offset and hand-pulled prints; a glossary of "print" terminology; a signed statement of why you refuse to number your reproductions, if applicable; etc. The downside: dealers would probably be scared off and it's unclear how your print/reproduction salability in the future would be affected and for how long. The upside: You could become a consumer hero of sorts—I can just see the articles you could generate in publications nationwide on "A New Way of Dealing Art" if you worked hard enough at getting the word out. This approach is certainly marketable but maverick—and maverick marketing sometimes takes longer than currently accepted, tried-and-true approaches.

Use the Reproductions as Promos

Using your reproductions as self-promotion devices is another good long-term strategy. You can send one or both prints in lieu of a slide packet to a very selective, targeted list of galleries with whom you would like to work. Your cover letter would explain that the reproductions give a good idea of the scale, color, and mood of the work you do. What the heck, you've already paid to have them printed—buy a few tubes and mail out a couple a day. Follow up with a couple of phone calls a day.

Or you can give away the reproductions as gifts, glorified Christmas cards, even premiums. People love surprises, presents, and freebies; people love to get more than they have bargained for.

Moral questions are tough. As I have said before, professionalism is not a whole lot different from courtesy. Professional behavior lets people know you value your clients' patronage enough to tell them the truth—the whole truth—about their investment.

Behind the Scenes of Reproducing Artwork Mechanically

Barbara Dougherty

Marketing art is a challenge that requires first and foremost a willingness to gather and retain information. To the artist who has hardly enough time in a day for creative tasks this reality is frustrating. A future as a successful artist, however, can be sacrificed by entrusting to others too many significant decisions.

Such significant decisions are involved in the process of printing images. Whether the product is a business card, postcard, brochure, catalog sheet, book page, advertisement, or a printed reproduction, the end result will have an impact on an artist's future opportunities.

It is critical to learn the process and the language of printing images. Keep in mind that the technology is changing and expanding rapidly in this field and that it will be an ongoing educational task. The alternative to this undertaking is to purchase reproduced products at too high a cost and risk the distribution of products that misrepresent your artistic intentions.

There are four media frequently used for making prints: photo-offset lithography, serigraphy, a photographic process called Cibachrome, and gidee or iris prints. The first step in each of these processes is to take a color transparency of the original painting.

For photo-offset lithography, a color separation must be made from the color transparency by a scanning computer that renders the image on four different pieces of film, separating out four colors: yellow, red, blue, and black. These are used to make plates for printing. A color separation can be expensive, particularly if flaws from the image or in the transparency must be corrected. For instance, a 16"x20" separation may cost $400, but if it is proofed the cost can be higher—and I do not recommend having a print made without first seeing a proof of the color separation. NOTE: Separations must be the same size as the intended finished printed image.

A printer does not always do its own color separations. If your printer contracts out the separations for you, it may cost you more than if you contract this yourself, as a printer will generally mark up the price. The downside of contracting for your own color separations is that the printer can claim that flaws in the final print job are not his responsibility, but that they are in the color separation. On the other hand, the same claim can be made of the photography given to the color separator.

The process of photo-offset lithography involves the use of printing ink and a wide variety of papers. The more permanent the ink, the finer the line screen of the color separation, and the heavier and better the paper, the better the print. Companies that create prints can have presses that print the four inks one at a time, two at a time, or all at once. In my experience the presses that do not print all the ink at once give a better color saturation but are less likely to make a print that looks like the original. The inks also must be cleaned from the press after use and because of that fact, cannot be made totally permanent. It is common advice from an art dealer that if you purchase a limited edition lithograph for investment you should store it carefully in the dark in a portfolio to avoid fading. On the average, a photo-offset lithograph can be made for $1 to $3 each if at least 1,000 images are made at a time.

The process of the serigraph involves using a different silk screen to print each color. The serigraphs of my work published by Colliers were made by a noted artist, Gary Hinte. He made thirty-four screens and used thirty-four different inks to print the images. The result: beautiful and permanent prints that did not look much like my original paintings. These prints were rated as permanent because of the nature of the silk screen inks. The cost of two different images, 350 prints of each, totalled $6,000.

The third process of reproduction is Cibachrome. In the 1980s this was not as popular as photo-offset lithography or serigraphy. The advantage of Cibachrome is that it is nearly permanent, it resists fading, and it can look very much like the original painting if the work is done well. The process is a photographic process. The average price of one 16"x20" Cibachrome print from a good photo lab is $40. The fourth and newest method is a "gidee" print using the computer and a digital scan of the image. This process can cost between $40 and about $200 for a 16"x20" depending on the quality of the scan, paper, and inks.

Always—and this is always—do your own press checks. Nobody but you really knows what your work should look like.

Press Checks

Press checks are your opportunity to team up with the technicians to produce good quality reproductions of your work. If you have respect for the people running the presses and work together to produce your product, you will have an easier time communicating your subjective likes and dislikes.

The color proofs of a separator should be viewed under correct lighting—this would be daylight simulated, or 5,000 degrees Kelvin. When you do a press check, your task is to like or dislike the item placed before you. You are using the color proof as a guide to the finished product; if you like the color proof but dislike the printed item you should tell this to the printer.

A careful viewing of the printed image begins by examining type and other solid black linework and making sure the ink is dark and clear, not smudged or too thin. Next look closely at the paper stock and make sure it is exactly what you specified. Look at the overall color of the image. Is it strong? flat? matched? smooth? Does it have pinholes or hickeys? If you find flaws that are not in the color proofs, then they should not be in the printed image.

As an artist viewing changes in colors, you might be tempted to try to correct color changes by the observation of alteration of color. Do not do this with press technicians; the science of mixing inks is different than mixing paints. The secret in having well-made products produced on mechanical presses is good communication. Good communication is easier if you simply relate your observations: Saying "this is too blue" can be much more successful than telling the technician to add red.

If the printer claims there is no way he can correct work you are displeased with, here are some things you can look for:

- Check to see that the printing is within the registration marks.
- There is a star target on the printed sheet. Check to see that the center of the targets is equal in all four colors all across the sheet without distortion.
- Check to see if the overlay of all three process colors is black.

If any of these things show up as inconsistent, then it is likely that the printing technician can improve the quality of the work.

Getting Information

The hardest part of negotiating with printers is finding the answers to your questions. I have two strategies for dealing with printers.

First, I subscribe to trade magazines for the printing industry. The advertisements and the language give me a good reference. The magazine I like best, published in Los Angeles, is *The Horsetrader*, P.O. Box 11712, Santa Ana, CA 92711, 714-921-3120. This magazine is full of advertisements that provide a basis of the costs of doing printing production services.

Second, I have a trusted colleague in the industry. My friend has worked for many different companies on the West Coast. In addition to answering my questions, she has helped me find printers for my various production projects. The money I pay her for her expertise is saved by reduced printing costs. She is willing to talk with other artists; her name is Rolanne Stafford and she can be reached at 503-227-2778.

In this article I have only briefly explained some very complicated procedures and projects. Reproducing images—whether a single postcard or as a book or as a photograph—is the opening of another Pandora's Box. The only antidote to the maladies is to seek knowledge, share experience, and never forget that your reproduced image is often your only foot in the door.

My Experience with Reproductions

Three years ago I went to a gallery and purchased a limited edition print by a very well-known artist. I paid $1,300 for the print and made sure I received a certificate of authenticity. My print was hand-signed and numbered 10/80. My purchase was intended to be an investment.

One year later, the prices of this artist's prints had more than doubled. So I decided to consign my print to a gallery that sells this artist's work—but the piece did not sell. I moved it to another gallery in a different locale, but the print still did not sell. I discovered there were so many works of this artist available that there was no market at a high price.

My experience is similar to the experience of many art collectors: Limited edition prints might not be a wise investment.

An art agent told me that the 1990s will probably be thought of as the decade of the limited edition print. The artist and the art marketplace found themselves with a product that could be reproduced time after time for purchase by everyone. The vision of the artists was that income from prints would free them to spend more time on their original work. Also, with the new income they could raise the price of the original paintings. The greatest benefit of the print was that it advertised the artist. In the 1980s, many artists became exceptionally well known by the marketing of prints: John Stobart, Bev Doolittle, and Eyvind Earle, to name just a few.

While the marketplace burgeoned in the 1980s, there were few obligations that the seller of prints had to the customer. "Original print" no longer meant created by the artist; the term was used to mean print production supervised by the artist. There were no federal laws to regulate the number of prints in a limited edition. Eventually, some states, including California and New York, passed fine art print laws that forbade the selling of limited edition prints without a disclosure form stating the edition size, print process, and date of the print run and the medium of the original art.

Today, art agents and galleries are urging artists to approach the print marketplace with caution. A couple of years ago I was in Carmel, California in early November. It is a gallery town. Even in the off-season and on weekdays this little coastal village is busy with tourists who have come to visit its seventy art galleries. Surprisingly, in the old established galleries there were no prints for sale, and sales of original work had been good this year. The sentiment expressed in these galleries was that original work would not sell if prints were available. The smaller galleries usually sold both prints and originals—and they had the most complaints about the bad economy and poor sales.

The exception was the smaller galleries that were owned by artists. The largest exhibits in these galleries were of the artist/owner and they were all having a successful year. The artist/owners said that this was made possible by limited edition prints that were affordable. The most common statement made by artists and gallery agents alike was that the sale and distribution of prints is an enormous project that can hurt the artist—an artist might profit monetarily but can suffer in artistic development.

This was in fact my experience in the 1980s. In 1982, two different companies published prints of my work. Unsigned prints were sold by Ira Roberts Publishing and limited edition serigraph prints were published and distributed by Colliers of Los Angeles. Although I made careful contracts with both companies at a cost of about $500 in legal fees, my total earnings from these published prints were only around $2,000 in royalties.

However, since there was a wide distribution of my work I felt I was being paid while receiving free advertising. The experience of being published mostly gave me the insight that people really were willing to purchase reproductions.

Thinking I might produce my own prints, I went to see Flavia Weedon, the owner of Roserich Designs, a family project that markets Weedon's paintings as prints and greeting cards. First I told Flavia that neither of the published prints of my work looked like my original paintings. Flavia said that I just had to get used to that—the pigments and processes of reproduction are so different from the process of the creation of an original painting that no perfect reproduction can be made. The goal, she said, was for a good image, not an identical image.

Next I asked Flavia if an artist could profit by producing his own prints. She said that the problem was not print production, it was print distribution. Before starting her own company, Flavia's work had been marketed by Hallmark Greeting Cards. Thinking she could be more successful on her own, she created her own family business that included framing and advertising promotion and employed twenty-two full-time people. Flavia felt that she had given away too much of her painting time to confront the problems of marketing her prints once they were produced. She told me she knew of artists who had paid to have one or two lithograph editions of their work produced, only to sell twenty-five to fifty images, leaving hundreds in storage.

In spite of Flavia's advice, I decided in 1983 to create my own limited edition prints. I decided to make Cibachrome prints of my paintings, although I had never done this type of work before. I invested about $2,000 in equipment and after a few months of learning I began making reproductions. The cost of an individual 16"x20" print, doing the work myself, was about $8. I was excited about being able to present the image as completely my own work. I scheduled two days a week for this work and in that time I could produce twenty-five framed prints of twenty-five different paintings. I learned about my own painting studying my work and the prints of my work in the darkroom. I found that the public liked these prints and that if I framed them I could easily sell them.

Within the course of a year I had mastered the production techniques and was selling an average of ten framed prints a week at $125 each. At $8 a print for production and $15 for framing materials, not counting labor, my weekly net profit was $1,000.

And then I lost my sales outlet. The art show in Santa Barbara where I marketed my work prides itself on being a show where no reproductions are sold. My Cibachrome prints were allowed in 1983 because they were photographs. Since I did all the work myself, I met the criterion that all work must be the original work of the exhibitor. When my prints began to sell very well, the administration of the show decided that the Cibachrome reproductions of my paintings were not the same as other photographs and could not be sold. At first I was outraged and tried to appeal the decision, but the appeals process became so involved that I finally decided to abide by the new ruling.

To my surprise I discovered that I had been spending an enormous amount of time each week making and marketing those prints. After the ruling, I began to put that time back into the making of original paintings. Today I am very grateful and I do believe I am a better artist than I would have been had I continued to invest time in prints.

Artists must be cautious about anything that takes time away from the creative process. The gallery owners, agents, and artists I have talked with agree that the effort to create and market prints will take valuable time and detract from the task of making your next new original work of art. As agent of my own art, I have found that all the marketing projects take time—time that could be used to paint. While artists must be their own agents at times to be successful artists, I think the key to success is careful management of time, resources, and energy.

What About Print Reps?

Alan Bamberger

An artist wrote to me with the following scenario. "A company approached me with an offer to represent me and market my art. For a fee of several thousand dollars, they will create a mailer that includes a color brochure, an 8"x10" photograph of my work, a cover letter, and a resumé. I will receive several hundred mailers for my own use and, in addition, the company will mail out over 500 to dealers, galleries, publishers, consultants, and others who they claim will have an interest in my work. For about the same money, probably less, I can put together a pretty decent mailer myself. Which do you think I should do?"

Regarding this company, and other companies offering services-for-fees, here are four steps to take before doing business with them.

1. Check them out before giving them any money in the same way that you would check out anyone else who you were thinking about paying several thousand dollars to for services rendered. This process primarily involves interviewing references provided to you directly by the company. A legitimate organization with a successful track record should have no hesitation about giving references—if they are at all reluctant, think seriously about taking your business elsewhere.

2. Ask to see at least two sample mailers they have created for other artists. Observe the similarities and differences between each one. If, for example, the mailers are similar in terms of layout, wording, and other respects, having the company do your marketing is probably not a good idea, because they are not individually customizing, but rather are running an assembly line type of operation. It also means that the names on the company's mailing list are receiving identical mailer after identical mailer and are most likely not taking the company or its artists very seriously. Variety between mailers is what you're looking for.

3. Interview at least two artists who have done business with this company and find out how satisfied they are with the results. In particular, question them about how much business they got as a direct result of the company's mailings. Ask whether, or how quickly, they recouped their investments. Also ask how the company is to do business with in terms of promptness, cooperation, quality of work, and so on.

4. Interview at least two clients that the company regularly mails to and find out how likely they are to get involved with the artists in question. Ask whether mailers are sent individually or packaged together—the more mailers that are packaged together, the less attention each artist receives. Find out approximately how many artists they have received material on, how many they have contacted, how much business has resulted, how successful any relationships have been, and so on. In addition, find out what they think of this company in general.

Regarding producing and distributing a mailer on your own—your second option—this is a good idea only if you really enjoy designing promotional materials, marketing yourself, and accepting the numerous challenges that this assignment presents. Keep in mind that in addition to the money involved, you'll also be spending a good deal of time not only in designing the materials and having them produced, but also in locating names of potential customers, doing mailings, making follow-up calls, and so on.

The third option is continuing to make contacts with potential buyers in the same manner that you always have. In most cases, galleries, consultants, agents, publishers, and collectors are only marginally more responsive to slick presentations than they are to standard resumés, bios, cover letters, photographs or slides of work, and other artist information. They are able to recognize art that interests them regardless of its packaging, assuming that the packaging meets basic neatness and clarity criteria. They are well aware of what artists have to go through in order to get their work shown, and they do not expect artists to invest hundreds or thousands of dollars in professional printed marketing presentations. What's most important in getting your work out there is making contact with as many potential buyers as possible, regardless of how many rejections and other variations on "thanks but no thanks" you receive. Sooner or later, good things will happen.

Postcards and Note Cards

Barbara Dougherty

Sometimes I feel like a racehorse with blinders on my eyes. On the track I see only one way to go and it's the same way thousands of others have gone before me.

This year I tried to take the blinders off by trying alternative marketing strategies. I was looking for high impact and, of course, low cost.

I am a collector. I collect American flags, baseball cards, and art. Although I never watch a baseball game, I enjoy a few days out of every year sitting mindlessly with stacks of baseball cards sorting them by date, kind, and number, checking their current value and imagining the worth of my growing collection. I do this after times of intensive art projects. The mindless sorting somehow makes order of the chaos. Earlier this year, an article in a magazine for collectors inspired a component of my art marketing plan.

The article was on collectible postcards, and not just those that had baseball subjects. It began with a description of the current value of collectible postcards. These, it said, are sometimes worth as much as $200. The description of the most collectible cards were those that are artist-signed. The definition of artist-signed was: displaying the signature or the initials of the artist on the face of the card. Postcards were divided by the article into four major periods: Pioneer Cards 1873-1898, Early Century 1899-1918, Mid-Century 1919-1969, and Late Century 1970 to present.

I have used postcards as business cards and in mailings, but I had never thought of selling my cards as collectibles. I liked the notion and I began a marketing program to sell reproductions of my paintings as Late Century collectible postcards. My goal was to create a further demand for my original artwork by using advertising which could itself generate additional income.

I contacted several companies whose printing specialty is postcards. I wanted to produce 5"x7" images that had good color quality and were coated with a postcard-grade plastic to keep the cards from fraying. When postcards are printed in multiples simultaneously, there is often poor color quality; this printing of many cards at once is called "ganging," or "gang printing," the images. However, if a company has a press dedicated to doing nothing but postcards, then adaptations are made that enhance individual image quality. I looked at many examples of printed cards and decided to use a company where the cost was 12¢ per image and they had postcard-dedicated presses. I chose to make six images with an initial press run of 4,000 of each image.

The next step was to design a plexiglass rack for my cards. The rack was made to sit on a counter without taking up a lot of space. I had holes made in the back so the rack could also be hung from a wall. I designed the rack with curves instead of angles. This design discrimination had come from a comment I had heard my father-in-law make about Hallmark card displays. He had been one of the first greeting card salesmen for his company and had noted that carefully designed curved racks had helped make the "Hallmark success."

I went with a drawn design to a plexiglass fabrication company. The owner agreed to make fifty racks for my project. He agreed to be paid a retail price for these racks as they sold. Each rack was to hold all of the six different images, fifty cards of each image.

While the racks and the postcards were being produced, I was working on my packaging system. I found a cardboard box company that sold white cardboard at a price that was the same as the normal brown corrugated kind. My box was 13"x10"x21". The cost per carton was 97¢. For padding for the rack I went to a van and storage company and bought 4'x8' sheets of Kraft wrapped padding that is usually used for packing dishes, at a cost of $1.50 a sheet. This material was as good as foam wrap or foam bubbles, which cost more and are environmentally unsound. Then I obtained shredded paper from a printing company to further protect the racks. The packaging for the postcards themselves was Ziploc bags; this would allow the extra images to be stored if they were not inserted in the rack. If I had used shrink wrap for the cards, the cost would have been less, but it might be less convenient for a merchant.

The next project was to create a label both for the rack and the boxes. I did the design on my computer and had it reproduced by a sign maker who screens onto clear self-adhesive plastic. One thousand labels cost $330 with 500 printed on clear plastic for the racks and 500 on white plastic for the boxes.

Once I made these product arrangements, I turned my attention to the task of record keeping. My decision was to make a packing slip in triplicate that would become the basis of my inventory. I also figured out a pricing schedule and the margins of profit involved in sales. My sales slip, which I designed on the computer, was also a mini-catalog because it described product options. I like a custom-designed sales or order form rather than a generic one, because the form can be used as a tool to give information and be an advertisement. Also, most people save their receipts, which therefore end up being important product literature.

Instead of offering separate items for sale, I offered an introductory package for $180. This included the rack, 300 cards, and one copy of a book of my artwork. Because the suggested retail price for the postcards was $1, I used in my sales approach the fact that the merchant would earn a 64 percent profit on the markup of the cards. Merchants are very sensitive to the amount of markup or the profit they can make from a product. Built into the $180 price for my introductory offer was also a margin that would allow me to pay sales representatives and distributors to market this package. If a sales representative sold one of the introductory packages I could offer a 20 percent commission, or $40. Also, I was prepared to offer a sales representative a commission on reorders of postcards.

The breakdown on my costs were: $36 for cards; $18 for rack; $3 for billing, labeling, and packaging; $5 for the production costs in the accompanying book; and $40 for sales commission, for a total of $102. By selling the package for $180, I made $78 while the merchant made $120.

After I had assembled the entire package of rack and cards and support materials, I ventured out on the road in California to try my hand at marketing my own art product. After a few weeks on the road and in my own town I had sold my cards and racks to galleries, bookstores, roadside agricultural stands, restaurants, florist shops, hotels, and vineyards. The best part of the experience was that retail merchants liked my product and were not offended by having it represented by the artist. This was especially effective if I introduced myself as the artist trying to experience the marketing of the product. It was simply exciting to be greeted by merchants who looked forward to an item they could sell for a dollar that was art.

After this degree of success, I placed an ad in a Los Angeles newspaper for sales representatives to sell my product. Placing the ad had not been planned early on, it just seemed to me at the time that if I was looking for a sales representative this was the way to do it. I was surprised by the number of calls, and I was able to arrange interviews with several applicants. I also spent a day with an experienced sales representative who had answered my ad. Together we took my cards to gift shops and stationery stores in the Los Angeles area. I found that the best approach to merchants was to let them see and touch the cards and be attracted to them in their own way rather than to babble a sales pitch. I learned this from my companion's experienced manner. His point of view was to let the cards sell themselves. This representative was impressed by the cards and the reaction of the merchants to them. However, since my product was new and I didn't have a lot of different images, he wanted an agreement to cover basic expenses if he was to represent my work. I could not afford an expense account for him so he suggested that I try to find sales accounts by attending wholesale product shows.

In October I did attend one of these weekend shows at the Los Angeles Convention Center. My product was well received, and I consummated orders. One of the things I learned at the show was that I needed a brochure to explain the cards and racks. Companies collect brochures at these shows and do their ordering from them later.

Is all this worthwhile? Well, I have not even sold all the initial fifty racks, but I have begun to hear from people who purchased my cards as collectibles and are interested in the original artwork. Also I gave some of my cards to a friend who is a photographer; she gave some of these to a prestigious event center in Orange County, California. The event center solicited my work for a show.

It is a different experience to sell art in forms other than the original work. It's as though there is something very established about an artist who has printed work available. The advantage of selling the postcard rather than a lithographic reproduction is that the postcard is a finished product in itself, whereas the lithographic reproduction usually requires framing.

As artists we rarely connect with the world of sales that exists around us for the distribution of other products, but the interaction with this marketplace can be valuable. I am awed once again that the strategies to market art can be as diverse as art itself.

Making Original Prints: Working with a Print Shop

Peggy Hadden

Kathy Caraccio is a master printer who owns a print shop in mid-Manhattan that has been self-supporting for nearly 20 years. Among her many accomplishments, she has printed a suite of works for Louise Nevelson through the Pace Gallery, one of New York City's most prestigious galleries. Many other artists have had the benefit of Kathy's expertise too. Recently, I spoke with her about how artists can work with a print shop like hers and what they need to know.

Kathy's shop is in the city's fur district, on a high floor, opposite an old Gothic church whose chimes resound at regular intervals. Although there is chaotic activity outside, inside all is tranquil, as interns and artists go about their work independently with little conversation.

The environment is both modern and centuries old. Brightly colored printing inks, the visual Mardi Gras of many different prints on the walls in a myriad of styles, the heavy solidity of hand-cranked Charles Brand presses waiting to be put to use—all contribute to an atmosphere not quite of this day and time.

Paper is everywhere—reams and stacks of Arches cover and Rives BFK—waiting to be soaked in trays of water, then blotted before going between the press bed and rollers to be imprinted by the etching or lithography plates, or aquatint or drypoint, which have been covered with artists' images. By the way, one of the ways you can spot a genuine hand-pulled print is by the impression, or indentation, made by the plate's edge into the softened paper. The sheet of paper, still damp, is then covered with a layer of tissue and placed between heavy boards in order to dry flat.

Later, they'll be signed and numbered if they are part of an edition, which the limited number of impressions made from one plate or set of plates is called. The numbers usually appear on the left side of the image, with a slash between them. The first, or top, number indicates which piece of the edition you're looking at, and the second, or bottom, number tells you how many impressions in all were pulled from that image. In other words, "15/50" theoretically means the fifteenth impression in an edition of fifty.

Kathy said, "it is a fallacy to believe that numbering relates to any quality difference throughout. Low numbers in an edition do have snob appeal because of the illusion that #1 was, in fact, printed first. Actually, prints are moved around so much in the printing and drying process, it would be very difficult to track one print and determine for sure that it was the first to be printed. The actual condition of the print—for example, clean margins, no curatorial repair—has more to do with the price it can bring than the lowness of its number. But generally, higher numbers of an edition should be as sound as lower ones." Also, artist proofs are generally worth less than prints that are numbered.

Kathy often works with artists who are unfamiliar with the specifics of the printmaking process. She likes to introduce them to what is possible by showing them the shop's print collection. Over the years, each artist who has worked in the shop has been asked to donate a print of each edition to this archive. The variety is staggering and offers the viewer a huge range of possibilities for ways to work. "I watch for what interests a new artist coming in, and this leads me to show other prints and ask a lot of questions." She visits artists' studios to see their work and begin to figure out how best to collaborate with each artist.

"Beginning with a new artist is the most expensive part for me," she says, "until I know the degree to which they want to get involved technically. Some artists want to do everything themselves. That makes them more expensive in terms of time for the shop initially—until they've gained finesse with their technique—but then more efficient to work with in the long run. Later, they'll work independently because they've learned how to get the effect they're after."

But the artist who wants to participate less is accommodated too, although "they are more expensive to the shop because they must always look to us for technical assistance. This is ultimately more costly for the artist, but we have worked with both types of artists and we're flexible."

Kathy is an active teacher of printmaking in various art schools in New York City and nationwide. She trains interns who receive credit from their institutions for independent study with her. She is also very encouraging to artists who want to experience working in a print shop but are unable to pay for instruction. She offers them the use of her facilities in exchange for their help in maintaining the print shop. Making monotypes is a good way to learn, because it is more spontaneous and requires less time to see the finished result. You can tell just from being present when other artists are working on their editions whether that is something you want to embark on.

Most print editions are now published, i.e., financially underwritten, by the artist. The days of a gallery paying for a print to be made are largely in the past, although the galleries love to have prints once they are made. Independent print publishers are pretty much on hold too and concentrating on moving their inventory.

"An artist will come to me and ask what editioning a print will cost," Kathy said, but pricing each job is as individual as an artist's work. "I usually estimate by the number of days that the shop and staff will be involved. We must figure on labor, materials, and platemaking and proofing, called 'p and p.' The figure we give the artist will yield them about four to five pieces of a 22"x30" color etching." Then the artist can show it to galleries and prospective buyers. The plates for the edition have been made and the artist can see what the finished print looks like. The cost of making an edition is the second part.

Altogether, the cost of making the print will represent about 20 percent of the total retail price of the print. If a gallery or retail print shop agrees to take several pieces to sell, they will take some part of the other 80 percent for their share. The balance will be yours. For example, let's say that you set your retail price at $100. If $20 is the cost to make the print, and the gallery wants $50 for their share, you have made $30. This might not seem like much if you are accustomed to receiving 50 percent or more when you sell a painting, but remember that you have more than one of each print to sell—up to 250 in a single edition. All of them will potentially yield you the same 30 percent profit—and, the more you can sell on your own, the higher your profit will be.

The average price for the preparation of an edition is about $2,000. This represents about one-third of the total cost the artist will incur. The other two-thirds covers labor and materials to make the edition itself. If you want an edition of 200 prints of one image, proofed for faults or damage, signed and numbered, the total cost will probably be near $6,000. While these estimates may vary from one part of the country to another, and from project to project, my intention with the example given here is to clarify what in general you are paying for in the production of a print.

Many artists work only in prints and have made excellent reputations for themselves in the field. Other artists, better known for paintings or sculpture, turn to prints as a less expensive way to attract new customers or sell to those who could never afford the artist's other one-of-a-kind work. Kathy feels, however, that the best reason for an artist to enter printmaking is for the personal growth that he can experience doing it.

So what about the market for selling prints? In recent years, some reversals have happened. Certainly, some prints languish for years or never sell. Your success in selling your print will depend largely on how determinedly you work at finding buyers.

What determines prices for an artist entering the print market today? Primarily, it has to do with that artist's reputation in other media. That is, if your paintings sell for $500-1,000 now, and you are experiencing some interest in your work, you might assume that a $100 print would bring some sales.

The appeal of, and knowledge about, handmade prints is definitely growing, in large part thanks to the availability of classes on the high school and university level in etching, aquatint, monotype, and lithography. There is also increased activity by galleries wishing to promote affordable art.

The quality of hand-pulled prints is easy to educate others about. The richness of the paper is beyond compare. The signature in pencil on a limited edition is an indication of the quality and care that have gone into the handmade print. They possess other unique qualities like texture, subtlety of detail, and color gradations that can only be achieved by pulling the print directly from the hand-cranked press—these are pleasures one experiences more and more over time.

"We still ink by hand-rubbing carbon black with linseed oil into copper plates in exactly the same way, and one of the most marvelous parts of being a master printer is knowing that I am directly linked to artists like Rembrandt and Dürer," Kathy says.

Kathy Caraccio may be reached at 208 W. 30th St., New York, NY 10001.

CHAPTER 10

Brochures and Catalogs: Developing Markets By Mail

An Introduction to Direct Mail

Carolyn Blakeslee

How long have you been wanting to reach a larger audience? How often have you dreamed of having the time, resources, and inventory to justify a direct mail promotion, catalog, and/or national advertising of your artwork?

This article sets forth a step-by-step action plan. This article will tell you how to identify your markets, produce a color brochure and/or catalog, accomplish a direct mail campaign, reach hundreds or thousands of people, and produce results at a reasonable cost.

If the thought of producing a brochure on your own is intimidating, then Step One is to join forces with several other artists with the intention of producing a group brochure and support team so you can all share the costs and efforts involved. Even if the thought of going solo is not intimidating, this approach might be worth consideration. Galleries and art consultants—portrait representatives, for instance—produce brochures of several different artists' works all the time. Think of this project as a co-op gallery by mail.

Perhaps the people with whom you want to associate work in styles and media similar to yours. Or, you might feel that presenting a wide variety of work, linked by a thematic or other thread, will get the best results.

Brochures and color postcards can be printed surprisingly inexpensively. You can get 2,000 postcards printed up for $200 or so (10¢ each). But with a little investigation, you can find firms who can produce, for example, 25,000 9"x12" high quality brochures, printed front and back on glossy paper, with typesetting, design, layout, and color separations of up to eight full-color images included, and folded into a standard three-leaf brochure format, for $3,000 (12¢ each) or less—several times the space for several more images, lots of copy, and lots of impact.

A directory of printers might be available in the reference section of your library. Find several printers who do the kind of work you're looking for, and ask several of them—at least 20—for samples and estimates. Believe it or not, only about half of them will respond. But after receiving a couple of weeks' worth of replies, you might find yourself laughing at the incredible variations in price—and you will be very happy you took the time to send off for as many estimates as possible.

Here are the economics. The above-outlined 25,000 brochures @$3,000 come out to 12¢ each. A Bulk Mail permit, available to anyone at any Post Office, will cost a one-time administrative fee ($85 as of this writing) plus a per-year charge (at this time $85), totaling $170 to get set up. It will then cost 22.6¢ (as of this writing) to mail each brochure. If you mail all 25,000, then the total mailing tab will be $5,650 plus the permit fees. (So far our subtotal is $8,820: $3,000 plus $170 plus $5,650.)

Next, you will need to compile or purchase quality lists of people to whom you will be sending your brochure: this is your target audience. More information on targeting them comes later in this article. Lists are available from mailing list brokers (in the Yellow Pages) as well as from most subscription publications. A quality list—an up-to-date list of people following your client profile—will run around $85 to $100 per thousand, and you can order the list(s) printed on self-adhesive labels and pre-sorted in Zip Code order. This Zip Code ordering is crucial for Third Class bulk mailings; your Post Office will give you details and instructions on how to prepare your mailing. So, your list of 25,000 will cost around $2,125.

So far your tab for printing, labels, and mailing is around $10,945.

You and your seven colleagues team up to produce and mail that brochure. Now the per-artist cost is $1,564—to reach 25,000 people directly, with a color brochure, not an ad buried in a publication. This is an investment, not a gamble, if it is done with proper attention to detail. Besides easing the per-artist monetary outlay, forming a consortium could help to alleviate participants' fears and generate credibility and mutual support. You will also be able to divide the time-consuming responsibilities of getting estimates, proofreading, obtaining the Postal permit, doing market research, obtaining lists, applying labels, bundling and mailing, etc.

Here are the statistics on direct mail campaigns. If a brochure is clean, attractive, and well-written, and is received by a reasonably carefully targeted group of people, the average rate of return is usually about 2%.

Before you compile or order lists, you must find out who your target audience is. If you don't know who your audience is, then some research will be necessary. Once you narrow down the field of prospective buyers (everyone), the goal is to contact a selected group (direct mail is just one way to contact them), nurture the establishment of your clientele, and develop relationships with individuals within your clientele until suddenly you find that many have become your friends and even passionate advocates—your "following." This process is fun—you are doing them the favor of letting them know about your artwork; you are offering them the chance to fall in love with your work and want to live with it.

To target your audience, you must first study yourself and your art. What kind of artwork are you producing? Do you produce small-scale watercolors you sell for $200 each? Do you do medium-sized portrait commissions in oils starting at $2,000? Do you make bronzes which you would like to place in corporate collections?

Each artist will have the best results with a particular kind of art appreciator. For example, if you do representational oil paintings with nautical themes, it would be futile for you to promote your work to people who love experimental media or abstract work. By the way, I believe there is no reason to tailor one's artwork to suit The Market. There is no reason for you to do any kind of art except the work you want to do, because there almost surely is a market for it. It is only a matter of discovering that market and letting them know you are alive.

Let's continue with the nautical example. Suppose you and seven other artists you know produce nautical artworks. One of you does limited edition hand-pulled prints. Another artist in your group does commissioned portraits of people's boats and/or the owners on it. Another does oil paintings of specific areas, like the Chesapeake Bay or the Florida Keys. Another does watercolor harbor scenes from a historical point of view. Another offers paintings of waterfowl. And so on.

Now for the market research part. To which 25,000 lucky people are you going to mail? You are not selling your wares, you are helping people become aware of your service and you are helping them to obtain it. What group is most likely to be assisted to discover and enjoy your product? For example, if you were cooped up in a law office 12 hours a day, wouldn't you love to have a large-scale painting of a sailing destination, complete with the proper mood and lighting, in your office?

One way of conducting market research is to go to the library and ask for a directory of trade associations. The purpose of trade associations is to assist their members to make their livings comfortably in their trades. If your trade is nautical art, perhaps there is a national association of nautical artists, or of nautical artists' organizations. Contact the appropriate organizations and see if they have data as to who is buying your kind of art. There will also be trade associations of marina owners, boat salespersons, and yacht clubs.

Get as specific as you can. Where do the buyers of your kind of art live—do they live on the coasts, near large lakes, or are they wannabes who live nowhere near water? Are they private individuals, or are they in charge of curating corporate collections? Do they buy from galleries, on their vacations, at art fairs, or have they demonstrated response to many ways of presenting artwork available for sale? How much, on the average, do they spend on artwork? Are your prices too high? Are your prices too low—just as frequent a turnoff?

Your research will yield a clear, concise mission statement which will save you time, money, and needless frustration. Here is a hypothetical description of your nautical artists' client profile.

The typical buyer of nautical art prefers medium-sized, representational, two-dimensional artwork with emotional appeal: dramatically stormy, sunny, etc. He often displays art in his office partly because of the prestige it offers him in his workplace, but he likes to display art at home as well. He takes an average of two weeks' vacation per year, usually to resorts on the water. Around 45, he is married. He and his wife hold upper-management jobs, and one or both of them own their own business. Their income is about $150,000 and they live in an upper-middle-class neighborhood outside a city along a navigable waterway. They own a sailboat and a second home. He buys nautical art because he enjoys its prestige, beauty, and escape value, but he also hopes for its eventual appreciation in monetary value. He is wary of spending more than $1,000 on an emerging artist but will drop up to $2,000 on an artwork which he feels is extraordinary. Normally, neither he nor his wife have the time or the inclination to visit galleries; however, they do so on vacations, and that is where they buy most of their art. He likes to read nautical publications, and would probably enjoy seeing a brochure which tastefully presents nautical art he has never seen before. He might not buy right away, but a year or two down the pike he might get around to it.

The shortened version of your client profile: "Professional men around the age of 45 from two-income families who own sailboats and live in the suburbs of cities on waterways." Your mission statement: "I provide (x) service to (client profile). They desire and enjoy my service because (x)."

How do you find your client profile/target audience? You talk to the trade association folks. You go to nautical art galleries' openings and people-watch. You go to an art expo or two and observe who hangs out at which booths, and you take notes when someone buys work similar to yours. You talk to marina personnel—in short, everyone you can think of and have time to approach. If you do portraits, what kinds of people buy portraits? Who buys large-scale interior tapestries? What kinds of people buy monumental large outdoor sculpture? Who will be most likely to buy—and love—your artwork?

Where do you obtain lists of 25,000 good prospects?

You might contact marina directors by letter, telling each what you wish to do; ask to borrow or rent the marina's membership list, and enclose a copy of the brochure you plan to send out. They might even offer to publicize your group in their newsletter, or offer you a show.

You could contact yachting magazines and rent their mailing lists.

Testing lists is a crucial direct mail business practice. One list might perform very well, another very poorly. The only way you will find out is to try it. But if a list boasts 100,000 names, you'll be out a huge amount of money if the list performs poorly. Therefore, the industry standard is to order a small quantity of names, usually 5,000, for the test. You will be required to provide a copy of your promotional material to the list owner and not deviate from what was approved. If the list performs well, you can then order the whole list and promote to the entire group. Aim for a consistent 2% response.

At the same time you are testing your lists, you should be sending news releases to yacht and sport boating publications about your art consortium and the services you provide. Releases should include photographs of some of the artworks and/or artists, or a brochure with a clear notation that reproducible photos of artworks and artists are available upon request. Releases should also be sent to resorts known for their sailing facilities; and, of course, to the marina directors. This way, you might be able to pick up some publicity in the press as your mailing hits.

Most of the people to whom you send your brochure will throw it away. However, a large number might find your brochure so attractive that they cannot bring themselves to throw it out. Your brochure is already "open;" there is no envelope or Letter from the Publisher to plow through; it is attractive and classy; you spent the time refining your brochure until it met your highest standards. Unlike a magazine ad, your brochure won't get filed away with back issues of anything. The recipients might put it into a pile to be gotten to later, but generally the response follows a bell curve—most of the people who are going to respond do so within two to six weeks of the mailing. So be prepared.

OK. Back to economics. Let's say your mailing generates an initially low response: only 1% of the recipients, or 250, send in an order. The orders are split fairly evenly among the eight of you. 250 divided by eight equals 31.25. So, with a low response, each of you has sold 31.25 artworks. Suppose your average selling price is $400. You have each grossed $12,500. Subtract your $1,564 for the brochure, money for framing and shipping. Also allow some time for some personal thank-you notes. These people obviously love your artwork and they will almost certainly enjoy the personal connection with you. Anyway, $12,500 minus the brochure, framing, and shipping costs, will probably net each of you around $9,000.

Many of those 31.25 people will turn into repeat clients. And who knows how many sales or commissions will come your way because they will recommend you to their associates?

There are, of course, alternatives to taking on seven quasi-partners. 25,000 high-quality postcards cost as little as $650. Postage for postcards is actually less than the Bulk rate—20¢ each, versus 22.6¢ each, as of this writing—and they will be delivered First Class. Using these numbers, your total investment will still come to $5,650. But suppose you are promoting, say, a signed offset reproduction which sells for $85 not including frame—far less than the $400 example outlined above. If just 1% of your postcard recipients place an order, you still gross $15,600.

Another approach, with or without artist-partners, is to print up a few or several hundred black-and-white brochures and a brief proposal for an exhibit, and mail your proposals to marina directors in your region or even nationwide. They could sponsor a month-long show of your group; they could sponsor a one-night installation of artwork for a special event they are holding; and so on. I have used the marina and nautical theme only as an example of carrying a theme through. The same principles can be applied to floral, medical, and a myriad of other styles and subject matter.

By no means is a direct mail campaign guaranteed. But it is very likely to produce good to excellent financial results if it is carefully planned and carried out.

Taking a personal risk—and that's what we're talking about here—is far better than chanting "What if." God did not intend that we be poor and unappreciated, nor that others be unable to see and thus share the fruits of our talents.

What Makes a Brochure Successful?

- Visual beauty. You are promoting a visual art experience. If your brochure is dowdy or amateurish, why would anyone want to buy your actual work?
- Contact information. If your brochure features several people, either agree in writing on who is responsible for being the contact, or print each person's information adjacent to his artwork.
- The inclusion of copyright symbols. Protect yourself. Include the copyright symbol (©), the year of the artwork's completion—the whole year, i.e. 1995, not '95—and your name (©1995 Carolyn Blakeslee). This information shouldn't be intrusive but it can't hurt to include it in tiny type underneath each image along with the rest of the caption information.
- Neatness and crispness. There is no room for typographical or grammatical errors. If you are not skilled in writing, editing, or layout, have a professional review your brochure before sending it to the printer. Have the printer send you a proof—it's worth the extra time and money.
- Clean, consistent design. Good color saturation, contrast, and a fine line-screen are musts. Blurry or coarse images are unacceptable. Often, color reproductions look classiest and most attractive set against a black background. Or, if you are aiming for a softer effect, a white background might be best. A crisp compromise is to box in each image.
- Attractive images. Your brochure should feature the best examples of your work.
- Simple, at-a-glance ad copy. Perhaps you could include a brief description of the work pictured, or quotes about your work from a review, a respected arts professional, and/or current owners of your artwork. Perhaps you should include highlights of your career or life, including goals and projects in progress. Why should people invest in you? Tell them! Also, sharing a select amount of personal data deepens the art experience for them. Seek the advice of a professional writer if need be.
- A list of your services, if applicable. Do you accept commissions? Do you do por-

traits? Are there other kinds of work you produce besides that which is illustrated in the brochure?

- Ease of ordering or commissioning work. Give clear pricing information and terms, or a statement that prices, further information, or references will be gladly furnished upon request. Words like "gladly" and "guarantee" mean a lot to someone who has never heard of you. Similarly, make it easy for the recipient to request further information and/or a portfolio review if he is not convinced on the basis of your brochure. You can probably talk your bank into letting you offer credit card capability, and 800 numbers are inexpensive—these two factors could increase your orders 50% or more.

- Guarantee of satisfaction. You can also be creative and offer other goodies besides a guarantee—for example, you can offer a trade-up option later on. Rentals or "on approval" plans can also work if handled carefully.

Brochures and Catalogs Make Great Promotional Tools

Alan Bamberger

Brochures and catalogs make great promotional tools. If you can afford it, go with a catalog rather than a brochure, preferably in the eight- to twenty-page range, assuming it's your first. Catalogs look more substantial than brochures, they're taken more seriously by readers, and they tend to end up on bookshelves and in files rather than in the trash.

A good catalog greatly enhances your ability to market your art. For one thing, it allows you to promote yourself without having to open your mouth—all you have to do is hand over a catalog. You can also use them to reach people who live too far away to visit, are difficult to reach by phone, or who need time to decide whether or not to buy your art. Finally, a catalog or a book is a credential in and of itself.

Keep the long term in mind and be aware that you are creating a record of your work that, if well thought out, will outlast you and serve to document certain aspects of your career for anyone researching your art in the future.

A conversation with an art librarian at a major art reference library will give you an instant idea of the scholarly value of many older art books and catalogs. If possible, make an effort to study examples of older publications that have turned out to be particularly useful research tools.

Regarding the structure of your catalog, the most important rule is to be concise and stick to the facts. People want to know who you are, what your art looks like, and what you've accomplished. Resist tendencies to dwell on the subtleties of your art or spell out personal philosophies in intricate detail. You'll lose readers.

A one- to three-page bio of well-constructed prose will usually do the trick. Include a statement of purpose or information about why you have chosen to become an artist only if it's brief and down-to-earth. If possible, try to get a respected art expert, critic, dealer, or personality to do the writing, or at least some of it—like the foreword, for instance. The more well-known figures you can associate with your art and your catalog, the better.

In addition to your bio and a list of exhibitions, you may wish to include a brief chronology of career-related events. Readers, especially researchers, prefer easy access to important dates, honors, awards, grants, people, and places. A listing of books, magazines, catalogs, and newspaper reviews that mention you or your art is also something to think about including.

Show all finished writing to a variety of people from different segments of the art community before you publish. Ask for their opinions and seriously consider everything they say. If you hear similar criticisms more than once, think about reworking the necessary paragraphs. You want your end product to be easy to understand and to have as broad an appeal as possible.

Color illustrations are always superior to black-and-white, but if color is too expensive, black-and-white will do just fine.

Include as many illustrations as you can comfortably afford. Your goal is to provide a comprehensive visual record of your work. Once again, getting a consensus as to which of your works should be reproduced is preferable to making all the selections yourself.

Also, whenever possible, list owners, dimensions of pieces, completion dates, places where they were exhibited, and other relevant specifics.

In addition to illustrations, provide a checklist of your major works. The closer your list approximates a *catalogue raisonné*, the better.

Things to avoid:

• Name dropping. Mentioning the world's great artists or art movements with the intention of forming some sort of evolutionary connection between you and them is self-defeating. Readers will not take this seriously. Only the passage of time and scholarly consensus determine the evolution of art and who the true greats are.

- Excess padding. Don't include the names of every single person who owns your work or every single place that has shown it. For example, mentioning that you once hung a painting at Bob's Pizza and Espresso can actually demean your work rather than promote it. (Not that Bob doesn't serve great food and drink.) Furthermore, people who regularly read about artists can spot excess padding in a heartbeat.

- Exaggeration. Tell it like it is and not like you want it to be. Misrepresenting yourself or your accomplishments can negate all the good you've tried to do for yourself, especially if you get caught at it.

Make Your Brochure a Marketing Bonanza

Constance Hallinan Lagan

If you don't have one, get one NOW. A brochure is your lifeline to financial success. Business cards are just not enough in today's world of high tech/high visual impact. "Yes, your brochure is more important than a business card," advises Dan Poynter, author of *The Self-Publishing Manual*. He adds, "Brochures provide you with an opportunity to say nice things about yourself that you can't say in face-to-face selling." I mean, can you imagine reading testimonials to customers at a wine-and-cheese opening!

Brochure production need not be costly. As a creative individual, you probably possess all the graphic and layout skills required to produce a dynamic, powerful brochure. You might need the assistance of a professional advertising copywriter to get your message stated concisely and effectively, but hiring a free-lancer will not cost nearly as much as hiring an advertising firm to do the entire job.

With a minimal investment of money and a few days' labor, you will generate a marketing tool that will attract new purchasers, impress gallery owners, spark media interest, and influence prospective investors. "Research indicates that the first piece of information a reader looks at when he receives a direct mail packet is the folder [brochure]," says Thomas Bivens, author of *Handbook for Public Relations Writing*. You will find your efforts well rewarded in the long term.

Begin your research by reading—really reading—your "junk" mail. Next, obtain copies of other artists' brochures by scouting galleries, cooperatives, museums, and anywhere art is sold. Request the brochures of artists whose work is being sold at each location.

Save those brochures that appeal to you for whatever reason: the copy, the layout, the style, the format, the paper weight, the paper color, the print font. These brochures will be your inspiration when you sit down to construct your own brochure.

Although brochures are not all the same, all effective brochures share certain characteristics that you will begin to recognize as you peruse more and more of them. To begin, they all have a theme that hits the reader right between the eyes. Some examples include:

- "Humor is the game and Harry is the name" —Comedian
- "No nodes are good nodes" —Speech therapist
- "Help . . . I have a closet full of clothes and nothing to wear!!" —Personal shopper
- "Power Programs = Success Stories" —Corporate trainer

In addition to your own unique theme, your brochure should include your logo, artistic statement, photos of your work, names of shows in which you have participated, a list of awards you have received, names of galleries where your work has been shown, commissions and client list (only with prior written permission of the buyer, of course), your portrait, testimonials (again, with written permission), any other pertinent bio information, and contact information (your address and telephone number).

"Brochures . . . are essential for any business for which the prospective customer needs detailed information," say Linda Pinson and Jerry Jinnett, authors of *The Home-Based Entrepreneur*. Be sure to work all the details into your brochure.

Even if you have an advanced college degree in English, even if you have won writing awards since you were eight years old, even if you entertain the hope of receiving a Pulitzer, submit your copy to a professional advertising copywriter for critiquing before going to press. The suggestions you will receive, even if they go against your artistic grain, are well worth considering if you want to succeed in the commercial marketplace.

After you have written, proofread, and edited your brochure copy, perhaps with the assistance of a professional advertising copywriter, you are ready to work on your layout. Read a few books on the topic and take another look at those brochures you have been collecting. If your computer has layout capabilities and a good graphics program, you may be able to complete this step on your own. If not, shop printers/typesetters until you find one who has talent, equipment, and a cost-cutting attitude to design your brochure for you.

Although the per-unit cost of each brochure goes down as the size of the print run goes up, do not be tempted to print thousands of your first brochure. It is a sure bet that within the first year after you produce your first brochure, you will want at least a dozen changes. Keep your initial runs small until you have all the glitches ironed out. Then, and only then, go for the 5,000 print run!

See you in print . . .

Suggested Reading
- Bly, Robert, *Create the Perfect Sales Piece*, John Wiley & Sons.
- Gregory, H., *How to Make Newsletters, Brochures & Other Good Stuff Without a Computer System*, Pinstripe Publishing.
- Holtz, Herman, *The Direct Marketer's Workbook*, John Wiley & Sons.
- Lewis, Herschell Gordon, *Direct Mail Copy That Sells*, Prentice-Hall.
- Miller, Marlene, *Business Guide to Print Promotion*, Iris Communication Group.
- Nash, Edward L., *Direct Marketing: Strategy, Planning, Execution*, McGraw-Hill.
- Rapp, Stan and Tom Collins, *Maximarketing: The New Direction in Promotion, Advertising, & Marketing Strategy*, McGraw-Hill Publishing Company.
- Stone, Bob, *Successful Direct Marketing Methods*.

Successfully Selling Art Through a Catalog: Interview with Larry K. Stephenson, Artist

Drew Steis

Larry K. Stephenson was born, reared, and educated in Oklahoma. He worked at furniture sales and oil and gas exploration before devoting himself to painting full-time more than eight years ago.

Today, Larry Stephenson is a successful artist with his own gallery, his own publishing house, a four-color, sixty-four page catalog, and international sales. His secret for success is posters.

"I believe that art is for everybody," Larry told *Art Calendar*. "If limited edition reproductions provide people the opportunity to enjoy a piece of artwork that they might otherwise not be able to enjoy, that is their decision. But the print market itself has gotten out of hand when you are selling—and I will not mention any artist's name— big numbers and calling it a 'limited edition.' It is not healthy for anyone except the people producing them."

Larry Stephenson decided to turn his 40"x60" watercolors of sunflowers, bluebirds, butterflies, canna lilies, irises and other flowers into quality posters. He credits his wife Sheryl for freeing him up to paint and always says "we" when discussing his business.

"My wife is a registered nurse and we decided in 1986 that she would support the family and I would paint full-time and it was kind of hand-to-mouth. "We went to the better juried art fairs in the beginning, but it takes you a while to get into the swing of things and get into the right shows. But by 1987 I knew which ones those were, targeted those shows and was well prepared, had professional slides done, and started to get into the shows I wanted to get into." Winter Park and Coconut Grove in Florida, and King Park and Boston Mills in Ohio, were shows Stephenson found helpful in selling his original art.

The idea to print posters grew out of his need to both please and make a living. "We decided that to make a living at this, and to make a lot of people happy at the same time, and provide them with an image they could enjoy on their walls, that multiples was the way to go and that we would be honest and up-front about it. They are posters, and what we do is we produce limited edition-quality reproduction in a poster format. The quality of our printing, the quality of our paper which is pH neutral, 80-lb. cover weight, has all the trappings of a limited edition print but at a price point that is the same if you walk into your local poster store and buy an image.

"We felt that art needs to be for everyone and if you paint a painting that has a lot of popularity, only one person can afford to buy that painting and enjoy it, putting aside the fact that not everyone has the money to purchase the original. So we wanted to actually provide an image at a price point that a lot of people could enjoy my work. At the same time it was a business decision because we felt that this was a good way for me to do exactly what I wanted to do in life and earn a reasonable living at it.

"A lot of things have happened in the poster market starting in the late 1980s. For one thing they are distributed worldwide at this point by several large poster companies. I am talking about high-quality posters, not the posters you see that come prepackaged on a piece of cardboard in your local record shop. I am talking about a quality poster that is aggressively marketed by a large distributor worldwide. These can be either framed with the poster lettering showing, or that can be matted over so that it becomes more of an art image."

In the first year, 1990, Stephenson printed two large posters and through a distributor sold about 800 of each of them.

"It was not a large number but we looked at it and realized the market was there and that we needed to make some changes in the design of our poster. We felt the image was good but that we could reduce the size of the lettering and the message that was on the poster. Clean that up and make it more attractive, standardize the size of the image so it would fit a standard poster frame, and also change the style of the actual image and print a little bit brighter colors. And we increased the amount of posters we sell so today we sell an awful lot of them."

By the next year, 1991, Sheryl was able to leave nursing to run the poster business full-time. They opened the Third Street Gallery in Ponca City, Oklahoma, a combined gallery of Larry's work and a frame shop. He printed twelve different poster images in his second year and again sold about 800 of each.

Larry charts the explosion of his business from Artexpo New York in 1993.

"By that time we had our line of posters, had done our homework, we had quality images, and all we had to find were the right contacts to distribute those images. I had a quality brochure, a tri-fold brochure that we were able to make additions to so there was room for expansion. And we had eighteen to twenty images."

But Larry Stephenson warns that fame and fortune did not come instantly.

"I would tell your readers that it is not instant gratification. You get exposure to the right people and a lot of people. But these people are not the type that come up and fall all over you with praise. They are businesspeople who look at your product and then take that home and analyze it and stew over it and maybe three months later you get a call. "That is really what we found. We got the exposure, made the business contacts, and then over a period of time sales developed.

"We found people in other parts of the industry, those who not necessarily produced posters. They produced greeting cards or stationery and they wanted to license our images for those products. We found distributors who wanted to distribute our posters as posters. We met with buyers for retail stores who began thinking about our product and that takes almost a year to get your images placed inside a big retail chain store-type situation."

His original art kept pace with the demand for his poster art. The price of his original watercolors climbed steadily from $300 to $1,200 in 1986, to $6,500 per work.

The idea for a catalog of Larry's work came as more and more people became interested in his art.

"We felt like we needed a way to tell the world out there what we are doing. We spent a lot of time designing that catalog and putting together what we consider a very sincere approach to what we are doing. We wanted to distribute it out there where it could reach a lot of people."

At a cost of around $1 each to produce, the catalog was sent to 24,000 readers of *Decor* magazine at an additional cost of around $8,500. And while Larry will not reveal his exact sales numbers, he reports that the response has been "excellent."

"In anticipation of that we put in a new telephone system, and in the first forty-five days after the catalog was mailed out both of our 800-numbers were ringing most of the time. These are orders that range in size from the Mom-and-Pop frame shop to companies that place sizable orders," he explained, adding that "it is not unusual to ship a thousand posters in an order."

Larry also declined to discuss what he wholesales his $15 to $30 unframed prints for. "Generally speaking the average price point in any kind of retail product like this is fifty percent of retail and sometimes our margin is less that than when we are dealing with quantity discounts." Poster publishers are known to mark as much as 75 percent off the retail price, so that both the distributor and the retailer can enjoy a 100 percent markup on what they have paid.

Larry Stephenson's advice to artists interested in the poster market is twofold. "Our images are uniquely ours. We haven't gone out and copied anyone else. That has been part of our success and I would encourage anyone who goes out to do anything in this business to at least be original, come up with their own ideas, follow their own conscience. That has been part of our success.

"But another part of it is that we have approached it in a very businesslike fashion. When I was teaching, I saw that we do a great job of teaching the students how to make their art, but nobody teaches them the business end of it. And there is a business end of it. You have got to be able to earn a living with whatever you do. You have got to come out with this college degree and apply it to the marketplace somewhere. Schools don't do a very good job of that.

"We are color people. To me, color is everything. I like bright, colorful work that is original. If you are going to do posters that are going to be sold to the public, it needs to be something that has a degree of marketability. You want to have something that has a certain degree of mass appeal but it also has uniqueness to it. And that is a tough nut to crack, I really don't know how to describe that any clearer."

Larry K. Stevens has now sold Third Street Gallery and is devoting himself to painting full-time.

The Postcard: Your Other Art Show

Peggy Hadden

If you have an exhibition coming up, you have a wonderful additional opportunity to reach lots of galleries, consultants, collectors, the art press, and just plain well-wishers when you send out your exhibition announcement.

There are many reasons for devoting time and attention to your card's design. The primary one is simply this: Lots more people will see your card than will see your show.

Here's an example. Recently I got a phone call from someone who had seen one of my cards posted to the wall above someone's desk at a museum. She contacted the owner of the gallery where the show had been held, who in turn called to alert me that she was interested in my work. He wasn't after a commission, either. The show announced by that card had occurred over two years ago. I use this event to stress how important a good card can be—she never saw my show.

Particularly during winter, the weather can affect show attendance. A strong card can bring a taste of your exhibition to those who cannot attend. A card with a strong visual image—your artwork—will long outlive the glow that your exhibition will give you. It will enhance office walls and living quarters all over town and beyond, making your exhibition continue long after the last painting has been taken off the wall.

It has been said that in New York City a critic will not come to see a show unless one of the artist's images is included on the show announcement. There are simply too many exhibitions competing for time for the critic to waste time on shows about which they don't have a clue.

Another point: suppose your work has changed a lot. People may come to your show expecting to see seascapes only to find that you are now into knotted ropes and conceptual art. Nothing wrong with that, except that people are creatures of habit, and might need a little time to absorb change. If your card arrives several weeks before the exhibition with images of your new work, the recipients might have time to digest this latest development in your work and might be intrigued to inspect the evolution in person. Also, critics and others who might have you pigeonholed will see that you have more than one side.

Let's think about creating a memorable card.

You might not want to include your name printed on the image side of your card. Let the art stand by itself and info concerning it goes on the back, right? WRONG. Here are several reasons.

- If you do abstract work, your name on the image side will help orient viewers to see your work as you intended them to see it—right-side-up.
- As time goes by, anyone who sees that card will also see your name. Name recognition is important, as I'm sure you already know. After you've created the name-included postcard we're talking about, later when you are part of a group show and no image goes with your name on the invitation, people will recall that they have seen your name and work in the past.
- People keep cards, sometimes for years. I have cards from as long ago as 1986. I was unfamiliar with some of these artists, but their imagery hooked me.

Typefaces are important. As artists, we tend to think that anything artistic is our cup of tea. After receiving many poorly planned exhibition cards over the years, I'm not so sure. A graphic artist who works with type and text shapes might be able to make the information you want to convey look neater and better designed. Quite simply, working with letters is another can of worms, and just because we've been trained as visual interpreters doesn't mean we naturally understand typefaces. We don't hesitate to use the services of a photographer, a framer, or a shipping company.

If money is a stumbling block, you might be able to arrange, as I did, to swap a piece of art in exchange for typesetting services. Sometimes the exhibition space where you are having your show will have a standard logo for their space and require that you use it. It's important to find a typeface, or set of letters, that works with that logo. They don't have to be the same, just compatible. You might want to use two typefaces: one for the exhibition's title, and another for the rest of the information about the dates, opening, and location. But be careful. Nothing will clutter up a card faster than too many typefaces in different styles. Usually, a maximum of three is all that can work harmoniously together. If this talk of typefaces is too involved for you, a graphic designer might save the day.

Proofread your text to be sure that everything is correct. In the rush to prepare for an exhibition, it is easy to overlook something small like this . . . until you find, as I once did, that the date on your card is wrong, and no one is going to be at your show! If you are working on a tight show budget or time schedule, this can prove disastrous. There is nothing you can do except have it reprinted. Ask someone who knows nothing about your show to read the card and then tell you what it said. The preparation time for a show can be such a stressful or exciting time that we forget about important details.

The paper stock you select is important in planning your card, too. Its weight will determine how well it travels through the mail and the shape it will be in when it arrives. We've all received announcements that must have looked great when they were smooth and new but haven't traveled well. Try for something at least as heavy as an average time card of the type used by many businesses for punching in and out by employees.

Card stock comes with either a glossy or matte surface. The gloss, or "coated," stock is more expensive, but it is probably preferable for showing off your artwork. You can also get stock with one side glossy, the other matte; this is my usual choice. The matte side is excellent for printing all your information about the show.

When planning your information layout, leave some white space, or blank areas, around the words. You'll be able to write a personal message or just give the reader a little breathing space. Conscientiously work to eliminate things you don't need, like the Zip Code at the exhibition space, or the size of your image, unless you feel it's relevant.

Also, ask your printer to run some of your postcards with blank backs, or with just your caption information. You'll be able to use them for correspondence for years to come.

All of this fussing over a postcard might seem like a waste of time until you look back after doing several of them and wish you had done them differently.

You care deeply about how your art is presented. It is a shame to shortchange yourself with poorly designed or hastily conceived cards. Keep in mind that for many who will receive your card, this is the only art from you that they will ever see.

Using Brochures to Find More Markets

Debora Meltz

"You need a gallery," an acquaintance remarked as she surveyed the pictures stacked three and four deep along my dining room wall.

"Gallery," I wisecracked. "I need a closet!"

"A closet is for storing things to keep them out of sight," she replied frostily. "I'm sure you didn't do all this work to hide it away."

I launched into a mournful litany of how difficult it was to sell artwork, how time-consuming and frustrating. My work, I explained, was not particularly salable, and the number of "alternative spaces" was limited, etc., etc.

"There is a market for your work and it is not going to come to your dining room. You're a smart girl. Go find it." That said, she changed the subject.

She was, of course, quite right. For years I had been going the usual route of entering competitions and submitting slides to galleries and alternative spaces I though might be interested in my work. My success was, euphemistically speaking, modest.

I had clipped an article from *Art Calendar*, written by Caroll Michels ("Rethinking Presentation Packages"), on marketing one's art with a large-scale mailing of brochures to as wide an audience as possible. Perhaps this was a way for me to find my market.

It was painfully evident from the pristine condition in which my slide packets were returned that the only thing the galleries were looking at was the stamped, self-addressed envelope. A brochure would, in a sense, "force" them to look at the work, could be discarded at no great loss to me if they were not interested, or filed for future reference. Yes, it might be a more effective, efficient, and productive marketing tool.

I was able to attend a workshop offered by Michels on developing a brochure and obtaining mailing lists. Within a month, I designed my brochure, had it printed, and was ready to go.

Michels recommended that individualized cover letters be included with the brochures as well as a self-addressed postcard the recipient could fill out requesting additional material.

I wrote a generic letter and, having a computer, did a "mail-merge."

Mailing lists were obtained from a variety of sources. The *Art in America Annual Gallery and Museum Guide* is invaluable.

Between January and June I mailed 1,462 brochure packets to curators, corporate consultants, private dealers, and galleries across the country. Here are the results:

- One hundred and nine returned as undeliverable
- Six responses from "vanity" situations, e.g., pay-to-show galleries, pay-for-inclusion publications, or wall space rentals
- Twenty-six "Thanks, but not for us . . . ," two of which referred me to other sources
- Eight personal letters of acknowledgment of receipt of the brochure
- Sixteen personal letters informing me they were including the brochure in their files
- Twenty-two requests for more information
- Three telephone requests for more information
- Nine packets of information about the recipient so I could decide whether or not to send further materials
- One phone call from a gentleman in California informing me that his gallery dealt in art-deco style works and asking if I would mind if he framed one of the reproductions from my brochure for himself
  And . . .
- Four invitations for one-person shows: one in January in Florida, another in May in California, a September exhibition in Florida, and a fourth to take place in the fall in West Virginia

For a total of eighty-nine responses.

I had been warned to expect a 1-2 percent response rate (a response is any reply) as this was the general rule for all direct mailings. With adjustment for the undeliverables, my response rate translated into a 6.6 percent.

Obviously, this approach is reasonably successful. Now, what did it cost? Please note: the prices listed below are not intended to serve as guidelines. I am merely reporting what I spent for the look I wanted. I had my letterhead and postcards printed in a color other than black, which added to the cost. Paper comes in a wide variety of colors, weights, textures, and prices. What I chose was not necessarily the "best buy" or the cheapest but it suited my particular needs.

- Two thousand brochures, 3-fold, full color on one side, B/W on the other: $2,013.00
- Two thousand Monarch 7"x10" letterhead: $148.00
- Two thousand envelopes 6"x9": $184.00
- Two thousand postcards printed both sides: $180.00
- Postage at 52¢ each: $423.98
- Total: $2,948.98

To be sure, this is not an insignificant amount of money and only time will tell whether I will recoup it. In addition to the cost, it was a mammoth undertaking. I looked upon it as my part-time job for several months. However, it did not detract from my studio time nearly as much as I had anticipated. I paid my son to enter my lists into the computer. My husband helped and the entire family stuffed, sealed, and stamped envelopes.

If you do not happen to have a computer-savvy son hanging about, you could hire a high school or college student for a few hours a week.

If you do not have a computer, there are businesses that specialize in doing mail-merges and printing letters and envelopes. This will significantly increase your cost, however, and if you're considering building your own mailing list anyway you should consider purchasing a computer.

Based on my experiences thus far, I can recommend some ways to cut expenses. While an individualized letter is a nicety, I did get responses from letters with no salutation. I do think that curators should get personalized letters. If the cover letter is not specifically addressed it could be photocopied onto your letterhead.

Mailing lists are available preprinted on pressure-sensitive labels. The "personal touch" is lost, but much time is saved. The postcard is not a necessity. Only about a dozen of my respondents used the postcard, and half of them included it with a personal letter.

Another option is to design your brochure as a self-mailer. You lose space for information and/or reproductions, but you would cut postage costs and eliminate the expense of letterheads and envelopes.

If you work in black and white, or if your work reproduces extremely well in black and white, your cost could be cut substantially.

Compare printing costs. Photocopy places should not be considered if you want a quality brochure. You will need real offset printing. There are printing companies that specialize in artists' brochures, but you may find that designing one yourself and having a good local printer do the work will be less expensive. Most print shops will work with you and help you design a brochure.

If you decide to undertake a mass mailing, I recommend the following:

Have at least twenty-five slide sheets ready to go when you begin the mailing. I had my slides computer-labeled and put in slide sheets. That way, when I got a request for more info, I had only to grab a sheet from a box. No laborious labeling and stuffing slides into those nasty little pockets.

Have updated, concise, and professional looking resumés and artist's statements ready to go out with your slides. Have plenty of resumés and statements on hand. Many places that return your slides will keep the support material on file with your brochure. Caroll Michels recommends including a brochure along with your slides to remind whoever requested your work why he or she wanted it in the first place.

A rubber stamp or labels with your name and address for the SASE are inexpensive and time-savers.

Get some good-looking "pocket folders" to put your slides and other material in. This will not only make a nice, neat packet, it will look good, protect your stuff, and if it is returned you have only to put in another SASE, change the cover letter, and it's ready to go out again.

Every response I received was gracious. Even the "no thanks" letters were encouraging and, in a few instances, asked not to be dropped from my mailing list but to see my work again in a year or so.

I'm still working on my mailing. I have about a thousand brochures yet to go and am hopeful that many out there that were unacknowledged escaped the circular file and may yet yield results.

One final note: Carry a bunch of brochures with you. I hand 'em out all over! You never know . . .

How to Get Retail Craft Stores for Your Craft by Mail

Karen Gamow

While this article was written primarily for crafters, especially those doing business in tourist/vacation spots, the principles can be adapted by almost anyone wanting to gain more outlets for his art by mail. Examples of other kinds of art that can be marketed this way are not limited to multiples, greeting cards or stationery, jewelry, or wearables. But remember to do your research carefully before you mail, keep track of mailings, make your follow-up calls, get paid up front whenever possible, and use contracts.

There are several simple steps to take to find retail outlets for your craft item. Here is a brief outline, and below I'll talk about each item in greater detail.

Step 1. Identify your market. Does your work sell best in country stores? craft galleries? nautical shops?

Step 2. Design a mailing packet. The packet should include a cover letter, a fact sheet about your product, a good photograph and/or a sample of your work, a photo or drawing of your display if you use one.

Step 3. Buy a mailing list, or create your own, of stores that would be most likely to be interested in your craft.

Step 4. Mail your packet at a time of year when your potential stores are buying.

Step 5. Set up an easy card file system to keep track of follow-up phone calls, and then make those calls.

Identifying Your Market

This is an important first step. When you sell at craft shows, ask your better customers what types of stores your work could be sold in, and test market on your own. Travel, look in the phone book, and brainstorm with friends, naming all the types of shops in which your craft might sell: country craft shops, bath shops, bookstores, galleries, furniture stores, floral boutiques, department stores, baby or maternity shops, health food stores—the list is almost endless. Once you more narrowly define your market, you'll be able to do the necessary research, or buy an already existing list, and start mailing information about your craft to those buyers.

It is important to experiment. Your market might not be what you think. We ended up personally hitting the road, and visiting more than a thousand gift shops, getting our product into many of them, and tracking sales to see which stores did best. In our own craft company, we've learned over time that our work sells best in country stores, historical museums, botanical gardens, nautical shops, craft galleries, and a few other types of stores. And we were surprised to discover that we did poorly in basket shops, shops with a lot of glass craft items, and Hallmark and similar shops. We once thought hospital gift shops would be perfect, until we learned that most purchases there are made by hospital staff, not visitors—a small market indeed!

Designing the Mailing Packet

• The cover letter. The cover letter should be a friendly and brief introduction to your product, and also a strong selling tool. Address it personally to the owner or buyer whenever possible. In fact, the bigger the store, the more important it is to address the packet to the right person before you mail, as the packet often ends up on someone else's desk. However, if you can't get a buyer's name or are short of time, be sure to clearly mark the envelope "Attention: Buyer." A beginning like "I came across your shop recently, and thought our product would work well for you" gets right to the point. Then describe what you've enclosed in the packet, and list a few key selling points about your product. These can be borrowed and rephrased from your fact sheet. These key selling points are the most important part of the letter, as they whet the buyer's appetite to read further. Things to include might be, "Our work has been voted the best pottery in New York by the Association of Pottery Shop Owners" or "Our work wholesales for only $x each and retails for $xx," etc. Then, the last paragraph can close with a "Thank you for your time" and a mention that you will be calling to answer questions soon. The cover letter should be one page, and preferably somewhat short and punchy, since most buyers don't take the time to read unless they get interested.

• The fact sheet. The fact sheet includes everything you can think of about your product that might interest the buyer. Write those facts in order of importance to the buyer—remember that facts alone are boring. Here are a few samples from our fact sheet.

  • Our product is hand-signed, original photography, with each piece set in a beautiful 5"x7" textured mat.
  • Each photograph wholesales for $1.50 and retails for $3.00.
  • An order includes a wood-stained display rack that holds up to ninety images. The display fits easily onto a counter or table top (22" high, 18" wide, and 11" deep) and permits customers to browse through the photos comfortably. A display rack is $18. If you decide after the initial purchase not to reorder, we will be glad to buy back the rack for the full $18: our money back guarantee to you.
  • Customer satisfaction record: Fully 95 percent of all stores that make an initial purchase from us also reorder.

- Our minimum order is sixty photographs plus a display rack. An initial order is generally shipped out COD, with future orders net 30 days. You can expect an order to take about one week to arrive at your shop. A complete setup of sixty photographs, one display rack, and shipping is $119.

- Samples. A photo or sample of your work is essential. We send a sample, as our product is small enough to make it affordable. Most craft people send a photo of their work. Be sure you've taken a high-quality photo, and if you can afford it, two photos might be better—experiment and see. If you have a display rack that you offer to stores to display your craft, also include a photo or drawing of that. If you don't have a display for your work, and feel you need one, make some visits to stores, and learn what types of displays are available. We found it cheapest to design our own and have a local cabinet shop make them up for us. You may decide to use plexiglass (ready-made displays are available by mail from manufacturers), wood, baskets, or something else. Whatever you use, be sure it suits your product, displays it well, isn't too large for a store to have on display, and is inexpensive. Try not to spend more than $20 on a display. And consider offering the display rack to the store for free, by offering free merchandise to offset the cost of the rack—e.g., if the display cost you $20, charge the store $20, but also give them two free items that retail for $10 each.

Obtaining the Mailing List

You may buy a good mailing list, or compile one yourself. One of the easiest ways to get a good mailing list is to buy one; the disadvantage is that mailing lists are generally rented on a one-time use basis only. Look in crafts newspapers to find ads for mailing lists that might meet your needs. Or talk with crafters at shows who may have leads for you. If your craft fits nicely into categories found in the Yellow Pages (like furniture stores, antiques stores, health food shops, floral boutiques, etc.), you can order good lists from companies that compile their lists directly from the Yellow Pages. Three such companies are American Business Lists, 402-331-7169; Edith Roman, 800-223-2194; and Burnett, 800-223-7777.

We were never able to find a country craft store list, since country gifts are a subset of "gifts" in the Yellow Pages. And so we traveled, clipped ads in tourist magazines, and visited state information bureaus for help. (NOTE: If you think your craft item would sell well in country theme or nautical gift shops, we make available our mailing list, which we compiled over the last five years of travel and painstaking research. Most are our own customers, and are high sales volume shops located in the most visited tourist spots in the United States.

If you find that your work is too specialized to find a ready-made list, you will need to travel or otherwise dig deeper to find good leads. But for most categories you are likely to pick, a good list can be found. The reference librarian at a large urban or university library can be of invaluable help. At the reference desk you'll find directories of chain store buyers, department store buyers by department, catalog and mail order retailers, and even whole volumes of people who buy specialty items for large grocery store chains. Go wild at the library—you will find unexpected treasures. Also ask about on-line databases, and see if something at the library can meet your needs. Be prepared to pay for on-line service, usually a fee per name found. A great resource is PhoneFiche, found in major libraries, which has many or all major Yellow Pages on microfiche. You can make copies of pages yourself, going to areas you know are good for your product. We made a comprehensive list of all tourist towns in the U.S., selectively copied fiche pages for "gift shop" Yellow Pages, and then made calls within each town to find the most appropriate shops.

Timing Your Mailing

Call several buyers of stores appropriate for you, and ask when they do their buying.

We found that most shops catering to local customers buy in January and in June. There is some flexibility, but you want to increase your chances of the buyer saying yes, so mailing during these times is most advisable.

For shops that do most of their business with tourists, they often pick up new lines from January through April for the summer and fall tourist seasons, and they often don't have much of a Christmas season. Really major attractions, like Disney World and other theme parks, will buy even earlier, e.g., November for the following summer season.

Following Up by Phone

Once you've sent your packet out, you can wait for orders to come in—if you wait for orders, you can expect a one- to three-percent response rate. Or, you can call each store lead within about three days of the time they have received your letter—when you call, your rate of sales will probably more than triple! Our response rate is 20-25 percent.

Here's an easy system for keeping track of phone calls. It is simple, inexpensive, and foolproof. Put each store name and phone number on an index card. Buy an index card file box. Get index card dividers and label seven of them for each day of the week, "Monday" through "Sunday." Then make twelve dividers for each month of the year, and four dividers labeled "Week One," "Week Two," "Week Three," and "Week Four." Put the dividers into a card file box so that Monday-Sunday is first, then the months next. Now, put the "Week One" through "Week Four" dividers into the current month. Whenever you have a call to make later, file it into the right month (if the buyer says to call back in April, make notes of the conversation and put the card into the April section of the box). When April comes, take out all the cards for April and sort them into their proper weeks. When that week comes up, take the cards and sort them out "Monday" through "Sunday," whichever day was the requested day for the call. Then, each morning, there are your calls for the day—just pull the stack and get on the phone. If people say the buyer is out until May 15, put the card into May; on May 1, you'll go through the May cards and put that one into "Week Three"; and at the beginning of the third week, you'll place the card into the right day of the week.

What to say on the phone? "Hi, this is Joe with Pottery Crafts. I just wanted to see if you had received my letter, and the photo of our blue hippopotamus pottery a few days ago." Of course he will say yes if the packet grabbed his attention, to which you may reply, "Would you be interested in trying our work in your shop this season?" If there is some interest, or even hesitation, now is the time to gently list one or two key points about the work, usually the most magnetic selling points of your product. I often close the sale by asking what date they'd like to receive the order. And finally I say, "Our standard policy is to send the first order COD, and all future orders net 30. Will that work for you?" Ninety-eight percent of the time people say yes. If people say no, get some credit references and a home phone number (many shops close during part of the year) before you agree to ship the first order net 30. We have very few problems with our customers, but all the problems we do have usually show up on the first order, so it's wise to be careful and gather plenty of information at that time.

If the customer says he can't decide, or wants to wait a few months before buying anything, ask, "Would you mind if I called you back in May?" Thank him, and be sure to put the card in the right spot in your box.

Watch the sales start to roll in, and get your shipments out quickly, and you'll see your wholesale business blossom.

How to Do a Bulk Mailing

Carolyn Blakeslee

This article will tell you how to do a fairly small bulk mailing—200 to 2,000 pieces—a typical mailing which might be done by an artist or arts center. Bulk mail is less expensive than first class postage. As of 1995, a brochure, or publisher's letter and response packet, usually costs no more than 22.6¢ apiece to mail, rather than 32¢ to 55¢ each at the first class rate.

In order to mail at bulk rates, you will need to purchase a permit at your post office ($85/year plus an initial application fee) and either print an indicia on your mailing piece or purchase bulk mailing stamps to affix to your brochure.

What are the disadvantages?

The primary disadvantage: Bulk mail gets lower priority at the post office than first class mail. A piece can take as long as three weeks to arrive at its destination. However, if you can print out your list using barcodes and Zip-Plus-Four, your piece could be delivered in just a couple of days.

Secondly, you won't get address corrections unless you place the words "ADDRESS CORRECTION REQUESTED" under your return address. Even if you have this printed, the post office won't always return address corrections. Furthermore, you'll have to pay 50¢ for each piece returned. If you want to do an address correction on your list, the best way is to send a postcard via first class mail; the cost of a first class postcard stamp, 20¢, is actually less than the basic 22.6¢ per-piece rate for bulk mail, and you won't need to pay the 50¢ per-correction fee.

What are the minimum numbers needed to do a mailing?

For a bulk mailing, the total number of pieces must be at least 200.

Why does the mailer get a discount?

The mailer does some of the post office's work:
• Sorting each piece into Zip Code order

- Rubber-banding the pieces into bundles directed to a specific mailing area, i.e. a specific state, area, city, Zip Code, or even a specific neighborhood
- Labeling the bundles appropriately
- Sacking the bundles into gray postal mailing sacks so they are ready to go directly to the destination
- Labeling the sacks appropriately
- Counting the pieces, doing paperwork to reflect the counts, and submitting the paperwork with the mailing and with payment

What is Zip Code order?

Brochures must be labeled with the lowest Zip Code (00001) facing up at the top of a stack, and the highest Zip Code (99999) at the bottom. All brochures must face the same way and must be neatly bundled.

How are bundles bundled?

To make a bundle, groupings of brochures are rubber-banded together. A thick rubber band is placed in the middle of the bundle, holding it together one way, and another rubber band goes around it perpendicularly to the first one.

A bundle must consist of ten or more pieces. The bundle should not be more than 3" thick, or else postal employees cannot pick up the bundle easily, and the bundle may therefore be refused.

Once rubber-banded, how are the bundles labeled?

Each bundle of ten or more pieces receives a sticker indicating its approximate destination. Bundles may be labeled in the following ways.
- Ten or more going to the same Zip Code: "D," a red sticker which means "Direct."
- An area, also known as a "Sectional Center Facility," consists of several Zip Codes, but all of the Zip Codes begin with the same three digits. For example, in Northern Virginia, 22003 is Annandale, 22041 is Falls Church, 22066 is Great Falls, 22070 is Herndon, and so on. If there are ten or more pieces going to the Zip Codes starting with "220," but there are not ten or more going to one specific Zip Code, then these may be bundled into a group marked with a "3," a green sticker

which means "the first three digits of each Zip Code in this bundle are the same." As with all the kinds of bundles, they must be sorted from lowest to highest Zip Code.

- A state bundle consists of pieces that didn't have ten or more going to a specific Zip or three-digit area. This bundle receives an orange "S" sticker, for "state."
- Sometimes there are not enough brochures in a specific state to make even a state bundle. So these strays are grouped together, in a bundle labeled "MS," for "mixed states."

Once rubber-banded and labeled, how are bundles sacked?

Each sack must consist of 125 or more pieces. The 125 pieces may be separated into one bundle, or several. Each sack may go to:

- One Zip Code
- A specific city consisting of several Zip Codes. For example, San Francisco has several post offices with Zip Codes starting at 94101 and going well up into the 941's
- An "SCF," or an area with several cities and towns, but all bundles' Zip Codes in the bag begin with the same three digits
- A state
- Mixed states

How are the bags labeled?

If the bag goes to a specific Zip Code, the top line should read "City, ST, Zip Code." For example, if all 125+ pieces are going to 10011, the sack would be labeled "New York, NY 10011."

If the bag goes to a specific city, for example Washington, DC, it would be labeled "Washington, DC 200."

Conclusion

Your postmaster can assist you with labeling and other details of doing a bulk mailing. The post office publishes an illustrated booklet and a video that might help.

As one's mailing gets quite large—say, more than 10,000 pieces—or targeted in a very specific area, better postal discounts are available depending on the electronic capability generating your list: Zip+4, barcoding, and other automated functions can decrease your costs and improve the delivery time.

CHAPTER 11

Publishing a Book

Book Publishing Options

Alan Bamberger

An artist wrote to me with a project in mind. "I have a large collection of figurative, narrative prints I completed about five years ago. I'm interested in having them published as a book in a 'story without words' type format. How do I go about doing this?"

This artist has several options here. None of the options are easy, but all are accomplishable.

Option A: Trade Book. If you want your prints published in the form of a trade book like you would find in a bookstore, you'll have to approach publishers pretty much in the same manner as any unpublished author would. This involves first finding out the names of publishers who produce this kind of book and then making formal proposals to them. Look at the copyright pages of books that are similar to what you have in mind. Other good resources for locating names include graphic artists, printmakers, literary or artist agents who have experience in this area, and graphics departments of universities, libraries, and museums.

Once you've made up your list, either write or call editors and ask whether they would be interested in seeing a proposal for your book. If they are not, ask whether they can refer you to any publishers who might be. Don't be discouraged by rejections—you might receive fifty "no's" before you receive a "yes."

When you have caught the interest of a publisher, photocopy the first twenty or so of your prints and submit them as they would appear in finished order. Also include a summary or outline explaining your story from beginning to end. Publishers who want to see more will request the entire manuscript.

Option B: Limited Edition. If you want your prints published as originals in a limited edition artist book format, you'll have to cross over into a fairly obscure area of the art/book world called "fine press" publishing. The main problems associated with this option are cost related. Not only do you have up-front printing and binding costs, but you also have to work your own profit into the picture. With so many originals that have to be printed for each book, the selling price gets pretty high pretty fast. Add to this the fact that collectors who buy art in book form are usually not accustomed to paying the high prices that art collectors pay.

To locate fine presses, check with the people and institutions mentioned above. Here are some artists' organizations that might be helpful: Center for Book Arts, 626 Broadway, 5th Fl., New York, NY 10012; Minnesota Center for Book Arts, 24 N. Third St., Minneapolis, MN 55401; Pacific Center for Book Arts, 6020A Adeline St., Oakland, CA 94608; Women's Studio Workshop, P.O. Box 489, Rosendale, NY 12472. In addition, check your local Yellow Pages or those of nearby major cities under the heading "Bookbinders"—these professionals can often provide you with the names of fine presses. The great majority of fine presses you contact will be interested in publishing your prints as a book, but not at their expense. Unless your prints are truly outstanding and a publisher gets really excited about them, expect to foot most or all of the bill yourself.

Option C: Do-It-Yourself. Your third option involves doing as much of the work as possible on your own. If you have a printing press, print all the prints yourself. If you don't, then beg, borrow, or barter to use someone else's. Then join forces with a bookbinder and perhaps a designer with fine press experience and work with them to produce a finished product. You may be able to hammer out an arrangement among yourselves where little or no money changes hands up-front and you all share in the final profits. Your chances of negotiating this outcome increase when all of you have comparable levels of expertise in your chosen fields.

Publishing My Own Book

Barbara Dougherty

A successful artist once told me to look forward to unstable economic times. It is a time in which to compete for opportunity and a time to do promotions. He said, "Be radical when others are being conservative, do more work when others are slacking." His attitude was the basis for my 1992 artist agenda, and it was a year of success and failure. My success was in having my work acknowledged, my failure was the diminished sales of my paintings.

The agenda for 1992 was to continue a project that was begun in 1990: to produce a book of my paintings. I have observed that in this country there is a great respect for books. People read them, collect them, and listen to their authors on radio and television. In fact, among academic professionals it is "publish or perish."

As artists we call ourselves published if reproductions of our work are made and distributed. However, the publishing "mystique" seems to apply more to writers who publish books than artists who publish images. Writers seem to get the invitations to interviews and publicity more often than an artist who has published images.

The creation of my first book, *Harvest California*, was the hardest and best project I have ever undertaken. The difficulties were:

1. Clarifying my ideas so they could become a cohesive presentation
2. Understanding the technology of book production
3. Negotiating with printing industry professionals
4. Allowing myself to invest in such an expensive project

By 1991, I had produced 1,300 hardcover copies of *Harvest California*. The book had eighty-eight pages including thirty-eight full-page color plates. The total cost to produce each book was $28. With the book in hand, 1991 became the best sales year I had ever had both for paintings and for books. I priced the book at $40 and sold most copies at my exhibitions. I also had placed it in local bookstores and then advertised the book and the stores on television. This marketing experiment sold about two books a week. I had intended to try to find a publishing company that would help me produce more books and possibly fund the creation of future work. I was going to approach companies with my completely produced book, the results of my initial local marketing, and some notable reviews. However, the year went by too quickly—I was painting full-time and did not have enough time for approaching companies.

In December 1991, I shared the book and my paintings with a longtime customer. He purchased a painting and called me after a week saying he and his wife wanted to invest in creating a publishing company for my books. During 1992 the company published postcards of my work and cookbooks with my images on the covers. It has done mailings and advertising and made contacts that I would never have made on my own. Also the company took my paintings and books to trade shows at the Los Angeles Convention Center. During this time, I did all the paintings and most of the text for my next volume called *In Search of a Sunflower*.

Unfortunately, I have never received any royalties from the company, and 1992 was an incredibly difficult year in which to sell paintings. However, the opportunities which emerged were notable. I signed a contract for a three-month show in a large event center in Orange County, California. I was approached by organizations to have my images on their annual reports, and for a while I was able to afford to operate a gallery featuring my work. Also, both B. Dalton and Walden Bookstores purchased my books.

The down side is that I have worked more hours doing support and promotion work than painting and that I am involved with more people than ever before who do not understand the sensibilities of artists. In addition, marketing books is far more tedious and difficult than marketing paintings. There are tens of thousands of new books produced and marketed every year in this country.

A friend, who is an artist, has recently had a similar experience. One of his patrons felt that in these times promoting the artist's work offered at least as much as any other investment he could make. This patron has published and distributed reproductions of this artist's work. The project has become large. The market he has entered is attractive and very promising. The prints were even distributed to Sea World in San Diego. I have watched the artist have his time taken up by promotions while his time to paint eroded. He made the supposition I had made—that successful promotion will lead to more time to paint. It is improbable. And this is the insight that I must carry into my plans and agenda for future years.

The world and this country need artists that have the strength and the singularity of vision to know that the best gift they can give is the commitment to making the images because images are the magic. An artist should never lose sight of the first obligation—an artist is the only one who can make the art!

The fact is that our population likes art and wants to support it. Not everyone can buy a painting and the purchase of paintings has become too much like the purchase of furniture—meant to look good in the home or office. Artists need to be able to do art without the concern of selling art. But perhaps producing a book is a way of giving the public the opportunity to pay to view our art. Paying to view can keep us working.

PART 3

Getting Into Print

Happy Medium #6, 1994, sagger-fired, 22" x 20" x 5", Cheryl Herr-Rains,
Alma, Michigan

CHAPTER 12

Getting Press Coverage

Getting Into Print: News Releases

Carolyn Blakeslee

A news release, also known as a press release if it is meant for print media only, is a statement prepared for and distributed to the news media.

News releases are written by Vice Presidents of Publicity for community organizations, by every P.R. firm, by every Communications Officer—in short, by every person or organization wishing to publicize his event.

It's a trade-off: the media gets its news, and you and your event obtain free publicity via press or air time.

Sometimes an editor will print your story verbatim as you submitted it, and sometimes he will call you for further information.

No matter which approach the editors take, you will get coverage in at least some of the media you contact if you send out professional-looking and -sounding news releases.

You could even get an interview or a full-blown story if you play your cards right.

Almost every event is news to one entity or another. Do you use an unusual medium to produce your art, say, discarded Michelin tires? For that matter, do you work for Michelin and produce pastel paintings at night? Then the Michelin corporate magazine and the other tire trade magazines should hear about your artwork and your shows. The editors of those magazines might feel that the story about your art will provide a human interest break to readers who are usually fed company and technical information.

Have you been in touch with your *alma mater* lately? with the old hometown paper you used to do cartoons for? with the people who produce the magazine you used to work for? with your local newspaper?

Almost every profit-making and nonprofit organization produces a newsletter, magazine, or other printed matter. They are constantly in search of news.

However, editors have a love/hate relationship with news releases. Their publications cannot exist without them, but there is always a pile of releases to read through, and many if not most of the releases which come over editors' desks end up in the circular file.

Why? Let's use *Art Calendar* as an example. As you know, *Art Calendar* publishes listings of upcoming professional opportunities for visual artists. We do not publish listings of current shows, although we are glad to list shows in the Classifieds. The press release we receive on anything other than upcoming enterable, or otherwise professional, events usually gets discarded. Don't get me wrong, we like to receive those releases—it is a great pleasure to see the names of *Art Calendar* subscribers on lists of winners, grantees, authors, etc., and occasionally these releases lead to an interview. But with very few exceptions, the only releases which get published here have to do with upcoming grants, juried shows, artist colony deadlines, etc., to which artists may apply.

It's amazing how many releases *Art Calendar* receives on plays, concerts, and dance performances—events which have nothing to do with our content. The people sending out those releases simply haven't bothered to familiarize themselves with our publication or to ask for guidelines.

The bigger the magazine/paper/TV/radio station, the more news releases the editors have to go through, and the less attention any release is likely to get, unless it is well written, targeted and tailored.

Troubleshooting

There are several reasons a news release will not make it into print or TV/radio/cable air time:

- It was sloppy. Sloppiness and ugliness of presentation reflect on you and your event.
- It was poorly written, with grammatical and spelling errors.
- It was less than intriguing and imaginative.
- It was imaginative all right, but unprofessionally so.
- It failed to grab the attention of the editor, i.e., it was boring.
- It was not directed to the proper editor.
- It was not appropriate for the publication/ TV/cable/radio station. It really helps

to be familiar with the style and content of the publication, station, or program to whom you're sending your release.

- The writer failed to discover that the medium to which he sent the release charges an advertising fee for making such information available to the public.
- There was not enough room that day, week or month to run the item because other stories took priority.
- It arrived too close to, or past, the deadline.
- The editor knows the person who wrote the release and doesn't like him. This is unlikely but possible. If this ever happens to you just keep sending news releases frequently and send duplicate releases to other appropriate editors on the staff. One person can't make or break you.
- The writer did not provide contact ("For further information please contact . . . ") information.
- The event was just not judged to be newsworthy.

Tailoring and Targeting

How do you know which media your news is appropriate for? Such knowledge comes only with paying attention. For example, only by regularly reading the critics do you know what kinds of shows, and which galleries, they cover. In fact, you may choose to continue to send releases to all of them even if you know that some of them will never come—that is just another step in getting your name known out there.

The first task is to figure out exactly what is newsworthy about your event. For example, will proceeds of your art show benefit AIDS victims? Then you should be in touch with every single news medium in the area, including major and community magazines and newspapers, radio talk shows, and radio and TV newscasters. You should also be in touch with organizations concerned about AIDS and let them know what you are up to. They may be able to help you with publicity, emotional support, maybe even information on how to get some volunteers to assist. In short, the more people you get involved, the more momentum you can create for your event.

If your show is about wildlife, contact the regional wildlife organizations about your show and make sure they print an item in their newsletters.

If your show is about portraiture, perhaps you will want to contact the society columns and society magazines.

Is it newsworthy that your art league will be having Mr. X speak at your meeting, open to the public, next month? An item about the lecture will perhaps draw a one-line listing here and there. But it is doubtful that people will care unless it comes across in the news release that Mr. X is a dynamic speaker whose program is worth the time and may, in fact, be worth a longer blurb or even an article.

The next task is to write the news release in such a way that the editor is likely to decide that it is worth running. You know your event is newsworthy. You must convince the editors of that—usually without your even getting to speak to them.

Format and Flash

The challenge is to produce a release which is engaging, follows the rules of format, and is visually appealing.

First, a news release must be neatly typed in a non-italic typeface and double-spaced, so the editor can read it quickly and edit it easily.

Your release should be photocopied or printed onto letterhead stationery. If you do not have letterhead, neatly type your name, address, and telephone number at the top.

In the left-hand top of your page just beneath your letterhead, you should have the current date including the year; as in a letter, this is the date you are sending the release. Just below that date, you should type "FOR IMMEDIATE RELEASE." This tells the editor he may print it any time from the minute he receives it. Or, if you would prefer that it be printed later, type "FOR RELEASE [fill in the appropriate date]."

In the top right-hand corner, directly across from the Release/Date information, type "For Further Information, Contact [fill in a name, address, and a telephone number reachable during the day so the editor can call that person for clarification or further information]." The address is not necessary if the address on the letterhead is where an inquiry for further information should be mailed. Fax and e-mail info never hurts.

The following, centered, should appear at the bottom of each page except the last: "- more -". And at the very end of your release text, even if it is a one-page release, should appear: "- End -".

Be sure to tell Who, What, When, and Where—as well as How Much and Whom to Call for Reservations or Information if applicable. Why's, How's, and histories may be necessary to your story; or, they may add interest and that dash of flash. For example, if you have shown at the Museum of Modern Art or if your work is in so-and-so's major collection, that background information might be appropriate, even crucial, in your news release.

However, producing a professional news release requires walking a fine line between the flash and the fire. An editor who receives a beautifully packaged release full of self-adulation probably will not run that item. For example, "Artist X is an unrecognized genius who paints wonderful, swirling, surrealist canvases answering the cosmic questions. Through this show he seeks to find a financial sponsor who will rescue him from underappreciation on the part of the masses of blithering humanity." Believe it or not, *Art Calendar* has received a couple of releases like that. It's OK to address spiritual or lofty approaches in your news releases, but be reasonable.

Spell correctly. And if you have any doubts about grammar or punctuation, *The Elements of Style* by E. B. White and William Strunk is an excellent manual to consult. An occasional error will not hurt. But a page full of glaring mistakes will go into the waste basket—its writer does not appear to be professional and therefore his event probably isn't either.

So much for format and visual content. Now for stylistic content.

Writing is learnable. Pay attention to newspaper and magazine writing. Each writer, and each journal, has an editorial thrust; each writer or journal generally covers a different kind of news.

Each also has a different style. As you produce your releases, you may decide to hand-tailor them to appeal to the editorial tone of each journal to whom you will send your releases. One magazine will be urban, cool, and up-tempo; another neighborhood paper will be hip yet homey; the next publication will be society. Then there are the intellectual mags, daily newspapers, etc.

When you send information to your community paper, make sure your news is of interest to members of the community. For example, if you are publicizing a show taking place in California and you live in Virginia, your news release should certainly say that you live in [your community] and the show features paintings of your son, who attends [your community high school]. Otherwise, who would care about a show across the country?

Sending Photographs

Local papers are more likely to run photographs of artworks because they are more interested in local artists than the larger papers are.

But always send photographs anyway.

When you send a photograph, make sure it is a crisp, accurate reproduction of your work of art. A snapshot will not do, nor will interfering background. Editors prefer 5"x7" or 8"x10" black-and-white glossies. Make sure you include complete caption information, written lightly on the back so it will not show through. Slides are appropriate for large magazines and any other publications which regularly use color illustrations. Enclose a SASE and you will probably get your photo or slides back.

Conclusion

The worst press is no press.

Publicizing Yourself: Steps Toward More Than 15 Minutes of Fame

Beth Surdut

Talent and luck are not the total ingredients in the recipe for artistic survival. The media is a necessary and surprisingly friendly component if approached with a coherent printable product. Free press can boost sales more than an expensive advertisement, perhaps because of a certain validity or credibility associated with an editor's choice. I suggest the following steps because of the results. More publications have said yes to me than no—many more.

Packaging Yourself

Remember that your slides or prints, articles, and resumé may well be the only contact a writer has with your artwork. Your press release and slides need to offer all the information. Don't expect a writer or a staff photographer to do the work for you. Most publications will be content to use the high-quality slides you provide. Others will have staff photographers. Rarely, an editor will ask for specific last-minute photography at your expense. The more you provide, the stronger the chance for you to be well represented.

Homework

When I began this current round of promotion, I had already been published in a variety of periodicals. When I first sought this kind of recognition I contacted community newspapers by calling, explaining my profession, and asking for the arts editor or the appropriate writer. I explained that I would like to send a package of information about my work. I had the package ready to mail immediately while the contact was fresh.

Before mailing, check your sources for correct address and contact person. Although there are current periodical listings available in the library, offices and editors change. Look in current issues for this information. See who is writing in any department that might use your work. If your artwork is applicable in more than one section of the same magazine, send separate packages to each one, tailoring the contents to specific interests if necessary. Do not assume one package will be passed around, even if you suggest that in your cover letter. One publishing company may have three magazines that could be appropriate showcases. These must be handled individually, although if one says yes you may use that fact for leverage. Although free-lance writers might be assigned to you, the initial proposal is best sent to someone on the staff. Consider calling, both prior to the mailing to ascertain the best person and prepare them and afterwards ostensibly to make sure the package arrived at the right desk. Occasionally, I have received a return receipt only to find that my slides were still in the company mailroom. This calling routine might border on nagging, but it works. If a prestigious or exciting project comes to fruition after the first mailing, send a follow-up letter.

I have found many of the editors and their staff to be delightful and communicative. A sense of humor can ease the solicitation process as does an awareness of deadlines. Although I have spent many hours and some dollars in plotting my media blitz, I realize that an interested editor might file the information for many months, contacting me either when there is space or an appropriate theme. One magazine responded when I coincidentally called two weeks before the deadline of a group article, I was to be featured in without my knowledge. The writer was "so glad" I called. She needed more transparencies of items specific to the article, which would appear in five months. Many magazines plan months in advance, especially if they are courting advertisers for a certain theme. Another editor suggested printing in September or October, asked me to call in July, then called me in June to confirm for the August issue—he contacted me the day before deadline! If you keep sufficient materials on hand, send the information well in advance of a proposed publication date to comfortably achieve your goal.

The Package

Fine presentation is everything. Talent is not enough. To hold all of the following stuff I use a folder with pockets for presentation, as there are odd-sized materials to compile. Make life easy. These people do not have the inclination to chase piles of paper dumped out of an envelope. Here are the elements of your presentation package.

• Resumé. Put your name, address, and telephone number(s) at the top. Begin with a short statement of what you do and why. As an artist, you have the license to excite the mind—go for it! The rest of this document is dry. List your accomplishments, the owners of your artwork, the sellers and other supporters (grants), your education (not necessarily formal), and influences. Travel and experimentation are my teachers.

• Slides. Publications almost always print from slides or transparencies. Send only high-quality duplicates—you may never see them again. I usually send eight (more to an arts publication). Send no more than twenty. Label the slides clearly and legibly with the title, size, your name, and a copyright notice (©) and year (e.g., ©1992 Beth Surdut). CLEARLY DESIGNATE THE TOP—I have seen beautiful upside-down reproductions.

• Photos or color copies. Slides, gorgeous though they may be, are teeny-tiny items that will be viewed with a squint instead of a loupe, shown by available light instead of a slide projector. Thus, larger format representations of your work are needed along with the slides. I send a postcard of one of my paintings and at least one color "sell sheet" consisting of a collage of photos that I have laid out and reprinted via a color copier. I suggest 5"x7" photos if you are sending photographic prints. Include a shot of the artist at work.

• Articles. I include one black-and-white newspaper article that is very informative and has a photo of me at work. I also include any article that resembles in format the particular space I want. Many local publications have a "Finds" or "Best Buys" column, usually in color, that shows one painting and a caption or paragraph with a description and contact information. If you have been in one, send a copy. If you were included with other items that do not complement your artwork, cut and paste, including the magazine's logo and date from the front cover. If none of the interviews are representative of the image you wish to present, use excerpts, listing the titles and dates in your resumé.

• Cover letter/News release. State the highlights of your resumé in the form of a letter or article that could be printed as an advertisement. This does not necessarily have to be in the first person. My approach is an enticing review of a visit to my studio. You may need a friend to write the first draft for you to edit. There is a fine line between honest self-promotion and egotistical posturing. If you're talented—which is why you're doing this—then say so, but find a diplomatic way to state it as fact. (Good luck.) At the top of your letter, clearly list yourself as the contact person. Include an address and telephone number even though this information appears on the resumé and return envelope. Within your letter, ask them to "please review the enclosed material for your publication. If the slides are useful, please retain them for your files. If not, there is a stamped envelope included for their return." Decide how much of the package you want returned. I opt for the slides. On the SASE note the name of the magazine in the upper left corner—a surprising number of people will neglect to add a return address even though they might contact you later; others might return the entire package. Remember, this is unsolicited material sent to busy people. One editor called the day he received the slides. He left a message telling me that he would return them after printing, probably in five months. This person deserves a big kiss.

Reality Check

Be available. Knowing that this is an exercise in future planning, plan for the future. If you are nomadic, rent a post office box and a phone number—a friend or voice mail. If there is an unavoidable change in your contact information, send a card to anyone who might need to reach you.

Keep extra components on hand. Prepare more than you need for the initial mailing; produce more slides, print more resumés, etc. Procrastination paralysis can set in and you'll lose a potentially great opportunity. Time, money, and the aggravation factor are better managed if another run to the printer's can be avoided.

Know advertising policies. Magazines vary in their advertising policies. There are publications that will not present a full-blown article unless an ad is purchased. If approached by an artist directly, there is more of a chance for totally free publicity. If a gallery carries your work, there may be a catch-22 situation involving the gallery buying an ad because you're featured, and you're being featured because the gallery buys an ad. I have been asked to buy an ad myself, but I have always declined. Having provided artwork, potential copy, and unpaid labor, enough has been contributed on my part—but do not say this aloud.

Start now. The best time to start this project is now if you are regularly producing artwork that you are proud of. Take photos and get out into the world. My first major newspaper article came out within a few months of my putting my work out on the market. I called them, and they were gracious enough to see me. The very small community newspapers are a viable venue because their purpose is specifically directed towards showcasing local news. You may start here to sell yourself and your work.

Deal with rejection blues and acceptance highs. Not everyone will see the merit of your artwork. If the local arts editor isn't a kindred spirit, try another paper or another department. For example, if you're making wearables, the fashion editor may gush while the fine arts editor turns away. If your statement or cover letter lacks clarity, you may remain the only one who understands what you're doing. Don't malign or insult. Don't beg or otherwise grovel. Did you send packages to everyone possible? Your artwork might not fit the "look" of the publication. Have you done your homework? Did you brainstorm with friends who are forthright? Your personal favorites might not be the most appropriate for printing. Ask for feedback. Upon acceptance, decide whether there are newer pieces you want published. Prior to deadline, not the last minute, offer the new slides to the writer. You might consider suggesting to the art director that a cover on the month you'll be inside would be great—this is a long shot, but worth trying. Don't be greedy. Usually the cover showcase alone would merit you monetary compensation; however, the magazine is giving you free space inside, so don't be gauche by asking for money.

Keep up your balancing act. Do you tell a rival publication that you're being published? I didn't; however, after one city magazine confirmed, the editor suggested I call the editor of another publication, an airline magazine (same publisher) and use the information. Thoughtful and effective. When one magazine asked where I sold my work, I approached a few places, told them I was going to be featured in the magazine, and so would they if they bought now. This worked like a charm.

After Publication

Be prepared for the glorious onslaught! Be prepared for two weeks of fame. Understand that some people will clip out an article and call you two years later.

One great benefit to sending many press packages simultaneously is a possible run of publicity spanning a few months' time. Not only will more people know of your existence, but repetition jogs the memories, piques curiosity, and affirms your success. My current mailing has resulted in August, October, and two November publications so far. I will, of course, include these in a revised package to send on the next round.

Although the time and money spent could have been applied to painting, I feel the allotment to publicity is necessary and gratifying, especially after discussing my project after the fact with the head of a public relations firm who would have charged me a $1,500/month retainer to do the same things I did.

After you've been published, write a brief thank-you note to the writer and thank him for the article.

Passport to Fame: The Media Packet

Constance Hallinan Lagan

Many small-business owners engaged in the creative industries fail to appreciate the value of publicity and its link to long-term business survival, as demonstrated by increased sales and expanded market share, until it is too late.

Publicity puts someone else's stamp of approval on you and your work. When book publishers, magazine editors, network newscasters, public service announcers, and cable television program coordinators provide you with editorial space or air time, readers and listeners receive the impression that you must have something of value to offer. Unlike advertising, where potential customers realize that if you are paying for an advertisement you are only going to say good things about your work and yourself, publicity leaves others with the idea that an unbiased party feels you are "good."

The backbone of your publicity campaign is your media packet. The appearance and substance of this media packet is as crucial to your marketing success as the quality of your art portfolio. Although media packets are very costly and time-consuming to develop, if you devote as much time, energy, enthusiasm, and creativity to its development as you do to your actual artwork, then you will find fame—and maybe even fortune.

If you believe in the power of publicity to help you achieve name recognition, thereby increasing your sales, but you are unwilling or unable to publicize yourself, consider hiring a professional public relations firm. However, most creative individuals can generate their own media packets. So why not try it yourself—and learn as you go.

Your media packet should include as many of the following items as possible:
- Cover letter
- Bio
- One or more new press releases
- Clips of published press releases
- Clips of any other media coverage you have received
- One or more photographs of you
- One or more photographs of your work
- Tear sheets of your published articles and/or designs
- Testimonial letters (with permission of the authors)
- Letters of recommendation (with permission of the authors)
- Client list (with permission of your clients)
- Business card
- Catalog
- Brochure
- Self-addressed, stamped postcard

Package these items in a twin-pocket portfolio, complete with business card holder. Laminated, stain- and moisture-resistant portfolios serve you best.

Since the weight of most media packets places them in the priority mail category used by the U.S. Postal Service ($3.00 up to two pounds), I find United Parcel Service more economical in most cases. The UPS charge also includes insurance while the USPS does not.

Since the cost of producing and mailing a media packet is considerable, I do request the recipient acknowledge receipt. I enclose a self-addressed, stamped postcard which I ask the recipient to return to me. If this postcard is not returned to me, I follow up with a phone call. When I use UPS delivery, I seldom discover the media packet was not received. But on the rare occasion that this has happened, UPS has reimbursed me for the declared value I entered on the UPS shipping record.

Send your media packet locally, regionally, nationally, and globally to book publishers, magazine editors, network newscasters, public service announcers, and cable television program coordinators. Refer to *Ayer Directory of Publications*, *Gale's Directory*, *Ulrich's International Periodical Directory*, *The Standard Periodical*

Directory, U.S. Publicity Directory, Standard Rates & Data Service, Bacon's Publicity Checker, Writer's Market (current edition), and *Artist's Market* (current edition) for contact information. And do not overlook staff and free-lance writers; you will find listings for writers specializing in art in *Working Press of the Nation*. Most urban and suburban libraries carry these directories in their reference sections.

Do not hesitate to toot your own horn. If you do it often enough, others will begin to toot right along with you. And even after you have become well known, do not ease up on the publicity efforts. My grandmother would often repeat a caveat she had heard growing up: "Don't rest on your laurels too long—or you will find yourself sitting on poison ivy."

Be patient, be persistent—and you will be famous.

The Local Art Critic Speaks

Roberta Morgan

I review shows that are on display in Montgomery County, Maryland, the county that my newspapers cover. I'm not a famous writer for a large city newspaper, but someone like me will write about your work long before the big-name critics do. In this article I will offer a behind-the-scenes look at how a local art critic covers her beat and how an artist has a better shot at having his work reviewed.

My readers are primarily people who are trying to decide whether it's worth it to make a trip to the local art center this weekend. If they find my opinions reliable, and if they find themselves learning about the work they see, then I will have done my job.

I tour spaces within the county, but when the same artists have a show in Washington, D.C.—the closest major city—I don't follow them there. When scheduling my reviews, I focus on the spaces I visit. This actually works in favor of a new artist, because this space-oriented approach tends to channel me more toward the works of people I haven't heard of.

To feature shows while they are on view, my editor and I must plan my column as much as two months ahead of time. This means that interesting work I hear about in spaces I cover can be missed in my column if I don't hear about it early enough.

In fact, I find that the timeliness of a press release can be its most important feature. I get a flood of news releases, and my editor gets even more. I rarely read more than a few paragraphs in each, looking for the basics of time and place—the same information you would put on an invitation—and a paragraph about what the work looks like and why. Therefore, extra information like your resumé, aesthetic manifestos, bios, or a statement about your work really doesn't help me very much, and doesn't help your chances of getting reviewed.

Color photographs aren't helpful to me; if your show makes it to my schedule, I will look at the work itself, and I happen to believe in writing about work that I see rather than work I am trying to remember with a photograph. The basics of my reviews I jot down in the gallery to avoid any confusion I might have once I'm distanced from the work.

However, sending good black-and-white photographs is a good idea because one of them has a fair chance of being reproduced with the review.

Let me tell you one more story about press releases. There is a small space in Montgomery County that is a little farther for me to drive to. But because of their press releases, I regularly plan on reviewing their shows. The news releases start coming three months before a show is installed, and fresh copies of the original press release come each week. Sometimes I get annoyed by this flood of the same thing I've already seen, and maybe it is environmentally insensitive, but you have to admit, it does the job. I always know what the space is showing and when.

I work to see a show as early as possible, usually before the opening. I like to see the show alone so I can sit there and write about the art. I tend to avoid openings of shows I write about, even when they are the first opportunity to see work, because openings are a terrible environment for contemplation and writing.

Once, my editor had a lengthy phone call from a distressed artist who hadn't seen me at her opening, and was therefore sure that we had decided to pass her show by. My editor explained that my review of the artist's show was sitting on her desk and that she was in fact reading it when the artist called!

For some artists the problem isn't getting reviewed, it's that they don't like the review they get. (I personally don't really mind talking with an artist about my impressions of the work, though I doubt if most other critics want that type of letter or phone call.) I have noticed from such discussions that most artists who are offended by a review have taken my words in the most negative way—a way that actually distorts what I have written.

But sometimes there is no such consolation. The critic genuinely hates the work and the artist must live with that. Remember that the value of critical opinion is its honesty, and every artist will face both sides of that.

Bear in mind that even a carefully written opinion is an opinion, nothing more. Some things that are said will be valid, some will not be, and artists must decide for themselves which is which. However, the things that will hurt the most are the things that are a little bit true, and you don't want to discard a statement because of the hurt without benefiting from the truth it contains.

One thing an artist can't say to me is that I don't know what it's like to be an artist. In fact, I spend more time painting than writing. This is often the case for local critics—usually they are artists with a sideline.

Writing reviews can be a good exercise for visual artists. The exercise offers an opportunity for the artist actually to practice those things you hope for in a critic. Artists who write reviews help to relieve the perennial problem of good work never getting the proper coverage. An extra benefit is that artist-critics get to know other artists and gallery administrators and become known by them as well.

If you would like to try writing reviews, take some writing samples to the editor of a local newspaper. Together you should be able to come up with a plan that is good for everybody. Beware of conflicts of interest—remember that your job is to present an objective view to the public. It is unethical to use a review column to promote your friends. Stick to writing about work you only know professionally.

The process starts there, and you will want to work at improving your reviews once you start writing them. Read the work of other critics and learn from them. Sometimes you will be able to talk with other art writers, and that can help you grow as well. Instead of being an artist longing to be written about, you will have become someone with a different perspective on the whole issue.

Collecting Your Press Coverage: Using Clipping Services

Peggy Hadden

Let's suppose you have been given a show of your work some distance from your home. After you have mailed out your press releases to the newspaper, radio and television outlets in the local vicinity of the exhibition and written notes to local critics asking them to see the show (and hopefully review it), you hit a stone wall. With the exception of the gallery personnel where you are exhibiting, you have no one to watch the press and see if your publicity has been effective. Unless you buy all the papers in the area every day while your show is up, you could miss a great review of your work.

Because one good word leads to the next, you can't afford to miss a positive review. That review could lead to another exhibition or an offer by a local gallery to carry your work. At the least, you'll want to include the press clipping in your presentation portfolio so you can impress people who might then be more inclined to help you if they read a positive review. What to do?

I, too, have experienced the above scenario. Because of what I've learned, I have good news for you.

Thinking back, I remembered once working as a temp—trying, as an artist, to support myself by working odd hours whenever I had the time—and being sent to work for a large public relations firm. My job consisted of gluing newspaper articles, which had been neatly clipped, into big photo albums. These albums were being prepared for the client to validate the public relations firm's activities on their behalf. I noticed that these clippings all had little paper tags with names and addresses of clipping services on them. Ever on the lookout for career information for myself, I wondered: Could an individual hire a service like this? What would it cost?

A visit to my favorite periodical—the local Yellow Pages—led me to search under "Newspapers," for listings for newspaper clipping services. Newspaper clipping services watch the papers in their area for items that their clients have told them to watch for. A phone call to one of the services I found connected me to a woman whose son happened to be an artist. (We are everywhere!) She explained the entire process to me—I was delighted to learn that clipping services are very flexible and affordable. They are there for the length of time you need them, at reasonable rates, and then, when no longer needed, they're gone until you need them the next time.

My experience with an out-of-town exhibition happened in an area of New Jersey made up of many small towns, mostly served by weekly papers. It would have been impossible to follow my news release and watch for reviews during the month my show was up. If I bought every paper in the locality of my exhibition every time they published for the length of time the show was up, it would have been a lot of money and I still would have needed to travel constantly to be where those papers are available.

Clipping services are everywhere. The New Jersey Clipping Service, the one I used, covers the press in New York, Pennsylvania, New England, and Washington, DC, and works with a national clipping service that keeps an eye on the press nationwide. Ruth Book, the vice president and general manager, said, "Often we'll request a copy of your press release and circulate it to our readers to familiarize them with your information. If your exhibition has a name, we'll look for that, too. We check for anything that carries the name of the artist, as well as the name of the gallery or exhibition space. Then we also check listings by date under the 'culture' column. Finally, we look under general information, in the local 'happenings' or 'goings on' columns. We cover daily papers, weeklies, special Sunday editions, college newspapers, the ethnic press, the religious papers, and magazines. Among magazines, we can watch the trade and consumer titles, as well as those for general interest readers."

The more information you can give your clipping service, the more likely they will be to spot all your coverage. Be sure to give them a list of critics to whom you have written and a copy of any photographs you have sent out.

The charges for using a clipping service depend on what you want. If you need them to watch the entire Northeast, including college papers, for instance, the charge would be different than if they were watching only papers for one city. The minimum length of time for which they will work is one month regionally, and three months for national coverage. This could include art magazines, whose publication time is traditionally slower than that of newspapers. There is a small clipping charge (about 50¢) for each item found and sent to you. The cost would run about $100 a month for regional coverage, $400 for a national watch. You receive clippings from a service about two weeks after publication.

Interestingly, clipping services are also able to track radio and TV coverage. Say, for example, you traveled to the opening of your show and the local TV station's camera crew was there, or that you were interviewed for the local station. Or you were in a show with several artists who presented a half-hour panel discussion on the works in the exhibition. The coverage might be caught if you had a friend in the area with a VCR, but usually events like this are lost forever once they have occurred. There might have been comments or discussion about your work that you wish you could have saved. By contacting a clipping service in the area, before or even shortly after the film clip was aired, you'll enjoy the satisfaction of knowing that you can view and evaluate the clip later, at your leisure.

Services like this are valuable to the artist, because it can stretch your "staff" when you can't be everywhere at once. Even if you don't presently have a situation in front of you where this information could come in handy, file it for the future. You never know.

CHAPTER 13

Getting Your Artwork into Magazines

"Exhibiting" Your Work in Magazines

Debora Meltz

In the last two years I have had six solo shows and participated in several group exhibitions around the country—and I have not sold a single piece. Clearly I am not doing this for the money. All my solo shows were at nonprofit spaces or college galleries, all of whose audiences are notoriously "financially challenged."

If, like me, you are an artist because you love making art, and because you find it marginally more satisfying than hitting yourself over the head with a brick, it is likely that your primary objective is having your work seen. The big question is how to get it seen. And where.

Experience, as well as common sense, tells us that commercial galleries are not interested in artwork that doesn't sell. Nonprofit spaces are too few and underfunded.

Stop thinking of gallery-style shows as the only venue for artwork. There are many other ways of getting your work seen.

For example, many publications use fine art to accompany articles or to illustrate the covers. Now, don't wrinkle your nose and think, "Aacckk, illustration." Wrong. Using the system I'm writing about, you're not being commissioned to produce a work for a specific article or topic. Your art is being chosen to complement the text, not illustrate it. Besides, what's so terrible about illustration anyway? Some of the most interesting and intriguing art around is or was considered to be illustration. The commercial publishing world has always used fine art as illustration, often preferring the Old Masters because they don't have to be paid.

I learned about "showing" my work in magazines unexpectedly. A few years ago I was contacted by an editor who had seen my brochure at the home of a friend who works for an arts organization.

I was a bit leery of how my work would be utilized and reproduced. Would it be cropped to fit the space? Would the quality of the reproduction be good? Would the feeling, meaning, or visual impact of the work be altered? Yes, yes, and no. The work was cropped, but in such a way as not to alter any of its essence. I was consulted and asked for my input. My work was accorded respect, and so was I.

The finished product was excellent and, to tell the truth, it was exciting to see my work in print in this context. The magazine also printed a little blurb about me and my artwork at the end of the article. And—get this—I got paid!

I have had other work used in magazines, as well as on the cover of a quarterly publication. I was concerned about the cover copy competing with or ruining the appearance of my work, but the end result looked fine. The editor had taken pains to integrate the image with the type in such a way as to encroach upon the artwork as little as possible. It was obvious that a good deal of care and consideration had gone into planning the cover.

Finding publications that will use your work is pretty much the same as finding exhibition spaces: You have to do research. Many fine magazines are special interest or regional. Pick up a copy of *The Writer's Market* and browse through it for publications whose subject matter or message seem to fit with your work. Then, when you find one or more good prospects, request a copy of the magazine(s). Many publications will send you a sample issue upon request, sometimes free of charge. That way you can see whether your work really would fit in and whether the magazine is one in which you would want your work to appear.

Send a brochure or a small packet of photographs to the editor with a cover letter suggesting that your work might be appropriate for the publication. You can note that the excellent quality of the magazine's art inspired you to send samples of your own work. Keep the letter concise and to-the-point, but be sure to make it clear that you are a fine artist and are offering work that already exists rather than looking for an assignment or commission.

Don't send slides. You want to grab the editor's attention quickly and easily. Slides require effort on the part of the recipient. If the magazine is interested in your work, the editor will request slides or transparencies.

It is not necessary, and it may be counterproductive, to send support materials like a resumé, statement, etc. Magazines are not galleries, so they are interested in what your work looks like, not your track record. Don't clutter up your presentation. Again, if the editor is interested, he will ask for more information.

Include a business-sized stamped self-addressed envelope (SASE) for the editor's response. It is preferable to send material that you don't need returned—personally, I send a brochure which I invite the editor to keep for future reference—but if you want it back, be sure the return envelope is large enough and has sufficient postage. Always, always send a SASE.

A few magazines reproduce art for its own sake. Some will even do a folio of artwork, and a brief profile of the artist, if the editor thinks readers will find it of interest. If you have a particular piece or a body of work that has a specific message you think might appeal to the readership of a particular publication, put together a compact presentation packet of photographs along with a brief commentary on the work.

Magazines that publish poetry, fiction, and essays are often on the lookout for interesting art. They tend to print only in black and white, so bear that in mind if such a publication wants to use your work. I have had color pieces reproduced quite satisfactorily in black and white, so don't dismiss it out of hand. Remember, the point is to get your work seen. The quality of the reproduction will depend in large part on the quality of the slide or print you give the magazine.

As someone who has done a fair amount of editing, I would like to stress that editors are swamped with all sorts of stuff and are chronically short on time. Make your presentation simple, attractive, and user-friendly.

Magazines and periodicals generally work at least six months in advance. An editor will often file something he finds interesting and get around to responding to it a year or more later. Don't bother querying the magazine about your submission. You will only annoy the assistant editor.

If you get a positive response, great. If you receive a negative reply, don't cross that publication off your list. Make a note of the name of the editor and check back in about a year. Also, the turnover rate in publishing can reach whirlwind proportions, and the next editor might love your work.

A publication is under no obligation to reply in any manner to unsolicited material, even if you've enclosed a SASE, so send off your material and forget about it.

Payment for your work will vary from one publication to another. Some will actually pay real money, some not much, and others will pay only in copies. Some of the smaller, more limited publications are so strapped for funds that you will get only one copy and you'll have to purchase more if you want them.

I look upon work published as a form of advertising. It isn't unheard of for an editor to be contacted in regard to the artwork printed in a magazine, especially if a line or two about the artist is included. Other publications might wish to use your work. One editor bought a poster of a piece of mind that she had seen in my photo packet.

Magazines and periodicals can provide an excellent, relatively easy way to reach an audience that might otherwise never see your work.

Before you submit anything, make sure it is copyrighted.

Also, I have been asked only for, and will grant only, one-time rights. Be sure the magazine understands that as a fine artist you own, will continue to own, will continue to exhibit, and own the copyright and all other rights on, the artwork. This has never presented a problem for me. In fact, the publications I've dealt with have been delighted that the works reproduced in their magazines were being exhibited concurrently.

If you have any doubts or questions, consult a legal guide for artists; *The Writer's Market* has a section on contracts and rights; and/or consult a qualified attorney.

Giving Artists Exposure: The Open Studios Press

Drew Steis

When Herbert Gliick and his wife, Althea, travel by automobile, they like to stop at roadside diners for meals. They consult the guide *Road Food*, by Michael and Jane Stearn, a region-by-region review of the cuisine of small diners and roadside restaurants.

Gliick, once publisher of the popular *Offshore* magazine for boaters, is also an art collector. He wondered why the concept of a regional guide to good food could not be used to highlight the works of artists, region by region.

Thus was born the New England *New American Paintings*, the first of a planned series of seven regional books—a no-fees, no-strings showcase for emerging artists in America.

"Collecting each edition of *New American Paintings* over the months and years should enable an art lover to follow the evolution of painting by many of the most talented emerging artists in America—subject, of course, to the vagaries of juries which will change from region to region, edition to edition," the introduction to the first edition reads. "It also should enable the collector to discover talent at its source. Addresses and telephone numbers are included for each artist."

There are no entry fees, jury fees, commissions on sales, or any other costs to the artists selected for inclusion in the publication. Each artist is given a two-page spread with four or more four-color reproductions of his or her art, a brief biographical narrative, a photograph of the artist, and the artist's signature. The publisher pays for color separations and even gives the participating artist one free copy of the book.

A Massachusetts artist told *Art Calendar* she had "sales and a one-person show as a result of being selected for the first edition." Her gallery in Boston is now selling the book.

"The first edition was the hardest," said Steven Zevitas, editor of the series, and a painter himself. "We had a lot of calls initially from artists wary of vanity book publishers. When we first started the project there was going to be a cost to the artist. The artist would not pay to be in the book but would bear the cost and responsibility of having the color separations of their work made. Once we heard how uncomfortable artists were with vanity publications, we dropped that idea because we wanted to establish our credibility and attract more artists to the project. So we charge no fees to the artist whatsoever."

Artists were solicited by a direct mailing of 6,000 names gathered from recommendations made by local and state arts agencies, gallery directors, art critics, consultants, agents, collectors, and friends. Zevitas made numerous studio and gallery visits scouting for candidates. An in-house jury was set up to help principal juror Joseph Thompson, who is executive director of the Massachusetts Museum of Contemporary Art in North Adams, MA. His selections were augmented by a panel consisting of a Boston area art collector, an art therapist, a professional illustrator, publisher Gliick, and editor Zevitas.

The work resulted in a practical guide to painters of all styles in the New England area. Prices of the work shown are included, as the introduction notes, "for guidance only, and reflect what the artist would ask for a particular work [at the time of publication]. The works shown are not necessarily for sale, although most were when the competition began." Prices of work shown range from $240 to $32,000 with the majority of work priced between $1,000 and $2,500.

"We sent out about a thousand books over time to collectors, curators, critics, journalists," Zevitas said. "Almost half of the initial printing of six thousand has been sold or is in the distribution chain. We are moving ahead with the next books."

"Artists working around the country rely on their immediate geographic area for galleries, local shows and competitions, and exposure to the market," said Zevitas. "Part of the use of this book is to give artists a way to show their work to people outside of their geographic area—to let collectors in Texas and California see the work of outstanding and up-and-coming Boston and New England artists."

The Open Studios Press is interested in hearing from painters in all of those regions. Send a sheet of 35mm slides, resumé, and SASE to Steven Zevitas, Editor, The Open Studios Press, 66 Central St, Wellesley, MA 02181. Please remember that individual submissions will not be acknowledged but that all materials will eventually be returned. If your work is selected for inclusion in one of the upcoming editions you will be contacted before publication. Copies of the New England and Mid-Atlantic editions can be ordered at the above address.

Interview with C. D. Clarke, Sporting Artist: Painting for the Hunting and Fishing Trade

Drew Steis

C. D. Clarke started out studying forestry but turned to art. Today, in his forties, he is an award-winning landscape artist who is well on his way to establishing an international reputation for his sporting art.

Clarke, an avid hunter and fisherman, is also serious about his art. He talks openly about how he developed both his art and his art marketing plan.

Clarke credits his knowledge of hunting and fishing for the success of his sporting art. He has successfully combined his love of the outdoors with a career as a painter. Well known for his landscapes, his watercolors have been run on the covers of two major historical nonfiction books. The night before this interview, he had just returned to the United States after a two-week, expenses-paid painting and fishing trip to the out islands of the Bahamas, where he was helping his host, one of his most loyal collectors, map out anchorages and fishing spots for future expeditions.

"I have always had two strong interests: art and the outdoors. I started out in college going for the outdoors end in a program that would have put me into the Forestry School at Syracuse University. After one semester I realized that forestry was chemistry and math so I turned to art." He then devoted himself full-time to painting.

The grand-nephew of Ethel Nixon, whose abstract oils hang in the Canadian National Gallery, and a cousin of Albert Murray, the well-known portrait artist, Clarke also counts the watercolorist Ogden Pleissner among his teachers and mentors.

"I did nothing but art for three years but then I got out of art school and had the same problem a lot of art students have. You're kind of flung out on the street without the support base art school is. All of a sudden you're not among other artists. There is no teacher giving you assignments—you're completely on your own. Not only do you have no way of knowing how to market your work and make a living at it, in many cases you don't really know what you want to do in terms of your painting. There are no assignments, no figure drawing classes eight hours a day twice a week. That's what happened to me. I just didn't have the discipline to put together a studio and paint every day, to get out every day and do landscapes on location the way I do now. There was probably a good year or two after art school when I sort of floundered around working part-time jobs and didn't know what the hell I was going to do. I think I was fooling myself that I was an artist while not really creating much and certainly not marketing."

Clarke worked as a waiter, tree planter at a nursery, and as a ceramist's assistant. But he continued to paint.

"I had to pull myself up by my own bootstraps. I said, Listen buddy, if you want to be an artist you'd better get a move on. I started painting on location in watercolor just everything around me here on the Eastern Shore. That's really what saved me—the discipline of forcing myself to go out in the field and paint every day. It didn't matter how the paintings came out, just do them. I had a lot of encouragement from Al Murray. He encouraged me to just paint and that's what I did. And that's when I learned to enjoy the process of watercolor and also learn everything I could about landscape. I got a lot out of Syracuse University but none of my knowledge that I use now as a landscape painter came from Syracuse other than maybe basic drawing skills. All my knowledge of light and how things should be recorded and responded to in the outdoors came from those years of working outdoors on location. That's the most important thing an artist can do. I can't imagine a more valuable thing than having a required class where students have to take whatever medium they want out into the field and paint. It is required that they draw and paint the figure, it should be required that they go into the landscape. It shouldn't matter whether they are abstract painters or whatever, because what you learn about light and color is indispensable."

Marketing came "after getting my painting in line. It was fired by guilt mostly. You're almost 30 years old, and what are you doing with yourself? I know there are artists who are strong enough people that they can just paint and not care whether they ever sell or not. I wasn't one of those. There was enough Puritan work ethic in me that I felt I had to make money in this."

Clarke credits his wife Iris with supporting him both emotionally and financially during his early career. Fame and fortune did not come overnight.

"There was such an evolution in my work as I was painting outdoors because a year later it all seemed like garbage so I wouldn't even want it included in my body of work. I was doing hundreds of watercolors a year. I was frequently doing two a day and I can remember days when I would do four. I still have a few pieces I've kept, and there are a few in collections from those early years, that I still consider almost as good as I can do now. But they're one out of fifty." He threw away about three-quarters of the work from those years.

"The art I started marketing seriously on a national level was sporting art. I guess like water I take the path of least resistance. I could see conceptually a marketing plan for selling sporting work—first getting my work into national magazines that sold sporting art and that would expose me to a lot of people who are potential collectors of sporting work. I have gone after that market the hardest and had the most success with it."

C. D. Clarke's first break came after sending a series of slides to *Gray's Sporting Journal*.

"I think with the first group of slides I sent them I got very lucky. They were doing a photo essay on the decline of black ducks and the fact that there were still people who hunted black duck marshes for the tradition of it. One of the paintings I submitted happened to be a still life of a single hanging dead black duck and it just fit so perfectly with the theme of their article that they grabbed it. It also happened to be one of those early paintings that was ahead of its time. I can still look at it, even though it was five or six years ago, and say yeah, that's a nice painting."

The lucky timing of that unsolicited submission led to the sale of the original painting to a Texas collector two weeks after the magazine was published. "It was a thrilling experience and looking back on it, it really inspired me to keep going. As weak-kneed as I was in marketing and unsure of myself, that was the very positive push that told me yes, this is the right thing to do. You can make it."

The art director of *Gray's* recommended several New England galleries that might be interested in representing Clarke. On a trip to the area, Clarke was steered by a gallery owner to the offices of *Fly Rod and Reel* magazine, where the editor promptly used the first of a continuing series of his work. Then *Field and Stream* began to use his work. Clarke's work has accompanied articles on everything from salmon fishing to bird hunting to big game rifles. Sportsmen began to offer him commissions of everything from their favorite hunting dog to on-location portraits of sportsmen in the field, in streams and ponds, marshes and lakes.

"This shows the one-thing-leads-to-another approach that has characterized the marketing I've done, the networking."

While continuing to illustrate sporting articles for several magazines, Clarke began showing his work at a number of prestigious juried exhibitions including the Adirondacks National Watercolor Exhibition, the Gold Room show at the Easton Waterfowl Festival, and at the American Museum of Fly Fishing. At one of these exhibitions he met a major collector and sportsman who invited Clarke to paint in Canada and the Florida Keys. That collector remains a friend today and has recommended Clarke's work to other wealthy sportsmen.

Admiration for his watercolors of bone fishing on the Florida flats resulted in his original paintings being selected two years in a row as the Grand Prize in the prestigious Annual Celebrity Red Bone Fishing Tournament in Islamorada, Florida.

Clarke has hunted, fished, and painted all over the United States and in foreign climes ranging from Scotland to Chile and Argentina. Not only does the travel help produce subject matter for painting, it also provides part of his formula for success. "Credibility—building credibility—is everything. It may repulse a lot of artists that credibility is important—that your work isn't just judged on its artistic basis. But it helps me to be able to say that I've been to these places because that is where other great sporting artists do their work."

C. D. Clarke lets past and potential collectors know of his recent trips and paintings via an occasional newsletter and a glossy four-color brochure. He estimates that a quarter to a half of his sales are to repeat customers.

His advice to other artists is to "keep your mind open, keep your eyes open. Look for markets, compile good contact lists. Network, network, network. That has been the key because eventually, if you keep track of those things, the pieces to the puzzle start to fit together. And the more they fit together, the stronger the structure is, and the more sales develop.

"The perfect example of this was yesterday when I was leaving the Bahamas. I met some people with fly rod cases at the airport. This is how things fit together. I gave them my promo piece which lists things like work published in *Gray's*, *Fly Rod and Reel*, *Field and Stream*—which is credibility. These people know a good friend of mine, and I find out one of them is on the board of Orvis, the fishing equipment manufacturer which is involved with the American Museum of Fly Fishing where I know people. They know people I know, they fit into my plan in six or seven different ways. I got a card, another name for my mailing list. They have my promo piece. They know because of our fishing conversation that I know the sport, they have a sense that I am a credible artist because they not only saw some of my work but read that I am established.

"The potential for a sale there—because of all these things, because of the people I know, because of my knowledge of the sport, because of the credibility I've built up by being published—the chance of a sale there is pretty good. But without all of the pieces, that strength in the possibility of a sale doesn't exist. There is a real synapse of how it all works.

"One can say that maybe I would have done more paintings if I had stayed at home but that is not networking and that is how, at least for me, it seems to be working. I think marketing schemes for artists evolve and you have to be flexible and open enough to see the structure as it forms on its own."

CHAPTER 14

Getting Your Writing into Magazines

The Art and Benefits of Wordsmithing

Constance Hallinan Lagan

Diversity demands creativity. To set forth in a different direction, to meander across new territory, to stray from the expected path is stimulating and often results in new visions, which eventually translate into original pieces of art or craft.

The immediate result of diversity, however, can also be financially rewarding, rendering additional sources of income. If you always colored outside the lines as a child, if you always found the fourth way when your high school teacher insisted there were only three solutions, if you broke all the rules and still rose on the corporate ladder, you are probably a prime candidate for diversity. Diversification requires the ability to see opportunity in chaos, challenge in difficulties, possibility in the impossible.

Diversify and consider writing for publication.

If you are like most of my artist/artisan clients, you might erroneously believe you have nothing to say (with words, that is). You have spent so much of your life creating visual impressions that the idea of creating with words seems foreign. However, you do have material galore waiting to be explored and shared—verbally. All you need to do is run that rake through your brain cells, combing marketable thoughts and ideas from unsalable ones.

Begin writing about what you know very well and eventually work your way into the unknown. One of the most rewarding ancillary benefits I have enjoyed as a writer is to be paid to learn. When a topic whets my appetite, I query an editor and often get the go-ahead to attend a concert in Manhattan, to travel to an out-of-state exhibit, to do research at the Yale Library—and I get paid to do this!

Finding editors who will be interested in your topics begins with researching the current issues of *The Writer's Market* and *Literary Marketplace*. Both publications list thousands of periodicals by subjects of interest. Information regarding rights purchased, manuscript length, payment policy, tips on querying, and much more is given with each listing.

Compile a list of publications you would enjoy writing for and send for each publication's writer's guidelines. These guidelines will provide additional information, such as topics covered in each upcoming issue (editorial calendars), deadlines, manuscript style, etc. Be sure to enclose a self-addressed stamped envelope (SASE) with your request.

After you have absorbed all the information available in *The Writer's Market*, *Literary Marketplace*, and the individual publications' writer's guidelines, compose a query letter. This one-page communication can begin with a real attention-getting opening: a startling statistic, a humorous quote, a shocking anecdote. Then outline your article briefly, including an approximate word count and tentative title. Include your publishing history, if you have one, along with clips of previously published works; if you have never been published, skip mentioning this fact. State your credentials for writing on the topic. Be sure to include a SASE.

If the editor is interested in perusing a completed manuscript, he will contact you. If he does request the article, remember that all he is agreeing to do is read, not buy. If the editor wants to purchase rights to your completed manuscript, you will negotiate rights and payment with him.

Before you know it, you will have your own byline.

And, perhaps to your everlasting astonishment, the thrill of reading your first byline may equal—even surpass—the excitement you experienced the first time you saw your artwork hung in a gallery or your craft work displayed in a permanent collection.

Books for More Information
- Burgett, Gordon, *Query Letters, Cover Letters: How They Sell Your Writing*, Communication Unlimited.
- Cool, Lisa Collier, *How to Write Irresistible Query Letters*, Writer's Digest Books.
- Cool, Lisa Collier, *How to Sell Every Magazine Article You Write*, Writer's Digest Books.
- Polking, Kirk, ed., *Writing A to Z*, Writer's Digest Books.

Magazines and Newsletters for More Information
- *Freelance Writer's Report*, Cassell Communications, Box 9844, Fort Lauderdale, FL 33310.

- *Publisher's Weekly*, 249 W. 17th St., New York, NY 10011.
- *The Writer*, 120 Boylston St., Boston, MA 02116.
- *Writer's Digest*, 1507 Dana Ave., Cincinnati, OH 45207.
- *Writer's Journal*, Minnesota Ink, Box 9148, St. Paul, MN 55109.

Trade Associations for More Information

- American Guild of Authors and Composers, 40 W. 57th St., New York, NY 10019.
- American Society of Journalists and Authors, 1501 Broadway, New York, NY 10036.
- Associated Business Writers of America, 1450 S. Havana St., Aurora, CO 80012.
- Comedy Writers Association, Box 023304, Brooklyn, NY 11202.
- Newsletter Association, 1341 G St., N.W., #700, Washington, DC 20004.
- P.E.N. American Center, 47 Fifth Ave., New York, NY 10003.
- Writers Guild of America, 555 W. 57th St., New York, NY 10019; 8955 Beverly Blvd., Los Angeles, CA 90048.

More on Writing for Publication

Carolyn Blakeslee

If an editor thinks enough of you to print your writing in her publication, recognize that she is giving you a tremendous career opportunity. The bona fide of publication can go a long way to boosting your art career. Please treat editors with respect. Editors are busy people with literally thousands of people to take care of, so limit your phone calls and demands.

Just as you should be familiar with the artwork a gallery is attracted to before you submit your portfolio to its director, you should be familiar with the look and feel of the magazines to which you want to submit work. After you've received the writer's guidelines, if you haven't actually seen a copy of the magazine, obtain one: Call area libraries to see if they subscribe to it, check the newsstands, or send a token courtesy amount (say, $5) to receive a sample issue. Pay attention to the magazine's editorial emphasis. For example, *Art Calendar* publishes profiles of artists, but they are much different from the interviews published in the other art magazines. *Art Calendar* artist interviews come from the point of view of how the artist has built a career, how he has managed to carve out a living in the arts, how he has built an exhibition record and schedule, the goals he has, and so on.

Learn what the publishing industry's ethical standards are. For example, if you write for *Art Calendar*, the height of insult would be to steal its listings for your own art league's newsletter.

Always inform an editor if your submission has been published before, if you are simultaneously submitting it elsewhere, or if you plan to submit it elsewhere within the next few months—if an editor accepts your article for publication thinking it's an original piece but finds out later that it was a reprint, your writing relationship with that magazine could end right there.

Even if you own the copyright on your article, inform the editor of the journal your article first appeared in whenever someone else wants to reprint your work; editors have a responsibility to be aware of where materials first published in their magazines go.

Be sure to use responsible journalism. Hearsay doesn't cut it; you need solid information that can be traced to reputable individuals. Integrity is essential.

Finally, your editors are genuinely interested in knowing what you're doing. Whenever you have an exhibition, give a lecture, receive an honor, or get published in another journal, let your editors know. Send them news releases and show invitations. Your activities in the field could lead to further activity with the publication(s) you write for—but your editors can't know what you're up to unless you tell them.

PART 4

Personal Appearances

The Tree of Life, 1997, oxidation fired to cone 06,
22" x 16" x 16", Doris H. Miller, San Antonio, Texas

CHAPTER 15

Low-Pressure Public Appearances

Take Your Work to Slide Nights

Peggy Hadden

Until recently, I'll admit, I was scared to go to an open slide night and show my work. In fact, I've decided my hesitation was pretty normal. Having attended several of these events, however, I've decided to stand up and vouch for them and, further, advise you of what they can offer you as an artist.

Slide nights are informal events planned by artists or artist-oriented groups so they can show their work and get feedback from other artists. If you are a newcomer to the area, slide nights are an excellent way to meet other artists. I think slide nights are tremendously underrated. Look at what you can gain by taking your work, and yourself, to an event like this:

• *Technical Help*. If a technical problem has you mystified, bring it along and ask for suggestions for solving it. At one slide night I attended, a question arose about how to keep works on paper from buckling. Within five minutes, there was more information brought out on ways to avoid buckling than I've seen in years of running to technical manuals and querying art supply manufacturers.

• *See What Other Artists Are Doing*. Slide nights usually attract artists of different ages and varying ranges of experience. If you haven't been to the galleries recently, this is a great way to catch up on new styles of working, aesthetic concerns being addressed, and just plain fads circulating in the art world. It's like hitting ten or fifteen galleries in an evening, all the time sitting down!

• *Get a Better Focus on Your Work*. By showing slides of your work, you will (a) see what your slides really look like, or how they can be improved, (b) get the immediate reaction of others who see lots of artwork and have the same problem you have getting artwork to come across on slides, and (c) find out which works others like best (probably not the ones you like!). Ask them why, and learn from what they tell you. You've been looking at these pieces so long, you might not be seeing the same painting they are.

• *Get Sharper at Seeing What Works.* When you see four or five slides from someone else, your ego is removed. It isn't your work. You can see stronger compositions vs. weaker ones. Now, go back to the studio and apply that objective knowledge to your own work. This works even if your art is completely different in style or media from another artist.

• *You Might Get Curatorial Ideas.* At the slide nights I attend most often, many ideas for group shows have been born on the spot. Quite simply, all the right elements are there to make it happen. I also know that curators working on future shows turn up at these nights to scout for just the right work to add to their show.

• *Make New Allies for Ways of Seeing/Showing Art.* There is so much conversation around the subject of art, you might hear ideas or articles discussed that completely agree with how you feel. You'll hear the pros and cons of ideas like showing work in alternative spaces, showing work in churches, and even taking work to poorer neighborhoods. This might give you a lot to think about—I met an artist who curates shows at a local food stamp center.

• *You Might Meet an Artist You Would Like to Work and/or Show With.* Stranger things have happened. Either his work is so completely different that the two of you might give a dynamic exhibition, or maybe you are addressing the same topic in two distinctly separate but equally vital ways. Even if you two only exchange studio visits, the relationship could prove beneficial to both of you.

Preparing for Slide Night

To get the maximum feedback and enjoyment from a slide night, here are some suggestions.

• Take fewer, rather than more, slides. Contact the person organizing the event; ask how many slides are shown on the average. If you take too many, you'll deprive yourself of other artists' responses and end up with less usable information.

• Show slides from one body of work. Mixing slides of sculpture, photographs, collage, and drawings will water down your presentation and the responses. Come back another night to present another group of work.

• Practice presenting your slides and anticipate the questions you'll get. Do this in front of a mirror so you don't stumble through the presentation later and get so nervous you forget the response. The idea of slide night is to rehearse for even more important presentations later.

• Be flexible—you'll learn more. I have found artists to be incredibly sensitive and caring audiences. At a slide night, you will be participating as both presenter and audience. What you give to other artists is as important as what you'll receive.

Now—go, listen, and have a good time!

Creative Networking

Constance Hallinan Lagan

What do threads holding patches together, electrical wires stretching between power lines, and railroad tracks extending from station to station all have in common with networks? They are all connectors. A creative network functions as a bridge between needs and means. It connects, providing solutions to problems and answers to questions. It connects, offering options, alternatives, and resources. It connects, empowering those on both ends of the connector with personal and career enhancement, enrichment and advancement.

When done creatively, networking creates an environment of giving. You introduce yourself to others in a way that indicates you are willing, even anxious, to help them reach their goals and that you hope they are likewise interested in assisting you to fulfill your aspirations.

Advantages

The advantages of networking are threefold. First, you reach more potential clients, suppliers, sponsors, and mentors through an ever-expanding number of network contacts (people who are spreading the word about your artistic talents) within a relatively short period of time than you ever could on your own in your entire lifetime. Second, you often find yourself riding on the coattails of those who have gone before you and who have established themselves in a positive light within their own circle of clients, suppliers, sponsors, and mentors. Third, you enjoy the intrinsic reward of knowing you have helped others.

Disadvantages

Yes, there can be a few disadvantages to networking if you do not beware of certain natural pitfalls. If you network indiscriminately, you risk being used by people who have no intention of reciprocating. You might also jeopardize your good name by being associated with someone who does not have a favorable reputation within his own, or your, circle.

The best protection against these two potentially disastrous situations is to develop and trust your intuitive sense. If you have any qualms or misgivings about a particular individual, do not add them to your network. Do not feel guilty for judging someone's networking potential based upon no more than an initial impression. There are literally millions of fantastic people with whom to network; there is no need to endanger your own credibility by being connected to someone with whom you do not feel comfortable. Especially avoid naysayers, gossipmongers, and those with questionable ethics.

Initiating a Networking Exchange

Whenever you find yourself in a new group of people, walk up to someone you have never met before and introduce yourself, using an effective, yet brief, tag line (description of who you are and what you do, e.g., "I am Joe Smithson and my photographs are currently on display at Uptown Art Gallery") while shaking hands. Ask what the other person does for a living. Try to find out what her concerns are—for example, finding wholesale art supply sources, developing a promising mentorship, locating upscale galleries that are open to new artists. Offer some bit of information that you feel might help her: a new wholesaler who recently exhibited at a trade show you attended, the name of a possible mentor, the title of a good gallery directory and its publisher's name.

Your goal, at this point, is to establish yourself as a person who wants to help and who has something to offer. Once this is apparent, the other person will want to assist you, too. Be sure to exchange business cards. After you move away from your network contact, jot notes on her business card—what you suggested, what she offered, how you foresee this relationship developing. Follow up with a phone call or letter within a few days, stating you enjoyed your encounter and offering additional assistance in the future. Finally, pin a note on your memo board to remind yourself to contact this person again in a few months.

Creative networking is never an "if-you-do-this-for-me-then-I-will-do-this-for-you" situation. Although there is a certain degree of structure to making the introduction, feeling out the needs of the other as well as ascertaining how they can help you, exchanging business cards, and following up, it should always remain a flexible, pleasant arrangement for everyone involved.

Suggested Reading:
- *Empower Through Networking* by Donna M. Reed, Resources for Women Press.
- *Is Networking For You?* by Barbara A. Stern, Prentice-Hall.
- *Networking* by Mary Scott Welch, Harcourt Brace Jovanovich.

CHAPTER 16

Speaking in Public

The Power of Public Appearances

Constance Hallinan Lagan

Contrary to what we have been told by Madison Avenue advertising moguls, products do not sell themselves. If they did, there would be no commercials, and those very same advertising moguls would be unemployed! No matter how beautiful and/or functional your work is, no matter how much soul you have invested in it, much more than the sight of your product will be required to move your product from your studio to the buyer's home or office. And the best advertisement for your own work is you—via public appearances.

A word-of-mouth recommendation is the best endorsement for any product. When it comes to products made by hand—to say nothing of the soul and heart—the most efficacious word-of-mouth recommendation emanates from the creator's (your own) mouth.

But what do I talk about during my public appearances?

Even if you considered Public Speaking 101 the crucible of your college career, when you realize how talking about yourself and your work results in sales, you will find yourself out in the garage, down in the basement, or up in the attic scouting for those old college notes. Public speaking is easy and it is fun. Since you will be informing others about what you know best—yourself and your product line, you know all the answers to every question anyone could ask. So what is there to fear?

Develop different angles, topics, and titles, so you can offer choices to your sponsors. I am a fiber artist. When I give lectures, some of the angles I use, leading into my low-key sales pitch, include the following:

- Nurturing creativity. This is a dialogue on how left-brain people can develop their right-brain function.

- Gift-giving in the corporate setting. This includes a discussion of global gift-giving and the appropriateness of different selections.
- Decorating with art/craft. This is a lecture/demo on how to embellish one's personal and/or professional space with artworks.
- Collector's corner. This is a trunk show featuring the high-end items in my product line.

Where do I make my public appearances?

All types of organizations are constantly seeking informed, entertaining, dependable speakers—especially when these speakers are willing to talk for the promotional benefits only (i.e., "*gratis*," or fee-free).

Potential outlets for your public speaking appearances include trade associations, nonprofit organizations, government agencies, churches and temples, women's groups, holistic centers, art leagues, craft guilds, arts and humanities councils, museums, schools, libraries, corporations, professional groups, bookstores, coffeehouses, and labor unions.

Can I really make a sales pitch during my public appearances?

When presenting program coordinators with your proposal, stress how members of their group will benefit from your presentation. Push the educational angle, such as how your audience will learn the history of a particular medium, the proper care of certain handwork, the financial advantages of collecting, and so on.

When you are actually in front of your audience, plug your own products but do it with subtlety. Since the organization is not paying you a fee, it expects you to include a brief sales pitch; just don't overdo it. Thirty minutes devoted to self-promotion in a 60-minute program is overdoing it.

On occasion, you may be able to arrange to sell your work following your public appearance. When requesting permission to do so, be sure to offer to donate a specific percentage of your gross sales to the group or to a charity of their choice. Never sell without prior approval.

Compile a mailing list by circulating slips of paper on which you ask the audience members to write their names, addresses, and telephone numbers. Inform your audience that these slips will be placed in a container from which a door prize winner will be drawn. This perk encourages participation. Give a merchandise credit as the door prize, thereby prompting at least one sale. Be sure to have pencils available for those who do not have pens with them. Also mention that you would greatly appreciate their jotting down the names of any other organizations which they think might be interested in sponsoring one of your free talks.

Distribute your business cards and promotional materials to each and every one in your audience. Hand out these items yourself or have an assistant do so—do not leave it to your audience to pick up materials on their way out. They forget, they are in a rush, they are deterred by lines, they get sidetracked by post-program conversations with you and members of the audience.

What do I do after my public appearance?

Follow up. With phone calls. With letters. With more phone calls. With more letters. To old sponsors. To new sponsors. To audience members. Persistence and perseverance pay plenty! Author Walter Elliott advises, "Perseverance is not a long race; it is many short races one after another."

"Tell Me About Your Work"

Peggy Hadden

Does an inquiry like this throw you into a panic? It used to make me completely tongue-tied. I think artists often have a very hard time explaining their artwork. For me it was difficult because it was a struggle to find the right words and because I cared about it so much. To this day, I know artists who get teary-eyed and mute when queried about their art.

Nevertheless, sooner or later you will find yourself asked to explain in 1,000 words what the pictures are all about.

Why is it so painful? Maybe because artists are visual people. Strong eye-hand coordination enables us to work with an object or idea until it appears perfect. But perhaps because we've worked so hard on polishing our visual sense we've neglected our verbal abilities.

A good goal for the balance of this year would be to strengthen your verbal skills as they relate to your visual ones.

Talking intelligently about your work—its content, the technical approach you have evolved, your use of color, anecdotes about how a work came to be created—can open many doors. It can produce more sales, arouse art world interest, or simply establish or strengthen your credibility with the public as a serious, thoughtful, eloquent artist.

We all know at least one artist who always has volumes to say about his work and the words seem to flow effortlessly. This was brought home to me one night a few summers ago as I watched a TV program spotlighting art in local neighborhoods. Several artists whose projects were being discussed were introduced. Within minutes it became clear how well they could talk about their art. Granted, they were well rehearsed for the broadcast. But I was devastated, thinking how poorly I communicated about a subject so terribly important to me. We are often alone for long hours in the studio and this, among other reasons mentioned here, may account for our seeming inability to interact with people as easily as others do. Verbal spontaneity withers. Introspection, much as we love it, becomes an albatross.

After mucking about in this depressing marsh for a day or two, I decided it was up to me to bridge this gap. I was looking for a nuts-and-bolts, inexpensive way to polish up my act. I decided to start conscientiously talking about my art out loud.

Since this idea scared me to death, I figured I'd better begin with strangers. Why fall on your face in front of people you know? A good available audience, I thought, might be senior citizens. I cooked up a talk stressing everyday language and simple facts about how I made my work. I avoided the baroque language of art school and the vague dressed-to-impress lingo of the art magazines. I used slides to demonstrate the talk and practiced in front of a full-length mirror. Finally, I called a nearby nursing home and asked to be connected with the activities office. When the woman in charge came on the phone, I introduced myself and launched into my idea. I proposed a short talk about my work, to last about 30 minutes with time for questions at the end. She was pleasant but unable to offer me any pay. I said this would be a new project and I needed feedback and that I would be willing to give the talk *gratis*. We set a date and I found myself committed to speak in public. It was not without apprehension.

How did it go? Well, some people fell asleep. Later, I learned that this often happens at an after-lunch program. Some people had difficulty hearing me. This we remedied with a microphone with which, I confess, I was not entirely at ease. But most of the audience loved it. They asked good questions and I learned a lot.

After that, I went to every nursing home I could find. The questions people asked tended to be similar so I got pretty good at answering them. The activities offices would print up colorful circulars, describing me in very flattering terms. Ask them for extras, as they are very good additions at the back of a portfolio.

Next, I tried the public library. They offer senior activities programming in the afternoons. I was paid $50 for a talk lasting an hour and a half, and I was invited back for paid speaking engagements at four other branches. The talks had some ups and downs. Attendance was somewhat dependent on the weather, and at times only three or four people showed up. Once a thunderstorm made much of my speech inaudible. Little by little, though, it became easier to do. I'd pick out someone who looked friendly and make eye contact, speaking directly to him until my initial nervousness was gone.

The most important thing these talks did was give me confidence. This kind of audience is usually seated informally and casually dressed so you don't feel as though you are addressing the United States Senate. Very often these groups convey a sense of gratitude that you've come to talk to them and this prompts me to try to be as good a speaker as possible. Many times people came forward and asked to be put on my mailing list.

But the benefits haven't stopped with love and admiration. The first nursing home where I spoke later sponsored me for a grant to paint murals for their dining room. I have received glowing letters from all of the organizations where I spoke, telling me how much they appreciated my talk. These letters, on letterhead, provide valuable evidence of my community involvement and I've included them in various grant applications as backup documentation.

A whole new category has opened up on my resumé. Called "Lectures and Talks," it gives me something else to broaden the conversation when I approach a gallery owner or museum personnel.

Books on public speaking can help with the form of your talk. You will find that having your own slide projector is helpful, but not essential, in ensuring that your slide carousel will fit properly and cords will reach outlets. Double-check to see that your slides are in the order in which you plan to use them and inserted so that you will get right-side-up images.

If you create at least two lectures a month I predict that in six months or less you will have conquered any reticence you feel when asked to talk about your work, and you will have gained the practice necessary to speak both eloquently and easily. You will also write better letters and artist's statements.

Giving a Gallery Talk

Alan Bamberger

The following has been spoken by nearly every artist: "I love creating art. I hate promoting myself and would much rather have others do it for me. A gallery that shows my work and has had reasonable success selling it is offering my first one-person show. Unfortunately, they want me to speak about how I do what I do to a group of their collectors. I've never done anything like this before and am wondering how I should deal with it other than run the other way."

If it's any comfort, you are by no means alone in your apprehension. You are experiencing a fear that more than 90 percent of all people list as their number one greatest fear: getting up before a group and speaking.

To be honest I have that same fear, but I go ahead and accept every single speaking engagement or interview I'm offered anyway. In fact, I even go out of my way to get them. You are your own best promoter, no matter how inexperienced you are. Be honored that you've been asked to do this, and get on with facing the challenge. You will be speaking about yourself and your art, the subject you know the best, and something you surely have no trouble talking about in casual circumstances.

For this more formal occasion, practice is the key. Figure out what you want to say and then start rehearsing. Take what you normally say to people when they ask you about your art, put it down on paper, and practice saying it over and over again until you virtually have things memorized—at least the major points you wish to cover.

Stand and speak in front of a mirror; speak in front of several trusted friends. If possible, have someone videotape you so you can see how you look. That way, you'll be able to modify anything you don't like about the way you present yourself. When you know what you're going to say ahead of time and are well prepared, once you get going you'll be just fine.

If you're still worried, fantasize a moment about the worst things that can possibly happen. Are you afraid you'll lose your train of thought? mispronounce a word? that your voice will shake a little? that someone will disagree with what you're saying? When you verbalize these fears, you see how inconsequential they are.

Your audience is on your side and every last one of them wants you to do a great job. This is a major opportunity for you. And the best part is that once the presentation is over, you'll experience an exhilaration you cannot experience any other way.

CHAPTER 17

High-Visibility Public Appearances

Organizing an Art Panel

Peggy Hadden

A good way to jump-start a becalmed career and become visible in your local art community is to create a panel to discuss an art topic. Planning a panel involves phone calls, letter writing, deep thought, and organizational skills. It is time-consuming. However, many benefits can be reaped.

Panels are offered all the time by nonprofit groups, museums, and art schools. Sometimes they come in a series, sometimes part of an all-day or all-week festival. Occasionally calls for proposals are published in these nonprofits' newsletters, but if you don't see them requested, contact an arts group that sponsors educational events.

Type up a one-page proposal letter, stating the topic with a short paragraph about why this subject needs to be discussed now. List the moderator and the names, or at least occupations, of the panelists you'd like to have. However, never list a person on anything you send out until you've contacted him and your invitation has been accepted. Mention additional parts of the program such as slide presentations, videos, or music that will add to the panel's investigation of the issue. Be flexible as to the date, but specify roughly when you will be available to present the event. You might suggest where or in what kind of location it could be held. In preparing this proposal, try to imagine the stumbling blocks this group might foresee, and offer them solutions.

Panels can offer real opportunities for learning. Unlike traditional educational situations with a teacher (the expert) and students (the novices), panels offer everyone a chance to listen and contribute equally. Watching panelists with various points of view focus on an issue is like watching TV. Their expertise is presented in a three-dimensional, back-and-forth manner which is much more immediate than getting the same information from a book. Challenges are answered on the spot, enabling everyone to see all sides of an issue.

One artist who has done several panels told me she has made many valuable contacts where doors were closed to her before. My experience was similar. My most recent panel was held in a commercial gallery, an arrangement made by my sponsoring nonprofit group. I developed relationships with the gallery owner and staff, so I felt comfortable to return later and show my slides.

In planning my panel, I thought of the best people to be panelists although I knew none of them personally. I sent each a letter, explaining my topic and why I thought he would be a good panelist. Every one of them said yes.

People participate in panels for a variety of reasons—public-spiritedness, the value of being seen as an expert, the publicity. There is almost never any pay, unless the sponsoring group can offer an honorarium. However, the elbows you'll be rubbing can almost certainly help you move your career forward.

Even if you are not inviting someone to participate on your panel, you could still call to ask their advice on a particular point. Under the umbrella of the nonprofit group sponsoring your event, you suddenly have a legitimate reason to ask for their expertise and they won't feel irritated in responding to your request.

Another benefit to organizing a panel is the potential elevation in your position in the arts community. When you are presented as a panel organizer, *voila!*, you are perceived as a mover, an expert, a person who gets things done. Depending on the type of topic you select, you may be seen as scholarly, involved in current art issues, gung-ho for educating the public on the arts, and so on. If the panel succeeds and draws a crowd, you may be asked to present it again in a prestigious place such as a museum. This links your name, through the mailings and publicity, to the museum. Even if you haven't yet exhibited your artwork there, the groundwork is being laid.

The Topic

Select something that is relevant, but not so political that fistfights will break out. Zoning problems, controversial artwork, and abstract vs. traditional art approaches might work on the op-ed page of the newspaper, but will prove to be difficult for a panel format. Likewise, inviting panelists who dislike each other may detract from your topic. However, select a topic where a variety of points of view are held.

The Panel

Invite panelists from more than one side of the issue. Avoid duplication. You might want someone who represents the historical perspective of your topic, like a writer or scholar. Another panelist who represents a newer or more radical view of the topic might add a different voice. Panelists from nonprofit groups, state or local arts offices, or granting sources will offer valuable perspectives in the discussion of almost any arts issue. Artists, well-known or not, will speak for many in your audience.

The perfect size for a panel is a moderator and four panelists. It's necessary to have a moderator—otherwise, your panel will not stay focused. An unfocused panel becomes four individuals just talking, not addressing the issues which build to a climax and conclude with a neatly wrapped-up discussion. If you don't want to moderate it yourself, ask someone who can keep a neutral point of view for the duration of the panel presentation. Media people are especially good in this role, as they are accustomed to asking questions and getting opposing points of view.

Remember that a panel is for discussion, but don't forget that your audience also wants to be entertained. Keep opinions brief. Don't be afraid to interrupt if someone's comments get long-winded. Interpose with a question, either to that panelist or to someone else.

The Balance

Consider gender, age differences, academic vs. streetwise education—many voices should be included. By leaving out obvious sides of the issue, you will ultimately weaken the entire panel, and this omission will reflect poorly on you.

The ideal panel lasts about one and a half hours. Attention spans will wander if it gets any longer. A question-and-answer period should follow, but keep its length to under 10 minutes. After 10 minutes, announce "This will be our last question, but please feel free to come up afterwards."

Be flexible in dealing with your topic. While you may know a great deal about your subject, the expertise in your audience may surprise you. At a panel I moderated about artists using TV to reach the public, it turned out that in my audience were four individuals who had public access cable programs of their own. Each offered insights that contributed much to the evening, yet I could not have prepared for their participation in advance.

If you plan to present slides, keep this segment short. You may need a technical person to help with the projector or screen. Before the big event, be sure cords reach plugs and slide carousels fit properly.

Likewise, if someone is shooting a video for you, be sure you've warned your panelists in advance and releases are signed by all concerned, to ensure that you have the rights to the tapes afterward.

You should think hard about whether to include slides of your own work. An artist/panel coordinator told me why she decided not to include her work among the slides accompanying her panel. She felt that her work didn't fit in with the other slides, and she felt she had saved herself possible embarrassment by opting to withhold her work. It is a serious decision that should not be left until the last minute.

Consider using microphones. In a large hall, they are essential. But in a packed room, whatever the size, they can make the difference between rapt attention and the annoyance that results from inaudible babble. Test the mikes beforehand—don't wait until the night of the event to discover that your wonderful panel can't be heard beyond the front row.

In preparing your panel, mail each panelist a short list of questions you might ask. Give them time to think about their answers a week or two in advance. It might be a good idea to meet briefly with them individually to tell them the order in which you will call on them or where you think their expertise will fit. I was told by one panel organizer that the single most important quality contributed by the moderator is confidence. This becomes contagious, and other panel members will actually gain confidence from your confidence.

Previous associations with business may be useful if you need special props for your presentation. A bank where I had curated an exhibition lent TVs and VCRs for use at the panel I mentioned earlier. The equipment substantially strengthened our presentation. When applying for special favors like this, be sure to emphasize the excellent publicity they will receive as a result of participating in your event. You will also benefit from their help in an interesting way: your sponsoring group will see you as someone who has valuable corporate support. By having your name connected with large and successful enterprises, your own reputation as an artist will shine.

A well-planned panel can bring you benefits far beyond the scope of the event.

Radio and Television Interviews: Are They Worth the Time?

Constance Hallinan Lagan

Commercial air time, when we have to pay for it, is very costly. "It is difficult to generalize about the cost of commercial production . . . . But it is safe to say that an advertiser paying the bills . . . is shelling out a big hunk of change," advises Huntley Baldwin, author of *How to Create Effective TV Commercials.*

Therefore, how can anyone question the value of radio and television interviews? Nothing can be less expensive than "free," right?

And yet many of my clients, when given the opportunity to receive free air time, complain because they have to rise at 5 a.m. to sit for an early morning talk show, want guarantees that the interview will produce income, and demand editorial license to review tapes before airing.

When offered the opportunity to sit for a radio or television interview, say "YES." And say it with enthusiasm and appreciation and with no strings attached. Very few artists or craftspeople can afford paid media exposure. By working cooperatively with program coordinators, newscasters, talk show hosts and others in the commercial media, you build name recognition, inspire consumer confidence, educate potential customers—and, in the long run, increase your bottom line. And you do it without any outlay of cash whatsoever.

Do not sit back and wait for the media to come pounding on your door, however. They will not. You must contact them. Compile local, regional, and national media lists and send an "interview announcement" to each name on these lists, stating that you are available for interviews and outlining your areas of expertise.

For some general guidance, consult the "interview announcement" I use—it has led to my being a guest on dozens of radio, cable, and television shows. Employ it as a guide to formatting your own "interview announcement." My interview announcement appears below.

Enclose a black-and-white photograph with your interview announcement along with any publicity clips you may have in your file. The media loves to interview individuals who have been interviewed elsewhere, whether on the air or in print. For a fantastic photo buy, contact Jem Photos—this firm has provided me with excellent quality 4"x5" black-and-white glossy photos, complete with name caption—100 copies for $29. Mention my name to John at Jem Photos, 3424 Butler St., Pittsburgh, PA 15201, 412-621-0331.

If you do not hear from the people to whom you sent your interview announcement, give them a polite call, asking if they have received your mailing and if they would like to schedule an interview.

If they book you, you are on your way to media fame.

If they do not bite, advise them you will stay in touch. And then do so, sending new press releases every few weeks. Since it is considered "editorially incorrect" to follow up on press releases, do not call to see if each press release has been received and considered.

But do be sure to send a complete media packet semi-annually. It is editorially correct to follow up on media packets, so sending them twice a year gives you a fantastic opportunity to touch base with old editors and to meet new ones.

Time spent sitting for interviews is time well invested. So I will hear you on the radio and see you on the tube real soon, right?

So you may see an example, I have included my own interview announcement below.

My Interview Announcement

CONSTANCE HALLINAN LAGAN, New York author, entrepreneur, lecturer, and trainer, is available for interviews. Her expertise in many fields makes her a lively and informed interviewee. She is well versed in the following topics: women's issues, entrepreneurship, home-based business, parenting concerns, personal enrichment, careers and motherhood, professional enhancement, small-business development.

Lagan has been a guest on WGBB Radio, People-Places-and-Things, Secrets of Success, Young at Heart, The Psychology Hour, Focus on Long Island, Spotlight on Long Island, Long Island News Tonight, Long Island Success, Newscaster 3, News 12 Long Island, Let's Talk, Straight Talk, and many other radio and television programs. Lagan has been interviewed by dozens of publications, including *The Women's Record, The New York Times, Family Circle, Newsday, Baby Talk, National Home Business Report* and *Homebased Entrepreneur.*

Lagan's byline has appeared in more than four dozen consumer and trade publications, including *Entrepreneur, Self-Employed America, Art Calendar, Income Opportunities, In Business, National Home Business Report, Behind Small Business, Craft & Needlework Age, The Crafts Report, Women's Circle, Long Island Parenting News, The Homemaker, See Saw* and *Parent Connections*.

Lagan is listed in *Feature Writer & Photographer Directory, Who's Who in U.S. Writers, Editors & Poets, Who's Who in Crafts, Who's Who of Emerging Leaders of America, World's Who's Who of Women, Who's Who of American Women*, and *Consultants & Consulting Organizations Directory*. Lagan is the author of *The Marketing Options Report* series. She has been awarded two grants to develop programming for The Staten Island Children's Museum, nominated as Homeworking Mother of the Year, and named to The Design Hall of Fame.

PART 5

Advertising

A Merciful Dance, 1995, oil on canvas, 48" x 52",
Elvi Jo Dougherty, Upper Fairmount, Maryland

CHAPTER 18

Print Ads

The Effectiveness of Space Ads in Magazines

Barbara Dougherty

Open up any art magazine and you'll find ads about shows, new images, and artists. How effective is print advertising for the artist?

When considering whether to advertise, some of the factors to consider include your goals, your budget, the audience you're trying to reach, your preparedness to respond to requests for further information, and your capability of meeting any commissions or production that might become necessary due to the demand for your work.

It will also help you to bone up on advertising in general. Each field develops its own trade lingo. In advertising, some of the buzzwords are "repetition," "researching the market," and "truth in advertising."

Repetition

"Repetition" can mean placing your ads in two or more sections of the same issue of a magazine, in consecutive or frequent issues, or in different media around the same time. Sometimes the purpose of advertising is to sell prints or gain attendance to a specific show, but the basic goal of repetition advertising is to make a name for the artist. By keeping the artist's name and an image before the public frequently, eventually collectors will get the message that the artist offers desirable work, has a market, and does good work. You gain the public's confidence through visibility.

Repetition advertising is sometimes called the Daniel Boone approach. The story goes that Boone was once trapped on mountain cliffs with enemy troops closing in. Boone was by himself, but he had several shotguns, which he placed a few yards from each other on the hilltop. He ran back and forth from gun to gun so it would appear that there were several other people with him. Thus the enemy thought there were several sharpshooters rather than one, and they were afraid to storm his hilltop.

The Daniel Boone approach, then, is to shoot several shots at the public from several different vantage points to give the public the impression that there's more of you than there really is—or, put more kindly and in a modern-day sense, that you are an established artist rather than a newcomer. Repetition advertising is also sometimes called the shotgun approach; with that many little bits of shot spraying all over the place, you're bound to hit the target.

Generally you'll get a price break if you place one or more ads, with the best per-ad price on a contract of a year or more. The most common contract is for the advertising to appear every other month if the magazine is a monthly. The hot concept is that "more often" is better than "bigger."

However, caution is in order. Though many businesses fail because they do not spend enough money on advertising, many others fail because they spend too much or buy inappropriate ad space.

Researching the Market

Though your per-ad cost will go down with frequency of insertion, will your results go up? It is always advisable to test advertising before going for a long-term contract, and it is critical to research which magazines will be best for your purposes.

Advertising to generate attendance at an event might be more effectively done in local newspapers and periodicals than in nationally circulated journals. A good public relations effort would augment that nicely, hopefully yielding interviews and articles about you.

If you are ready to make a name for yourself on the national level, study the different magazines whose pages are available to you. If you're a realist painter, then magazines that focus primarily on abstract art probably will not be a good place to advertise. If you notice that most of the ads in a particular publication are placed by galleries rather than artists, meaning that the ads are soliciting attendance at shows rather than new artists to represent, then it might be unlikely that your ad will generate new representation for you.

The ad sales staff will be able to answer any questions you might have. First, contact the magazines that appeal to you as possible advertising venues. Using your letterhead, write a letter to the magazines asking for a media kit. If the media kit's advertising rates, reader/audience profile, and looks appeal to you, it might be a good idea to talk with someone in the marketing or ad sales department. You should have specific questions ready and be polite—people who work in marketing usually have more obligations than time. However, these are the experts who know what will get response from their journal, and they want you to be able to get that response. Ask them what brings the highest response—get details on the best ad sizes, whether color is necessary, and what repetitions seem to work best. Ask if they think your work would be a good fit for their magazine.

There are often several options with journals. An ad can be among the printed pages, or it can be a blow-in, an additional page bound into the magazine, or a ride-along.

Once I advertised with our local cable television network. For $1,500, the company inserted into all of their 63,000 bills one of my four-color postcards announcing a show I was having. In addition to the ride-along, my investment earned me air time on the channel. This was the best advertising I could have done for the money for that occasion.

Besides considering the other media such as cable television, don't overlook non-art magazines for your print advertising. For example, *Architectural Digest*, a high-end magazine, often includes artists' ads. Portrait painters and bronze sculptors seem to advertise most often.

Truth in Advertising

It is very important not to advertise your name and your work until you're ready. If you are experimenting with various media, if you're trying different styles, or if you are not confident about your work, it might not be the right time to advertise.

One artist I know was told that in order to be a marketing success he should begin advertising in magazines. He did so, but five years later he had only tales of woe. The work he had advertised had been immature and derivative of other artists' work. Thus, his reputation was tainted and when he approached galleries he was told it would be too difficult for him to overcome his past reputation.

Besides being ready, it is critical to be truthful; public skepticism is allayed by the truth. The world loves an underdog and admires the truth. The Avis car rental firm used this to their advantage by using the advertising slogan "We're Number Two," referring to Hertz's claim that it was number one. The response ratings were so high that the slogan became a motto.

Design

Other principles of advertising should be considered when designing your ads. Logos work well to help the public visualize your identity.

Coupons can be effective and can help you judge response to your ad, but sometimes they are inappropriate.

Formal advertising is like dressing up for a formal affair—it's best to leave the gimmicks and frills in the closet. Consider the look of your advertising carefully. If your work is expensive, your ad should look expensive.

Some advertisers use endorsements, or goodwill, effectively. Absolut Vodka promotes artists as its advertising motif. This plan gives them a progressive reputation in the marketplace. Endorsement is often used in advertising. However, the public is generally skeptical of endorsement, so it should be done with great care.

Don't overlook the possibility of sharing advertising costs and effects with others. Possibly the local chamber of commerce would like to be seen as the sponsor of some cultural events; sharing ad costs and space with them can help your ad have greater impact.

Consider the placement of your ad. For instance, when a person picks up a book at a bookstore, statistics show that he spends an average of four seconds looking at the book's front cover and seven seconds checking out the back. Show the journal you want to advertise in to friends and acquaintances; ask them what in the journal drew their attention. Ask the marketing staff for advice on ad placement too.

Tracking

In order to judge the effectiveness of your advertising, you will need to keep track of the response.

If you advertise in different journals, a useful tool to keep track of your responses is to code your address. For example, my P.O. box number is 170; if I were to advertise in *Architectural Digest* I would list my address as P.O. Box 170-AD. That way I would know that all written inquiries bearing the code "AD" came from that magazine's ad.

It's a little more cumbersome to code your telephone number with an extension number. Also, this practice gets away from truth in advertising, as it gives the caller the impression you're a large company. Simply ask the caller where he saw your ad.

If you carefully track each ad by time spent researching, time and money spent designing the ad, and money spent on the ad space, versus the number of responses, quality of responses, and contacts made and income realized, you will have the basis for following years' marketing plans.

Pros and Cons of Artist Sourcebooks and Directories

Alan Bamberger

An artist wrote to me describing the following offer: "I recently received an invitation to be listed in a directory of artists. The fee for a listing is $300 or $750 if I want to include a color illustration of my work. I've heard that publishers sometimes list certain artists at no charge because they're well known. Since I'm getting better and better known, I think that I should ignore this invitation and wait until the publishers offer me a free listing. If I pay the money I'll feel like I'm selling out to a vanity publication. What do you think?"

This artist brings up several worthwhile issues here. The overriding question is whether to be included in directories at all, and if so, what kind—my cautionary note is to determine whether your inclusion in paid "vanity" books will do you any good. Keeping this caveat in mind, my opinion is that all artists should get themselves listed or included in as many books, catalogs, directories, and other mediums of communication as possible—the more your name gets out there, the greater your chances for shows, sales, reviews, publicity, invitations, and related benefits that come with being easily accessible to dealers, collectors, museums, and the arts community in general. Your task will be to discover which directories will benefit you.

Even more important than the short-term advantages are the long-term and distant future benefits. Suppose, for example, that someone buys one of your major paintings and lives with it all his life. When he passes away 30 years later, a close family member inherits it. Ten more years pass before that family member decides to redecorate the house and, in the process, disposes of the image. Let's further suppose that at some point during this 40-year stretch, all information about who you are, what your painting represents, and what you accomplished during your career is either lost, misplaced, or was never passed on by the owner in the first place.

With the assumption that you are listed in no major art books, catalogs, or directories, the following possible outcomes are all taken from real life experiences:

- The owner contacts several art dealers, museums, appraisers, or other art experts and gives them your name. None of them recognize it. He decides either to donate it to his favorite charity, throw it away, sell it at a garage sale, or store it in an unsafe place.
- The owner figures the painting isn't worth much because in all the time it has been in his family, no one has ever said a word about it. He sells it for next to nothing at a garage sale. The buyer is an amateur flea market dealer who tries to find out something about who you are, comes up empty-handed, and ends up trading the painting to a local secondhand shop owner for a small pottery vase.
- The owner calls in a hauler who takes the painting, tries to find out something about who you are, comes up empty-handed, and hauls the painting to the dump.
- The owner makes no attempt to find out anything and breaks or cuts the painting into small enough pieces to fit into the trash can.

Now let's assume you are listed in major art reference books. Here's what may happen:

- The owner contacts several art dealers, museums, appraisers, or other experts and gives them your name. All of them recognize it and can provide some biographical data; some additionally provide price information. The owner decides either to hang your painting in a prominent place in his home, put it up for sale at a local auction house, donate it to his favorite museum, or sell it through an established art gallery.
- The owner figures the painting isn't worth much because in all the time it has been in his family, no one has ever said a word about it. He sells it for next to nothing at a garage sale. The buyer is an amateur flea market dealer who tries to find out something about who you are, locates basic biographical and pricing information, and sells the painting to a local art dealer who either sells it privately or puts it up for sale at a local auction house.
- The owner calls in a hauler who takes the painting, tries to find out who you are, and has the same luck as the amateur flea market dealer.
- The owner makes no attempt to find out anything and breaks or cuts the painting into small enough pieces to fit into the trash can. Unfortunately, these things still happen. This outcome is highly unlikely, though, if you get your name out in the general public during your career.

The point of this example has been to illustrate how a simple procedure can safeguard your art from horrible fates. A surprising number of people, including haulers, flea marketers, garage sale junkies, secondhand shop owners, collectibles dealers, and estate liquidators, know how to use standard references to locate artists. In the long term, the easier you are to research, the more your art is generally worth, the more likely it is to be preserved for all time, and the more likely it is to eventually receive whatever recognition it deserves.

Regarding the issue of paid versus unpaid listings, paid ones tend to be more problematic and less effective over time than unpaid ones. Outside of being able to see your name and your art in print, paid listings offer little else in terms of career enhancement.

Determine whether a paid listing produces any benefits by getting hold of the most recent edition of whatever directory or dictionary is soliciting you and seeing whether artists whom you trust or respect are included. You might also make several random calls to other listees, find out what they expected or were promised when they signed on, and whether those expectations were met. In addition, call several major museum, public, and university library art departments—find out whether they shelve the directory and how frequently it is used. If you can't find it anywhere or no one uses it, paying for a page in it probably won't do you much good.

Who's Who in American Art, on the other hand, is an example of a directory that lists artists at no charge. It also happens to be one of the references most heavily used by people researching unfamiliar names and can be found in almost any major library art department. *WWAA* publishes every two years, and mails out applications approximately six months prior to publication of its next edition.

Your chances of being listed increase if you've had major exhibitions, public works commissions, noncommercial gallery and institutional show participation, and other significant accomplishments. Anyone may request an application, however. If interested, contact Reed Reference Publishing, 121 Chanlon Rd., New Providence, NJ 07974, 908-464-6800.

Also, the Open Studios Press publishes regional books featuring painters. There are absolutely no fees—no application fee, no advertising fee, no production fees. To be considered for one of their books, send a sheet of 35mm slides, resumé, and SASE to Open Studios Press, 66 Central Avenue, Wellesley, MA 02181. Please remember that individual submissions will not be acknowledged but that all materials will eventually be returned. If your work is selected for inclusion in one of the upcoming editions you will be contacted before publication. Copies of past editions can be ordered at the above address for $16.95 each plus $2 each for shipping and handling.

As for publishers of pay-per-inclusion books sometimes listing well-known artists at no charge, that does happen occasionally, but the purpose of the publisher offering the free listing is to enhance the prestige of the book. I understand your concern with selling out to commercialism in such a case, but assuming the publication is a respected reference, viewing your actions as furthering the ultimate cause of your art or saving pieces that might one day be headed for destruction could make paying fees more meaningful. Playing waiting games with publishers will only work to your detriment.

Buying Ad Space in Artist Sourcebooks

Carolyn Blakeslee

To pay to have your artwork published in a book—a good investment, or a waste of money? It depends. There have always been artists' sourcebooks. A few are just fine. A good sourcebook fulfills its function—it is received, valued, and used by people who buy and commission artwork.

If placed in a quality publication, your advertising is valuable for several reasons. It can generate new clients and commissions. It can be an important part of the process of producing name recognition. It can boost your career self-confidence. Finally, in addition to your ad's placement in the printed book, many sourcebooks give you several hundred copies of your printed page for use as a direct mail piece to send to past and prospective clients.

But there are a slew of sourcebooks on the market now. There are encyclopedias, directories, catalogs, surveys—of contemporary art, New York art, living artists, erotic art, West Coast artists, Florida artists, and so on. Some of the sourcebooks are of questionable quality and value, and a few are downright awful, even some that have been around for a while and are well known.

And who can forget the Les Krantz/American References fiasco? Krantz, an established publisher whose books had a reasonably good reputation, went out of business after collecting millions of dollars from 3,000 artists who were never able to recover their money to the tune of nearly a thousand dollars each. Yet he declared bankruptcy and is still out there, writing books for other publishers.

If you are considering buying ad space in a book, do not be flattered into buying impulsively. Evaluate the publisher and the offer first.

Judging the Prospectus

First, look at the prospectus or other advertising materials you received from the publisher.

Did you order the information? Was the material unsolicited? Did you receive duplicate solicitations? Duplicates indicate that the publisher has bought several mailing lists, meaning you were part of a large-scale solicitation. That is not necessarily bad, but do you feel the publisher cares about artists and the quality of the sourcebook, or do you think they're probably in it just for the money?

How does the presentation of the ad solicitation speak to you? Is the material attractive and well-written? Is the print job professional? Or is the material amateurish—riddled with editorial, grammatical, graphic, typographic errors? Poorly produced?

If their prospectus packet doesn't look good, the final book is unlikely to look much better.

Judging the Offer

There are two signs of a questionable operation: a prospectus that doesn't tell you up front what your costs will be, and an entry fee.

Sometimes publishers or galleries will lure artists gradually, reeling them in with promises of services and results. Once the artist is hooked and ready to sign, or even after, the hidden charges come out. A few vanity galleries operate this way, and so does an occasional publisher. It's very seductive: the letters are glowing, positive, congratulatory, sometimes even veiled behind a screen of European glamor if the letters are written by someone who is European and pretends not to speak English well. Often these letters seem quite personal. These publishers or galleries may also employ telemarketing, though at first it might seem like personal attention. Don't count on it—these people might be paid to sit there all day and sign on new artists, whether by phone or by mail. On the other hand, one sign of a good publisher is a sales representative who calls you to follow up or get further information from you. Pay attention to the tone of the telephone conversations. If you sense a high-pressure sales job going on, rather than a professional and respectful "Let's get the job done" attitude, you probably should avoid the situation. NOTE: If a disreputable gallery or vanity book has solicited you by mail, you have remedies through the postal system. If you have been solicited by telephone, the FCC has jurisdiction.

The second questionable practice associated with sourcebooks is the requirement of entry fees. Let's run some numbers. Suppose the entry fee is $22. The publisher mails out 100,000 brochures soliciting entries; each packet costs around 35¢ to print and bulk mail, so the promotion has cost $35,000. Suppose 3,000 artists decide to "enter." The artists' entry fees add up to $66,000. So the publisher has already made $31,000, on top of the hundreds of dollars each accepted artist will have to pay for his ad. One of the publisher's arguments will be that the entry fee money will be used to cover the costs associated with a quality publication. However, ad revenues should be sufficient to cover a quality publication without entry fees. Companies buying ads in magazines don't have to pay entry fees to be considered for an ad. The publisher's second argument will be that entry fees will screen out amateurs. However, many professional artists will not have anything to do with any competition that has an entry fee, and the jury process itself will screen out the amateurs anyway.

If the offer has passed muster, then you should order a copy of a previous book so you can judge its quality for yourself.

Judging the Sourcebook

When you get the book, look through it critically. Is it so striking you can't put it down, or do you feel like putting it on your "pile" and going through it later? aesthetically OK? editorially, grammatically, typographically OK? In captions, did the editors know to put vertical dimensions before horizontal before depth? Is the book consistent? Are the reproductions clear and clean?

Would you be proud to be in a similar book, or would you hide it from some of your dealers or collectors?

Would you want the other artists' artworks in your home or business?

Next, put yourself in the recipients' shoes. If you were a recipient or purchaser of the book, would you use it? Would you feel confident about commissioning the artists therein? Would you look forward to receiving this book every year or so?

Now for the acid test. Write or phone some artists in the book whose work is similar to yours. Ask them what their goals were and whether they were happy with the results of placing an ad in that sourcebook. After all, even if a book looks bad and is managed badly, if it produces results for the artists therein then maybe it is still worth considering.

Questions to Ask the Publisher

If there is no past sourcebook available, ask the publisher the following questions if they weren't addressed in the prospectus.

* What kind of paper will it be printed on?

Good coated stock—preferably smooth, glossy color litho paper—reproduces color more richly, and black-and-white has more contrast. For a book, heavy paper is better than magazine-weight paper. Ask the publisher to send you a paper sample or a sample page so you can see and feel it for yourself.

* At what line-screen will plates be reproduced?

Color images are printed via color separations, one color at a time, and black-and-white images via halftones. Simply speaking, halftones and color separations are screen-print negatives—the image is broken down into tiny dots through which the inks are forced, producing a printed image.

The lower the line-screen number, the fewer dots per inch, and the coarser the image will appear. Newspaper photos and comics, for instance, are extremely coarse, and are printed through line-screens well below 100. Halftones and color separations, to look good, should be at least 150 and preferably 200 lines.

If you are unfamiliar with line-screen terminology and differences, a visit to a print shop is a good idea. Most printers will be happy to show the results of printing with different line-screen/halftone resolutions. You might also ask to see some paper samples while you're there.

* How large will the book be?

There are some high-quality illustrators' and photographers' sourcebooks that are spiral-bound and fairly small. Generally, though, a cocktail-table-sized book will make more of an impression than a smaller book, and is more likely to be saved even after the next editions come out.

* How many pages will the book consist of? How many people is the publisher aiming to include?

Ask how many pages and how many people their previous editions have featured. If the publisher's policy is that each artist must take out a full-page ad, the book will probably look cleaner and be more effective for the included artists. If their policy is to squeeze several artists onto a page, they might be more interested in getting as much money as possible out of the project in any way they can, including talking artists who can't afford such advertising yet into spending the money anyway by taking smaller ads.

Whether there is a previous book available or not, you must know the answers to these questions:

- How many copies of the book will be printed?

Don't be dazzled by words like "circulation" or "readership." Ask specifically how many copies of the book will be printed. Weigh the number against the answers to the next groups of questions.

- How many copies of the book will be sent out free of charge?
    a. To what groups? curators, dealers, art consultants, interior decorators, architects, critics, developers?
    b. How many to each kind of group? If the publisher is targeting your market, then even a relatively small press run (a few thousand) might do you some good. For example, if you are interested in contacting architects and public art consultants, and the book will be sent to 10,000 of those people as well as 3,000 corporate buyers, buying a plate in the book might be a good investment for you. After all, if you had been meaning to send your materials to corporate art advisors around the country anyway, and the book will be sent to a few thousand art advisors, why not let someone else do the printing and mailing?
    c. Is their circulation audited? Not necessarily a big deal if it isn't, but if it is then you have more of a guarantee that the publisher is telling you the truth about the numbers.
- If the book will not be sent free of charge to anyone or to very many, be wary.

Ask whether a direct mail campaign will be carried out, and if so, how many brochures will be sent, to which groups of potential buyers. Figure that one to three out of every 100 will buy the book as a result of a direct mail campaign. It is a mistake to plan on any more—2 percent is an average response. Ask about how much advertising other than direct mail they plan to do, and how forcefully. Ditto for publicity campaigns.

If the print run isn't high, and/or the number of targeted free copies isn't high, then the book probably wouldn't do you much good. On the other hand if you think their direct mail campaign is likely to be aggressive and successful you could always test an ad just to give it a try.

• How often does the book come out?

The shelf life of a book is an important factor in your decision. An annual is good—people start to look forward to it every year.

Ask for—and get—all of the above in writing.

Your Goals

Now look at your own bottom line. What are your goals? What do you expect to get out of your investment? Does the book fulfill your needs?

Even the best sourcebooks have a few disadvantages. For one thing, there's a long lead time between placing your ad and the book's appearance. If a deposit or up-front payment is required, your money will be tied up for quite a while. For another thing, even if other artists' ads pull well for them, there is no guarantee that your ad will produce results for you.

Oh, well. Everything in life has its risks, including advertising. Just know the book and the publisher before you buy the space.

Advertorials: Paying to Be Interviewed?

Alan Bamberger

An artist wrote to me asking about the following situation. "The possibility exists that I can get written up in an art magazine. To increase the chances of this happening, someone at the magazine recommended that a display ad showing my work be purchased for the issue that would contain the article. This can either be done by me, someone who represents me, or a gallery where I show. Should I pursue this?"

Any time you have to pay for this kind of exposure, watch out. Publications with these sorts of editorial policies are not highly regarded in the art world. For one thing, the artists they feature are often chosen on the basis of their abilities to deliver advertising revenues and not necessarily for the quality of their art. Go through a couple of back issues of the magazine you're considering advertising in and you'll see that their article/advertisement pairing is a regular occurrence.

Another point to keep in mind: Most subscribers have little trouble figuring out when the buy-an-ad/get-an-article arrangement is in effect. Readers who become aware of this almost always discount such features as questionable or even ignore them altogether. Some readers are not aware that this is happening, of course, but they tend not to be art business movers and shakers.

The best procedure is to go after more genuine forms of recognition for your work. Participate in juried shows, apply for commissions and grants, get involved with artists who are advanced in their careers and who you can learn from, and do everything else in your power to keep your work in the public eye.

Most importantly, expand your resumé and continue to produce art. The better you get, the more your art will get around, and the more you'll be noticed.

Throughout your career, people will attempt to extract money from you in exchange for promises of fame, fortune, and varying degrees of publicity. My advice is to walk the other way and let the fame and fortune come as you earn it. There is no easy way to make it in the art business.

CHAPTER 19

TV, Billboards, Alternative Media

TV, Radio, and Billboard Advertising: An Overview

Barbara Dougherty

An artist with work to sell must be a marketer, like it or not. One of the components of marketing is advertising. Advertising, a part of the art of public relations, is basically communication. As an artist, you can get excited about applying design and creative techniques to the tasks of advertising your art.

Your resumé, for instance, is a form of communication that is an advertisement. Acknowledging this, you may find that your resumé is not just a bothersome task of making lists but instead a tool with which to greet certain potential clients. Other forms of advertising are:

- Print ads in magazines and newspapers
- Videos
- Postcards
- Brochures
- Catalogs
- Telemarketing
- Television
- Radio
- Lectures and other personal appearances
- Billboards
- Internet and CD-ROM

Successful advertising must tell the truth. In other words, if you have not participated in major exhibitions then don't create a list in a resumé that is meant to look as if you have. Major marketing firms learned long ago to use the truth to sell products and services. For example, Avis Rent-a-Car—a smaller agency than Hertz—created a very successful advertising campaign saying "We're Number Two." The concept and law of truth-in-advertising implores a marketer to remember that the public is skeptical of overrated claims; people prefer to have a way of recognizing and relating to a product or a person rather than an insupportable claim.

What is your claim? Who are you? I am an agricultural artist. Maybe you are a creator of temporary structures. Maybe you are a promoter of ugliness. This identification of yourself beyond your name is called positioning—it is a concept that will help you bring a visual image or another association to the mind of your potential client. People often love an underdog—so you do not need to be the best. Just be somebody the public can remember.

A common tool used by corporations to evoke public recall is the logo. Products are associated with logos: Ralston Purina's checkerboard, the Mr. Clean giant, the Chiquita sticker on bananas, and so on. An artist should have a logo. A logo will help you to be remembered and it should be simple, clear, and easy to reproduce. Any presentation that an artist makes with a logo on it will give that artist one more chance to plant a small seed in the memories of those who might offer an opportunity. If you don't feel capable of creating your own logo, I would say it is so important that you should hire someone to do it for you.

After your identity and logo are worked out, the next step is to do some marketing experiments. I recommend that you try techniques not traditionally used by artists. I think it's about time artists started making TV commercials as well as radio ads. I also think billboards can be very effective. Artists can use these and other traditional advertising tools to their benefit.

For the last three years, I have purchased air time on a cable network for a TV commercial showing me painting in a field of cultivated flowers. There are no voices in my commercial, only music. Superimposed is the text, "Share the passion for the vanishing agricultural lands with artist Barbara Dougherty." The benefits of this commercial, which costs me approximately $8 per appearance, are immense. We as artists can entertain and educate the public and stimulate the marketplace with creative, low-cost TV commercials.

One element of my commercial that has an impact is the "Share the Passion" slogan. Whenever my name is used on products bearing any of my images, I insist on this statement following my name. Professionals in the advertising business call this use of a slogan a "hook line" or a "tag line." An artist might resist using such a tool, feeling that the public will remember them by their visual images. But just think of the number of hours most people spend in front of a television, and the immense number and nature of other visual images encountered by people in their daily lives. Any help jogging the public's memory should not be overlooked. You might find that a logo and a slogan used in other ways, like on your car, might bring you recognition that galleries cannot always achieve—that is, causing people to know who you are.

We artists do not have to settle for the belief that the public only wants pretty art matching a color scheme. If we take on the task of letting the public know who we are, then they may want our art whether it is pretty or not. The public likes not only prettiness, but also prestige. If others know who you are, then your work has prestige—and it will sell.

Good advertising in the established manner can cost a lot. I am not suggesting here that an artist can do this haphazardly and gain benefits. A successful advertising program takes time, money, research, and sincerity.

The following is some information on the three advertising alternatives that I have mentioned above: TV commercials, radio ads, and billboards.

Television

Cable networks in your community offer commercial time at very low cost, and many of the cable programs are very popular. I find advertising at prime time on CNN effective. I often go to the store wearing the same jacket I wore on my commercial, and I hear people saying, "There's that artist!"

The production of TV commercials is an ever-changing technology. A great commercial can be produced at low cost using the new tools of transferring slides to CD (compact disc) and, on computer, editing in music and text.

Fact is, you are only looking for a 10- to 30-second message letting the public know who you are. You must think about the message—with art you might not be advertising to sell as much as to create an identity. The simpler the message, the more memorable it will be.

If you invest in the TV option, research the best times of day and year for advertising. Summer, for instance, might not be a good time to run commercials because of reruns and vacations. One way to market-research TV or other commercial advertising is to seek advice from professional ad agencies. Small local companies that advertise on TV might also be approachable with your questions about cost and impact.

Radio Commercials

Even though radio is an audio rather than a visual medium, it can be an effective tool for the visual artist seeking to gain a public identity.

An opportunity existing in practically every community in the country is the radio talk show. Artists competing for air time have a unique appeal to the public just because they are artists.

If you have trouble with the talk-show style of spontaneous and direct communication, a well-planned verbal commercial message might be the best alternative. One of the advantages to advertising on the radio is that if your commercial isn't working it is much easier to change than a TV commercial is.

As you negotiate to buy radio time, remember to research the time of day more people are listening. I find that buying a few carefully selected time slots is more effective than buying a lot more air time when fewer people are paying attention.

Music in a commercial can enhance the emotional effect of the presentation. However, if you use music in a commercial, whether for television or radio, you must make sure that you are not infringing on copyrights held by companies or musicians.

A radio commercial with a personal message can be a great way for an artist to gain an audience and develop a client list. Most important is to use your imagination, try to run your commercials at the best times, and be very prepared to respond to the public who responds to you.

Billboards

Not everyone can land an opportunity to paint a public mural. However, most communities do have outdoor sign space available for rent.

One advantage of a billboard over a mural is that you might be able to prepare the materials in a studio rather than on site. Another appealing option of the billboard is that it is a project that several artists could do well together.

If you compare the price of a billboard, which you might be able to rent for as little as $100 a month, to the cost of a one-day $100 display ad in a newspaper, the greater effort and risk might have a more meaningful result.

Whether in negotiating for air time or billboard space, as an artist you have an advantage. If you are not afraid to raise the question, the idea of having art advertised might be so pleasing to the people selling advertising space that they might create special contracts just for you. For instance, a town might look better if artwork is displayed on a billboard rather than the run-of-the-mill signs advertising new cars or the local radio station.

In choosing to advertise using this medium, weigh the question of higher viewership. One location might cost more than another but it might be worth the extra expenditure.

Advertising is not a new phenomenon, nor is advertising art. However, somehow the practices I am suggesting here have been eliminated from the common repertoire of artists' public relations efforts with the assumption that they cost too much and are too much trouble to create. This is a new day and a new age and artists must use the tools accessible to them, because it is clear that the old ways are not working for very many artists.

Surprise, You Can Afford to Advertise on Television

Barbara Dougherty

One of the benefits of writing for *Art Calendar* is the phone calls and inquiries I receive from other artists. Recently I spoke with two serious artists; both had years of art experience, yet they both felt frustrated with and unsuccessful in marketing their art. Both had good presentations and good credentials, but neither had a good mailing list. They also had limited budgets. They came to me with one very direct question: "What can I do to attract a buying public to a showing of my work?"

My suggestion to both was to advertise on television.

The fact is that both local cable and local independent television station advertising can be low in cost and high in response.

I started using TV commercials to advertise in February, 1991. Since then, I have been regularly greeted in public with: "Oh, you're the one I see on television." I have even been asked for an autograph. My first contract was for forty commercials to be shown on three stations during the three days prior to a local showing of my paintings. The cost of the contract was $200 and the cost of producing the commercial was $75. That amounted to $6.88 per commercial! When I reviewed the entry cards I had required for free admission to the show, I found that 300 of the 800 attendees said they had come because of seeing the commercial; the rest indicated the mailed invitation as their source. This was even though these stations in Santa Barbara reach only 62,000 viewers.

Clearly it is easier to attract a buying public by showing the artwork itself. I call this the need for visual advertising of visual art.

With television you can simultaneously use visual, audio, and written messages. And I have found that the technology is not that difficult.

The first step is to plan a 30-second commercial. It may be really helpful to spend some time studying commercials. If you do something that is not like other commercials, you get a better response. Therefore, don't let a television station that produces commercials suggest a format. If you do, you will find your spot is too much like many other spots already on the air.

One commercial I produced myself begins in a large field of planted daisies. Then you see me at my easel between the rows of flowers with my back to the viewer. I am painting a watercolor of the field. The camera pans over my shoulder and watches me paint some large brush strokes and then pans to a field worker. The audio throughout the spot is flute music I recorded with a street musician. Scrolling over the image in the same manner as credits at the end of a movie is the statement, "Share the passion for the vanishing agricultural fields with artist Barbara Dougherty." At the end of the commercial I created what is called in the business a "tag." That is when the screen fades to a solid blue color and in white letters my coming show is announced. There is no voice on my commercial and I have been told by creative directors at large advertising agencies that to their surprise it is very effective. Subsequently a local jewelry store used the same style for their new commercial.

After you plan your commercial, you have to decide whether you want to produce the commercial yourself or contract for this service. The best time to contract for production services is at the same time you contract for airings. Recently I negotiated a contract for television commercial advertising for the Santa Barbara weekly art and craft show. The contract was with a station with a 300-mile viewing area and 363,000 viewers. They produced the commercial according to my specifications for $450. This was inexpensive considering they had to do two on-site camera sessions, about three hours of editing, music overlay, voice, and written messages called "character generation." They also supplied me with a video master that I could use on other stations because I had written this requirement into the contract. I achieved a low cost for both commercial production and airing because I agreed to run the commercial for at least three months. They call this an extended time contract. The cost was $200 for twenty commercials a month. An additional factor that lowered the cost was that I did not specify the exact time these commercials had to be shown. I only specified a time bracket. The spots, at $10 each, were to be shown during the hours of 9 a.m.-12 p.m. Despite our low-cost approach, the commercial was well made and shown during programs like Oprah, Donahue, and the soap *Santa Barbara.*

Contracting for time and production takes the most time and I have learned to be extra cautious. Everything must be in writing. Like any other arrangement, it is important to be specific and review the billing. It might be proposed that you run your spots ROS, which means Run of Schedule. I never use ROS because that means the station can place your spots anywhere but they usually are aired between 2 and 3 A.M. Sunday morning.

In a contract there are also extra services that can be specified. For instance, while planning a 1992 show I made two separate contracts with our local cable company. One is for forty time-specified commercials at a cost of $400. Most of these spots will be aired during the evening news. I find this time arrangement gives me the best results. The other contract is to have a color postcard of one of my paintings and a show announcement included in the cable bills that go out to 62,000 homes the month prior to the show. The cost of the second contract is $1,500. I must provide the postcard or mailer of my own design. There will also be 200 commercials during this month on five stations, including CNN, telling people to look for the postcard.

Keep in mind that when you work with a sales representative on this type of project you spend a great amount of time together. Once I was given a sales representative whom I had trouble reaching by telephone. When I asked for a different representative that request was immediately granted. Remember that the salesperson usually gets paid a set commission on whatever you spend, so in effect you pay their salary and they should be working for you.

The cost of a television commercial project can be lowered by doing part of the production tasks yourself. While many professionals would discourage my methods, one way is to use one of the newest 8mm camcorders and tape your own footage. These recorders have such good visual resolution that the tape can be transferred to a larger format for editing and broadcasting. This can be done in a television station or video production facility where music and character generation can also be added. I have done this, and it usually takes only an hour of production time because I plan the visuals, the music, and the written words before I get there. The average cost of production time is $100 an hour. Remember, a commercial is usually only 30 seconds, so plan your message well.

Another alternative for exceptional visual clarity and low cost is to use an old 16mm movie camera. After your shoot, have a video replica of the 16mm negative made. This can be done at the same time the film is developed. This video replica costs about six cents a foot plus the film development charges. Film development cost can be high, but remember the commercial is only 30 seconds. Then, with the video footage, go to the production facility for editing and music and character generation. This costs about $100 in shooting costs and an additional $100 in production.

If you decide to do your own production, remember that it is hard to get a good image without exceptionally good lighting when using video equipment.

A commercial can be produced without an outside shoot by projecting the 35mm slides of your artwork and taping the image with a video camera or 16mm movie camera. When I do this, I treat the image as if it were a movie backdrop. I do this by letting the camera pan within the projected painting, rather than showing a piece as a finished product on a wall or easel. My point of view is to take the public into the image.

An overlooked resource for production of commercials and videos is the local public-access stations that are all across the country. I have taken two years of classes at one in Santa Barbara. The classes cost $10 each and I have learned to use good equipment and state-of-the-art techniques. I can use the studio and get help from professionals at the station.

The purpose of public access stations is to provide the local communities low-cost television time in order to promote the right to free speech. All these stations train people how to do the work and use the equipment. They specify that every project should not be commercial, yet within the guidelines are opportunities to pay for studio use when doing commercial work. You don't have to get involved yourself, but at these stations you can usually find people eager to help and participate in projects. My first and second video productions were seen as documentaries on artists and each was shown free more than ten times on our local Channel 19.

As a footnote to the above information, I have found that I can buy what is called public programming time on local stations for about $60 an hour. This means if you have produced a video or been a part of a taped interview program, purchasing these time slots is a good way to attract a local audience to a showing of your work.

The issue I confront in my life over and over again as I work at being a successful artist is whether or not to spend the time learning to use new technologies. The world is an obstacle course of these: computers, videos, faxes, etc., but as artists our imaginations can be larger than the technology. There are ways to tap into the resources and options these technologies provide without sacrificing the time to do your own creative work.

Using Billboards Effectively: Interview with William H. Turner, Sculptor

Drew Steis

Within an eighteen-mile stretch along Route 13 on the Chesapeake Bay's Eastern Shore, you can find copies of poor copies of Frederic Remington bronzes, do-it-yourself duck decoy carving sets, and the wonderful oasis of Turner Sculpture in Onley, Virginia.

"The difficulty is, many people think this is a tourist trap, and it is hard to convey that it is not," says William H. Turner. "What do you do, put up a sign that says 'This is not a tourist trap'? You can't just put up a sign that says 'world's greatest sculptor.'"

Turner Sculpture is definitely not a tourist trap. It is a father/son business which in 10 years has become the largest wildlife art gallery and the biggest personal foundry in America. With hundreds of works of original art on display and prices ranging from $45 for a bronze oyster shell to $75,000 for a life-sized, limited edition black bear, it is not the place to casually pick up a souvenir of your summer vacation.

And that is just fine with William Turner, the plain-speaking artist/craftsman who paid his way through dental school by selling his art. His style of doing business may be the most open and most trusting in America and it seems to work. Not only is he selling but he has only had two small thefts in 10 years.

"Here in our gallery anybody can come in off the street and take anything they want home. And when they get back home they can send us a check or send the piece back and that's the way we operate," Turner told *Art Calendar* during a recent tour of his gallery and foundry.

"We will give people their money back anytime they want. There is no point in not letting people try something. We will let people try it for a lifetime if they want—15 or 20 years and if you get tired of it, send it back. We'd love to get it."

This trust of his customers includes inviting potential buyers to stay at the Turner waterfront guest cottage on 180 acres of land. One artist who stayed there reported that he was also urged to eat the native wild ducks and geese filling the freezer.

It took many years for Turner Sculpture to find a successful way of doing business. His 4,000-square-foot gallery is somewhere between a museum and a comfortable living room with fountains, sofas, and soft lighting.

"I was sculpting long before dental school. I was doing porcelain and earthenware wildlife sculpture." Turner is very direct about his art and his success. No longer practicing dentistry, he devotes himself full-time to creating lifelike images of wild birds and animals in a complex of buildings along the busy Ocean Highway that runs down the thin strip of land between the Atlantic Ocean and the Chesapeake Bay.

Always interested in sculpture, Turner started out as a taxidermist. "When I was in my early teens I learned of a gentleman named Robert Rockwell who had worked for the American Museum of Natural History in New York who had retired near my home. He was reputed to be the world's greatest taxidermist and I was soon knocking on his door because I wanted to preserve some of the specimens that I had collected. But he always encouraged me to sculpt rather than do the taxidermy work."

Turner began with ceramic sculpture but soon included bronze figures. His first bronze, a fox and duck, was cast in New York City in a limited edition of five.

"The first few things I sold were just by happenstance. I had a few things in my dental office, a patient displayed others in her home where her affluent friends saw them. And you know how things mushroom in a geometric progression—you just have to get that seed started."

William Turner credits word of mouth for this success. "It is better to be a mediocre sculptor with good friends than a good sculptor with mediocre friends." Turner's porcelain figures of wildlife were soon very much in demand and were picked up by such retail stores as Neiman-Marcus, Cartier's, and J. E. Caldwell.

During this time he continued to create works in bronze, a medium he liked because it has "relatively few size and design limitations."

In 1982, Turner, with his son David and one other employee, opened Turner Sculpture devoted exclusively to bronze sculptures using the lost wax process. The firm has since added a foundry and now employs twenty-four people. Annual sales are more than a thousand pieces of sculpture and revenues are in the seven figure range.

Advertising his work has never been a problem. "Probably one of the most important things we have to help us in advertising is the least glamorous and that is highway signs. Sixty percent of the people who come into the gallery see our highway signs. After they come in here we give them an atmosphere that says we are good sculptors. We show them the casting and the foundry, they get to meet the sculptor. It is more personal than walking into a gallery in Palm Beach or New York where they wear pinstripe suits and the artist is someplace else."

Turner prices his work according to a complicated formula and may increase prices on a limited edition several times before it is sold out.

"The price we get for our work increases. I don't know whether the value increases, because nobody ever sells anything, so how can you tell? We look at the complexity of it and how long it is going to take us to do it and how much money we think we are going to have in it. Then we try to anticipate the demand before we will put a price on it. When it starts selling real well we'll start upping the price. We just had a Blue Heron that we started selling at $3,500 a copy a couple of years ago and when we got through an edition of thirty-five we were getting $9,000 a copy. I'm not saying it doubled in value, I don't make those claims. I'm just telling you what we got for them in the beginning and what we got for them at the end and they were just as easy to sell at $9,000 as they were at $3,500. Blue Herons are great sellers because I think a lot of affluent people see them where they live on the water."

In 1979, Anne Morrow Lindbergh, who had seen Turner's work, commissioned a life-size bald eagle for her husband's memorial and museum in Little Falls, Minnesota. Since then the Turners have created commissions ranging from life-size wolves for the American Museum of Natural History in New York to a life-size family of black bears for the Philadelphia Zoo. Barbara Bush was given a fox weathervane as a gift commissioned by the Congressional Club. Both father and son have works on exhibit at the prestigious Brookgreen Gardens in South Carolina, a Great Blue Heron by William and in 1990 a life-size alligator by David who then became the youngest sculptor ever to be represented there.

William Turner accepts public art commissions but he doesn't go looking for them. "We don't like to enter these competitions where you get all these committees and yuppies who have something to say about what's to be done. Then they get some hippie to do it who will get some stuff from a junkyard and weld it together. We don't like wasting a lot of time in competitions. If somebody wants us to do something they can come to us. We don't really go out seeking things. We like to make it known that we are available to do big pieces of sculpture."

Turner also has strong feelings about gallery representation. "We don't like dealing with galleries. A couple of real small galleries, who are friends of ours, handle our works. But these are all low-key galleries with super nice people. We don't get into the Madison and Fifth Avenue stuff.

"I had a gallery in Palm Beach that sold an awful lot of my work. In fact the last year the guy sold my work he sold $200,000 worth of my stuff but he was a pain to deal with. I had trouble with getting paid, though I eventually got most of it. He would try to hide things from me, it was just too much of a hassle. I finally had to take a sheriff and go get my sculptures out of the gallery. "I would rather deal with a nice person that I can trust and sell nothing than I would getting rich off of some jerk that I have to keep my eye on."

What Turner does rely on is people.

"Not much would be sold without the right people. Mr. Rockwell told me one time that every artist needs an angel. What he meant was some affluent, influential person that will push your work, buy it and get his friends to buy it. That is important to all artists, not just to sculptors but to painters and others. We get referrals for large commissions and we get calls in here every day from people who have seen our work in a friend's home."

Turner also credits his periodic newsletter filled with information about new editions and prices for helping with his success. "We also do a nice looking catalog. It is the type of catalog people would be reluctant to throw away—a tabletop type catalog."

He uses no paid advertising other than roadside billboards. His sales philosophy centers around the understanding of people. "The way we do our marketing is when people come in we essentially ignore them. We don't like to intimidate people. We like people to come in and enjoy themselves. Most people can't afford to buy anything but would still like to look around without a salesman looking over their shoulder. We like to leave people alone and if they want something, they'll find it."

In 10 years William Turner would like to be doing pretty much the same thing as he is doing today. "Sculpting a little bit, maybe painting a little more, getting out on the water more. I like fishing."

For the artist who is not ready to open his own gallery, Turner has useful advice. "The best way to market your work, really, is to have a show through a charitable organization. Have a solo show; that way, you give 'em some whiskey and the only work they can buy is your work. We generally give the organization a 25 percent commission and it's an event for them, a sales program and a community outreach event for us, and everyone is happy."

William and David Turner can be reached at Turner Sculpture, P. O. Box 128, Onley, Virginia 23418, 804-787-2818.

CHAPTER 20

The Computer Age: CD-ROM, the Internet

Imaging: The Mystery, The Language, The Resource

Barbara Dougherty

I have contracted a new disease: Tech-Ache. The symptoms are a headache associated with the arrival of new technologies. I usually medicate my Tech-Ache with a product that bears a warning from the Surgeon General. When the headache is subdued, or I am too numb to notice, then I go in search of information.

I began my latest search with the desire to transfer my paintings onto CD-ROM (Compact Disc, Read-Only Memory) for presentation to galleries and potential clients. Knowing a little about new computer technologies, I also thought it would be exceptional if I could computer enhance the images by removing blemishes and correcting color shifts in the photos. I visualized next adding descriptions of the work with slick computer typefaces.

My idea was born when I played with new software I bought recently on a computer CD. The art images were crisp and impressive.

In the past, I have been impressed with painting images transferred to video—I have in fact created video presentations of artwork. The drawback: video equipment, though abundant in the home, is not found frequently in the commercial establishments of the art marketplace. One reason to pursue CD imaging is that computers are abundant in these places, and are often accompanied by a CD-ROM drive—this allows viewing of CDs that contain pictures on a computer screen.

My search for answers led me through a maze of dungeons and dragons, mermaids and oceans. I encountered tech-monsters bigger and more powerful than the slyest gnome. But I survived and I'm ready to share with you what I discovered.

There are now companies called service bureaus. Some of these were the typesetting companies we went to a few years ago—but typesetting is now a job done mostly on personal computers rather than by these specialists. Thus, these companies have diversified with new services. An artist can take 35mm slides or 4"x5" transparencies to a service bureau and have the images scanned onto a CD. The most popular software for this application is Kodak Photo CD. There are currently various types of these—Master Photo CD, Pro Photo CD, Portfolio CD, and, soon to come, Print CD.

Not only service bureaus, but also some mail order art suppliers, offer image transfer services. One catalog company, Sax (800-558-6696), transfers to Kodak Portfolio CD. Most service bureaus can scan images with as little as a one-day turnaround time. The standard in the industry is that if you want a rush job you pay more.

Usually the images are scanned in at several different exposures, and a "thumbnail" index is provided. The quality of the image depends on the quality of the original photo and the quality of the scanning equipment. There are two common types of scanners: flatbed and drum. The drum scanner is usually higher quality and higher cost.

A scan can cost from as little as $1 to as much as $200. The scanned image can have remarkable quality, although it is not, of course, a perfect reproduction. The cost of the scan may include the production of a match print, which allows you to see the colors and resolution of your image. If the match print is made at the same time a scan is performed, it usually costs less than when done later. You need the match print to truly view the scanned image. If the match print is a disappointment, it may be that the scanner is not a high enough quality instrument.

However, your computer monitor might not allow you to truly view the image. Computer monitors vary immensely in quality, as television screens do; an image will look different on different monitors. The images on CD, though, can also be viewed on a television. Costing about $250 and up, some CD disc players can be connected to any television—portable television players cost about $400.

Resolution in a scan is measured in "dpi" (dots per square inch). Usual resolutions are 300 dpi, 600 dpi, and 1,200 dpi. Although a scanner may be capable of a high resolution, you might not need or be able to work with high resolution. Generally, the higher the scan's resolution, the more computer memory is required to handle the image. If the image will later be printed—for instance, in a brochure—you will want to inform the scanning technician of the intended reproduction size and line-screen (printed resolution quality) that will be used to make the final printed image.

The photo CD is technically an optical disc, which makes it quite versatile. Service bureaus can output images in several different formats. They can be transferred to computer and/or other optical discs that will not necessarily be playable in your CD-ROM drive—many other optical drives play optical discs that cannot be played in ordinary CD-ROM drives. You need to check this capability with the service bureau. Don't assume that the image on any optical disc will be compatible with your equipment.

A friend of mine is publishing her own children's book. She had a 4"x5" transparency scanned onto a disc via flatbed scanner. Then a computer artist used the software programs Adobe Illustrator and Quark XPress to add the book title and author to the image. He also used Adobe Photoshop to correct a color shift in the photo. The computer file was then taken back to the service bureau and output as a printed image. The cost to her was $100. The print will allow her to market her book before it is produced. Thus the new technology not only offers the capability of viewing on computer screens, it also offers new methods of making reproductions.

One new reproduction method uses a dry press. This process takes the computer image and, without color separations, allows it to be printed. NEC of Nashville is one of the companies leading in the application and development of this technology. NEC produces magazines like *Cosmopolitan* and *National Geographic Traveler*.

Computer artists who work with programs like Adobe Photoshop use service bureaus to have images scanned onto optical discs. They then take these image files and photo-retouch or add to the image artistically. They also use programs that are available on both Macintosh and IBM platforms to add graphics and text to the images. When they print these images, they have several different options.

Artists who do this work report that the quality of their work is dependent on both image input (scanning) and output (file transfer to computer storage or print). The options for output, in addition to dry press, include ordinary or laser computer printers. This output is relatively low quality compared to the output techniques available at service bureaus. Service bureaus usually have either Iris printers, dye sublimation printers, or they can do match prints of files. There are several types of Iris printers; some can print on any surface, including watercolor paper or fabric. In fact artists have gone to producing small editions of reproductions using Iris printers. The only issue raised about this has been the question of longevity, or how long the print will last. An Iris print can cost $50 and up. A common size of Iris print allows two 8"x10" images to be printed twice on one side. Dye sublimation prints can be more costly than Iris prints. Match prints—high-quality in-process prints not meant as a finished product in itself— can be more expensive also.

Well, at this point I can take a transparency and get it transferred to CD disc. I can view this image on a computer or a television monitor. I can adjust the image for viewing—close-up or cropping is possible. I can enhance the CD with an audio sound track. I can index and organize the images with software like Kodak Shoebox. I can integrate the images with text and graphics using other programs.

The disappointment is that I cannot easily take the images edited with text and graphics and put them back on a new CD. The machinery for the re-transfer to a new CD is scarce, and the process is costly. However, the product called Kodak Portfolio CD does have a limited ability to allow the user to add text and sound to the presentation. The less expensive alternative is to have my files of edited images output by a service bureau as film (transparency) and then re-scan the edited images back onto a new CD. The drawback, of course, is that the generations of transfer will weaken the images, and the cost is still high.

My Tech-Ache became very intense when I discovered the last bit of information. I was told that every ad agency under the sun craves the ability to create presentations the way I want to present my art. Everyone says it should be a service easily obtained in the near future. They say that my desire is just ahead of its time. So my next writing will be the Artist Lament—it will be a song that describes a showdown between a dying artist and the smoking gun of technology that is always either too far ahead or too far behind.

One more piece of the mystery of all this new technology that I tried to solve is to discover how one locates a service bureau and how to be assured of quality and fairness in negotiation. Whenever there is a new technology, there will be many problems and errors made before the consumer becomes educated. To avoid these pitfalls, consult the Association of Imaging Service Bureaus, an international trade association founded in 1990 and located in Greensboro, North Carolina (800-844-2472). You could also drop in on a printer or computer dealer in your area and ask for a recommendation of a scanning service.

A good practice when contracting with a company for the first time is to do one experimental scan and output before you contract for a large job.

Whenever I write articles that contain technical information, I get letters from others complaining about omissions or nonstandard practices I write about. I've been told I'm like a cook who doesn't use a careful recipe. Sure, I make bread—but my bread is made more by intuition than by information. This means that even if I'm brave in exploring these new territories, I'm not always completely accurate in my understanding. So take the information herein not as gospel, but as a primer to understand the language of a new opportunity, or as just a bit of an answer to the mystery. Just don't get a Tech-Ache over it.

Warning: Big Problems Ahead

Barbara Dougherty

A big new door has opened and a myriad of new opportunities and problems suddenly are confronting artists. The door opens to the electronic highway.

You can access your friend's computer through a modem. That friend can access other computers, and so on. Images can travel from one place to another in seconds.

Suddenly, you will be hearing that you can have the images of your visual art viewed by thousands of interested people who sit by their computers and see visually dynamic snapshots of your art. You will hear that you will be able to present images with the smallest of effort, and that you will therefore be able to make sales more easily than ever.

The actual process involves transforming images into digital messages by scanners. The scanned images then go into a digital file that can be sent on the airways through and into computers. With these images can go descriptions of artists, artwork, sales information, etc.

I have talked to many different companies all offering to do about the same thing. First they will do the scanning and create the sales info for you. Then they will link you to the electronic highway via software and modems; your images will be available to anyone whose computer accesses a certain telephone number. These services may involve initiation fees and maintenance fees costing from $5 to $5,000 or even more.

These are the things to consider:
- Who will really see your images? Do art buyers at this time really sit at their computers in hopes of finding a painting to buy? Or are the electronic highways navigated by tech-heads who want free information, free software, and perhaps free images?
- Your images can be downloaded as files to anyone's computer and could be used for any purpose. Although this practice may be a copyright violation, it is easy to do. It is not so easy to take the time and energy to do the policing that protects

your legal rights. At the very least, be sure that your images are scanned in at computer monitor resolution—this means they will look good while being viewed on the computer monitor, but they will look jagged if downloaded and printed out.

• The providers of the service of transmitting your images may ask you for a contract that keeps them from having any legal liability for the reproduction of your images in order to perform the scanning and transmission. Your signature on this document may in fact transfer your precious copyrights. Remember that copyright is the right to copy. You can't sign it away and keep it at the same time. Review the contract language carefully.

The field of computer communications is wide open to legal land mines that have yet to be decided. Besides the copyright questions touched on above, there will probably be many tests of law in the next several years or even decades as these cases weave their way through the technology, the courts, and appeals processes.

The time is now. The technology is here. Hold on to your hats—it's going to be a bumpy, bumpy ride.

CHAPTER 21

Getting Others to Show Your Slides

New Thoughts On Slide Registries

Peggy Hadden

There are several once-a-year jobs that will notify people that you and your art are alive and well. One of those tasks: to contact or to keep in touch with slide registries. Your state arts council should have a list of slide registries. Also consult the "Slide Registries" section of *Art Calendar* for registries that are farther away from you but will still accept your slides.

I think that slide registries are one of the most underused resources that artists have. Consider this: a whole group of largely nonprofit organizations, at no charge (or a minimal one) to you, will act on your behalf, showing your work to curators, gallery owners, private dealers, and potential buyers. What would that same service cost you if you had to construct it and fund it yourself? Yet we tend to take them for granted. We always have something more glamorous to take care of, and if there is something we don't have time to do, this is usually the area that has to wait. Like a good resumé, though, slide registries are out there working for you, an unpaid employee, while you may not have the time to handle these aspects of your career.

There are several preparatory steps you will need to take before participating in slide registries.

First-rate slides of your work are essential. I find that the cost of having slides made is less daunting if I can get them done as I finish each piece of work. If you suddenly have a bill from your photographer for slides of twenty artworks, that is going to take a real bite out of your budget. And you should analyze whether you can have dupes made for less than the photographer is charging you.

Next, the labeling process has to be tackled. The important part here is that your labels are thorough, correct, and legible. Measure those paintings, don't guess how big they are. Decide which twenty slides will make up your ideal slide sheet, then set about making multiples of that ideal. You will find that substitutions will most likely become necessary, but stick to the original plan as long as you can. Make as many sets as you can. Never send out your original slides, as you will need them again for more dupes and you don't want to be held up waiting for the return of slides before you can send more out. I've gotten slides back up to two years after they went out. That's putting others in control of your career, which they too often may seem to be anyway.

If you have decided to take your own slides, maybe this is finally the time that you should read up on how to do the best job. Or how about taking advantage of a class or a seminar specializing in art photography? A third option is to call a photographer whom you know and arrange for a tutorial or one-on-one session on how to capture your work at its very best. Caution: Artists traditionally dislike slides of their work. Don't expect the photographic reproduction to match your original. On the other hand, by correctly lighting your artwork, getting the best film type and correct f-stops, and eliminating unnecessary background distractions, you can produce slides that will serve your work well at the slide registries and can get positive results for you.

The next step in preparing for a visit to leave slides—and this is true no matter whether you are dropping them off or mailing them—is an up-to-date resumé. By up-to-date, I mean not only listing details of your last show, but a current phone number, address, and Zip Code. If you are moving, list both old and new addresses, first the current one and then, "after Nov 1st," and the new address. Nothing is worse than finding an artist whose work you want in a show you are curating, then discovering that he has disappeared. Even if you are unsure of where you'll be, put a "can also be reached c/o" phone number on your resumé. It is more professional and you won't miss an important contact.

The next step is optional. If you have many slide sheets that are identical as far as the slides you've included, it's a good idea to prepare a slide list, naming all of the slides you've included, with measurements and titles and media. In visiting registries as a freelance curator, I've found that the easier it is to look, the more inclined I am to do so. Include a copy of your slide sheet and resumé each place where you leave slides. Note: These are the parts that may disappear from your folder at the registry first, so stop by every three to six months to be sure that all of the parts you've included are still there, providing replacements if necessary.

Next, call to find out the days and times that these registries are open to accept new slides. One person is usually in charge of the slide file, and you should make every effort to get his name and give a favorable impression. This is a person who can be of great help to you and it is worth the small amount of time it takes to create a good impression. These people are often interns or volunteers and not the directors of organizations, who would usually get your attention. However, they sometimes curate shows of works from the slide files and they could include your work. They'll appreciate your attention, too.

The last step in getting your slides into a registry is the most important. I've been thinking about it a lot lately. You will receive a form to fill out from the registry concerning where your artworks fit. Categories will be listed like painting, drawing, sculpture, etc. which are fairly straightforward, but also others that are more ambiguous, like mixed media and collage. Ordinarily, I would check one of these, perhaps collage, since my work is largely collage with painted backgrounds. But think about it. How many curators come into a slide registry, planning a show of strictly collage work? Don't you think that more of them come in and are curating a painting show? Am I not cutting myself off from their consideration by "ghettoizing" myself into a marginal and much less-used area called collage? Put another way, whose slides have a better chance of being seen—an artist who puts the slides in a popular category like painting, or the one who chooses a category like collage or mixed media? It may seem like a minute point, but I believe we control our careers only up to a point, where more powerful figures can help or hinder us. So let's carefully consider where we put ourselves, and how we classify our work. If the guests at a registry don't see our slides, it may be because of the category we've chosen for them.

Take an extra set of slides and ask if you can put your work into more than one section of the file. Check off more than one category for your work.

Also, most slide files are set up so that two of your slides are put into a mixed carousel, allowing the viewer to see many artists' work at one sitting. That way, they can weed out work that is not of the style or content they specifically seek. You will need to bring two of your best slides for the carousel, as well as your sheet of twenty works. Be sure to include those two again on the sheet of twenty, so that they are visible in both places.

In an age of specialization, when bookstores are filled with books on how to write the best resumé, etc., we need to be very savvy, very aware of the small elements of difference that can help our work to be seen. There is a "best" way to accomplish tasks we have to do as artists and that way changes as we understand more about how the process works. We owe it to our work to do everything we can to give it the exposure it deserves.

How to Participate in Slide Registries

1. Write to the sponsoring organization and request guidelines, an application, and other pertinent information about the registry and the sponsoring agency. "Pertinent information" could include a brochure illustrating accepted artworks, a copy of the jurisdiction's Percent-for-Art legislation, and other helpful stuff.
2. Ask to be placed on the mailing list to receive Percent-for-Art and other announcements.
3. When you make your slides, pay attention to the slide registry's prospectus as well as other clues such as their illustrated brochure. You may wish to tailor your slides to feature your artworks only, your artworks installed, or a combination of both. If none of your artworks are actually installed in corporate or government locations, enlist a friend to lend his office walls to you for slide-making *in situ,* or to talk the management into accepting one or more of your pieces on loan. The organizations administering public art projects prefer to see artists with experience.
4. When you send in your packet, be sure to include a self-addressed stamped envelope (SASE), whether the guidelines specify it or not.
5. From time to time, send the registry a batch of new slides, an updated resumé, and—if required—an updated application form. There are two reasons to send in new slides from time to time:
   a. New slides keep the registry up-to-date on your new experience and/or your new styles and artwork available. Your slides might be less likely to stagnate in an "inactive" file.
   b. Slides can wear out. Slides can fade or change color after as little as one hour of cumulative projection time. Even slides stored in the dark can fade after just six months.
6. Always view your slides, projected, before sending them anywhere.

Working Effectively with Art Consultants

Peggy Hadden

With the arrival of the 1990s, the art world has made another of its periodic shifts. Many older, more established galleries have merged or closed; adventurous new ones have sprung up. Several artist-run cooperative spaces are in their third decade of successful operation, and alternative spaces, once the artist's other exhibition choice besides commercial galleries, have themselves become one of the strata of the art establishment. So, we now find ourselves with a variety of avenues for showing and selling our artwork. Among these choices, we should consider working with art consultants.

Art consultants function as small service companies, and often receive the confidence of other corporate organizations, while the individual artist may seem to be a small, unknown, and unpredictable element. In our slow-moving economy, corporate decisions to buy anything must be cautiously thought out and supported by objective opinions from outside "experts."

Another reason for working with consultants is that they have seen many of their traditional clients fade away because of the economy, so those who have stayed in business have aggressively pursued architects and interior designers as well as individual buyers to make up for other lost business.

While every gathering of artists produces a lurid tale of an artist's woes with an unethical art consultant, personally I have been rather fortunate in dealing with them. Certainly, one must seek out consultants who are, as best as can be determined, reputable. Ask for the names of other artists who have worked with them and check out their business methods. You would do as much in non-art dealings, such as in making a major purchase. If you are in doubt, a telephone call to the Better Business Bureau will tell you if there have been complaints about a consultant. I do not recommend that you pursue an arrangement with a consultant about whom you know absolutely nothing. But after some checking, armed with the names of several legitimate consultants, I think you'll agree that they are more accessible and less egotistical than most gallery owners.

Art consultants can offer the artist a non-gallery alternative that may turn out to be as lucrative, yet avoid the emotional wear and tear that preparing exhibitions for a gallery entails. For one thing, the consultant might be located some distance from you in another part of the country; though the geographical distance will require long-distance phone calls, faxing, and shipping, this may also allow you to keep your sanity and dignity through the whole transaction.

You can, and should, work with several consultants at one time. There are consultants who specialize in certain fields, such as hospitals, cruise ships, etc. I work with several consultants in different cities, as well as with one whose dealings are all in the Far East.

To initiate working with a consultant, send him a slide package that includes a cover letter, resumé, and retail price list. In the cover letter, indicate who referred you or where you got their name. State your interest in working with him and mention any corporate sales you have had. If you have worked with other reputable consultants, mention this—it can reassure your reader of your professionalism.

One of the major complaints of art consultants is that many of the artists they've dealt with were amateurish or unpolished in their business dealings. Problems include frequent price changes, poor record-keeping, and failure to communicate vital information such as address changes.

Indicate in your letter that you would welcome a studio visit if they are near you, or that you would be happy to come and show them samples of your work. If this is geographically impossible, you might offer to follow up the initial slides with more detailed photos or 4"x5" transparencies.

Close the letter by stating that you will call in a week to follow up and arrange an appointment. One week later, call to see if there is sufficient interest in your work to merit an appointment. Don't wait longer, as you'll give a better impression of promptness, and if they receive lots of mail (they almost certainly do), they might forget the strength of your first contact with them.

Appointments with consultants are generally more relaxed than with gallery personnel. The most a consultant can do is to offer to show your work in future slide presentations. The least they are able to do is tell you that for the clients they have now your work would not be appropriate. It is a more straightforward business transaction, avoiding personal likes or dislikes, than having a gallery owner pass judgment at a face-to-face encounter.

A price list for your work is crucial and should be typed and dated. You want to provide retail prices—that is, the price for which the work will finally be sold to the collector. Thus, regardless of what arrangement for commission is worked out, on the market your work has a stable, single price. This is to your advantage and should be maintained, no matter what. If you get the reputation for producing work that varies in price, you will always have difficulty getting the price you ask.

It is good market strategy, though, to mention that discounts can be arranged in the sale of three or more pieces. Many consultants' sales involve several pieces and this offer gives them an incentive to work with you. On the price list, state that all prices include dealers' commissions. Also note any works that are currently framed or where other expenses have been incurred. Figure these into your price. Even though consultants prefer to do their own framing, if the piece they want has been framed for a show or other event, you've still paid for the frame. If you include this added expense in your price in the first place, you will not find yourself at a loss later after the piece is sold and reframed by the consultant.

Another aspect to be considered in working with art consultants is the size of the work. Because consultants often work with clients who are looking for art for lobbies and conference rooms, art consultants usually prefer to show larger work. Many will not even consider work smaller than 24". When my 30"x60" works were shown, they sold well. When my work went through a small phase (8"x10"), I was told to call back when my work got bigger. Like those decorators who sell "books by the yard" for people's libraries, this seemed like art sold by the yard! They were apologetic about it, but pointed out that it took as much time and energy to sell small work as larger, and larger work usually brought a higher price. I found other outlets for selling my small works, but I include this anecdote so you won't be surprised. When I'm ready to work larger, I'll contact those consultants again.

Oh, yes—let's not forget subject matter. Consultants have no objection to trends in abstraction or realism, but they say they cannot sell nudity or politically sensitive art.

A consultant might want only your slides at first, as most of them work with their clients by first showing them a slide presentation of the kinds of work they have available. Needless to say, the quality of your slides is crucial here. A future sale depends on sharp, clear images that are well lit and have solid black or white backgrounds. If the client shows an interest in your work (he will probably be interested in several artists), the consultant will then ask you for several pieces on consignment. At this point a list should be drawn up of all works taken by the consultant for consideration—generally up to six or eight.

I would be loath to part with more than that for several reasons. Certainly for security, but also because these works will be out of circulation for some time and you don't want to miss other sale or exhibition possibilities.

Back to the consignment list, a legal document that makes the consultant responsible for the work until it is returned or sold and the artist is paid. The list contains retail prices and the amount of commission to be paid. It is signed by the consultant and copies are kept by both parties. It should be dated and marked "Received on Consignment." The artist should keep all consignment records in one notebook to avoid loss and to quickly see what works are out of the studio.

Art consultants charge for their services in several ways. Some charge the client a fixed fee, with no commission taken from the selling prices of the sold artwork. Some work with the retail prices set by the artists and then take commissions from those prices—up to 50 percent is common. Art consultants who take their clients to galleries are paid by the gallery—usually 10 percent—after the client has paid the full retail price. Yet another arrangement is for the consultant to charge the client an hourly fee and also to receive a 10 percent commission from the artist on sold work.

Artists must be careful to avoid giving different prices to different consultants or dealers who might be competing for the same sale. If slides of your work are shown at two different prices, needless to say it will be sold for the lowest price. This will alienate the consultant who was underbid.

Working successfully with art consultants is best accomplished by being well organized, always following up, and keeping complete and accurate records. Be sure to contact everyone who should be advised if you have an address or phone number change. Periodically check on the work that is out on consignment. You'll find that you gain respect from consultants for doing this, though it might seem hard to do at first. Call and say you are making a periodic check on all work that is out and ask when would be a good time to stop by. It is more likely to be accepted as standard professional practice if it is done regularly and will keep a consultant on the straight and narrow knowing that you check in periodically. Calling beforehand is more professional than just suddenly showing up at what could be a truly inopportune time.

Take your consignment list with you; if you find any discrepancy between what your list says and the work you see, ask for an explanation. If you are told that a piece is out being viewed for possible sale, get a date when its return or a sale confirmation is expected and when you can stop by to view it or get paid. Check for damage and bring anything that has changed to the consultant's attention. Works on paper are particularly fragile and might require special handling.

If you find that works you've left on consignment are not even being shown (for example, assistants aren't familiar with your work or your name), take it back. This isn't easy to do. However, you might find another buyer. At any rate, you won't be deluding yourself about possible sales when none are forthcoming. This system of keeping your work is absolutely professional and you should check all work that is out of the studio on loan or consignment at least once a year.

For many artists, showing and selling artwork through a commercial gallery is their ultimate goal. For others, a gallery might not offer them the best solution. What is rarely mentioned, but often true, is that a gallery owner may expect the artist to show up with his own following. This following is then expected to pay full gallery prices for works that they have been accustomed to buying for less in the artist's studio. Along with the attention a gallery can help to achieve for an artist's work, the artist will also find situations where personalities conflict, egos get bruised, and artists within a gallery will often (always?) compete for the attention of the gallery owner, not unlike small children in a nursery.

Again, we have more sales and exhibition choices than ever before. The important thing is to find what works best for you.

PART 6

Competing For Grants Effectively

Poetry Desk, 1997, typewriter, desk, neon, laser-etched acrylic,
11" x 19" x 24", Vincent Koloski, San Francisco, California

CHAPTER 22

Getting It Right from the Start: Careful Grant Proposals

Before You Write Your Grant Proposal: Interview with Dr. Judy Levine, Cause Effective

Peggy Hadden

Artists write proposals to get funding for projects they wish to create. Even if there is no specific project but the artist seeks funds to continue making art, the funder must be convinced that some accomplishment will be achieved by giving support to this artist at this time. In fund-raising, this is called the "Why now?" factor.

In order to create a winning proposal, certain factors must be addressed. Most proposal writing in the arts is done by arts organizations in order to maintain their framework, plan events, and provide artists with opportunities to create and exhibit their work. Many of the concepts used by arts organizations can be adapted for use by the individual artist in search of grant funding.

Dr. Judy Levine is a proposal and fund-raising expert in the arts. She has taught, written articles, and consulted on fund-raising with more than a hundred grassroots and mid-sized arts organizations. She spoke with me about individual artists and what they need to know in order to craft successful proposals. Her advice focused on what the organization or artist needs to do before the proposal writing even begins.

JL: Think of the proposal process as communication—a dialogue. In order not to be at a disadvantage, you first need to know whom you are addressing. You don't want to start off on the wrong foot, and first impressions stay with people a long time. Without knowing something about the recipient of your proposal, it's purely a chance thing that you'll get funded, no matter how convincing your proposal is. And the chances don't improve, no matter how many proposals you submit. You don't want to waste your time. So you want to improve your chances by knowing as much as possible about where you are seeking funds.

PH: Tell us a little about funding sources. Do they have any traits in common? Is there any way to tell if they'll choose one creative project over another?

JL: Every funder has particular things which they hope to accomplish with their money. This may even be legally binding, as when the funds that established the foundation came from a bequest in someone's will. That person wanted their funds to benefit certain causes or types of individuals. This is the funder's mandate, their objective. Even if they say they are giving to help needy artists, they may only give to artists who work in a certain style or who have reached a certain professional level. You, as an artist, also have a mandate, to create and exhibit your work.

Drawing two circles next to each other, Levine labeled one "Funder's Mandate" and the other "Your Mandate."

You need to make the two circles merge partially. Where there is an overlap, you and this funder have something in common and this is the area you must emphasize when proposing to this funder. Stress the project, not the artist. You want this to say "Don't fund me, fund my work." Saying things like "This will enable me to . . ." sounds like you're asking for money to do laundry.

PH: Where do arts organizations go to find out about potential funders and their interests?

JL: The Foundation Center is a funding resources library. They have collected an abundance of materials about possible funders, broken down in several ways, such as arts funders, funders who will only give within a certain state, etc. There are guidelines for creating better proposals, as well as a collection of funders' annual reports. Perhaps the most valuable information which they have are each foundation's IRS 990 forms. This form will list who the foundation gave funds to, as well as the names and addresses of the board of directors. The 990s are kept on microfilm and filed alphabetically. These are readable on microfiche machines, which are easy to operate and are located near the 990 files. The Foundation Center is connected by over 150 cooperating collections around the country. To find the one nearest you, call 1-800-424-9836 between 9 and 5 E.S.T. Monday through Friday.

To start your search for funding sources, go to the reference desk and ask for the latest edition of *The Foundation Center's Guide to Funding for Individuals*. Much of the material at the Foundation Center is intended for groups and lists funders who cannot give to individuals, so keep your focus on the materials that fit your requirements. Consult the examples at the front of the book to use it most effectively. Each funder is listed with a current address and contact person. You will also find the fund's total assets, how many grants they made last year, what their interests are, and how to apply. There are some particular things you can surmise from a listing. If the fund's name and the principal officer are the same, or if the last name is the same, it is probably a family foundation. Many family foundations don't employ a full-time staff person, but have their mail addressed to a post office box. These funders will be more difficult to approach, unless you know someone in the family. By checking on how many grants they gave last year and then looking up their IRS 990, you can tell if they only gave to a few people, maybe friends. If the 990 lists a number of artists as grant recipients, try to trace the connection. Are they all from one geographic area, or all of a certain age group? In your first exposure to this volume, try to make a list (ten to twenty at least) of possible sources for a grant. This phase is known as "identifying."

PH: Time-wise, what percentage of the whole process is taken to accomplish this?

JL: About five percent. After gathering the names of possibilities and checking the 990s, you will begin to eliminate. Now we'll begin the second phase—cultivating and refining your research. If there is a staff person named in the listing, call him up and introduce yourself. Ask how to proceed. Check on the deadline date—it might have changed since the listing went to press—and ask if particular forms are required. If there are guidelines, request these. The most important fact about this phone call is that you are establishing a relationship with the one person who can aid you most in guiding your proposal to the decision-making committee. If there are many proposals received, the staff person will read each one and write a cover-page summary. While a staff person does not have the power to fund you, they do have the power to eliminate your proposal from consideration. Ask if a meeting can be set up to show your work. If this person seems helpful, you might ask a question, such as "I notice from last year's list of recipients that all of them seem to come from one area and is this something that the foundation emphasizes?"

PH: At this stage of your proposal process, these people should be included on your mailing list and receive press releases about your work and any other distinctions you've received.

JL: Absolutely. You need to familiarize them with your work and your name. When your proposal arrives, it should be almost a confirmation of things they already know about you. I hate to send any request in cold. Cultivating is 90 percent of the proposal process. In the beginning you can invite them to events in which you are participating.

Ask them for things like their time, things they can say yes to. Then maybe you'll want to request in-kind services, such as printing your announcements for a show, which they can give you without money being involved, before you ask for funding for a project.

In cultivating possible funders, don't forget the support possible from your own circle of sources—people who have bought your work, vendors who sell you supplies, co-workers at your day job, your government representatives, other family members—all can be helpful in ways that you and they might not have thought. Just as one of the functions of board members of an arts organization is to speak up for their group to friends and possible funders, this function can be performed by one of your sources who can write an endorsement letter or make a phone call in your support and say all the good things that need to be said in praise of your work.

Another word about that meeting you are seeking with the foundation's staff person. It's a good idea to take someone with you—a supporter or collaborator—to provide an outside viewpoint and keep the conversation flowing. You should rehearse the scheduled meeting, planning what you want to stress, and making sure that you all have the same agenda. If the staff person is not able to encourage you in regard to your proposed project, see if they will suggest other funders you might try. If they offer this, ask if you may use their name ("so-and-so suggested that you might find my project interesting"), but never use a name without permission, as this is sure to come out and be embarrassing. These staff people are largely professionals in their fields and know one another.

The next part of your proposal process should involve long-term planning. A yearly list of whom you want to submit proposals to and those you will be cultivating will help you plan ahead so that when you suddenly get an exhibition and face unexpected expenses, there will be resources in place to help you. Plan also by devising a core proposal. You can tailor this for each project that comes up. Start with a full proposal, then reduce it to two pages, then to one page. These can be used in a variety of ways, depending on the size of the application required and good words and phrases concerning your work won't have to be thought up at the last minute. This solicitation phase is the actual "ask" and once you've got your core proposal done, should take only about two percent of your proposal process. Using the quotes of critics who liked your work is a good idea, too. Try stringing several quotes together linked in a written narrative. One advantage of this is that critics write for general audiences, and don't include things that the general public doesn't understand. The committee which reviews your proposal will likely be made up of people who do not come from the art world, so you'll want to eliminate jargon which only an insider would understand.

Here's another false step to avoid with a proposal. Don't include information which the funder does not need to know in order to fund you. It will cloud the focus you want them to have on your request. Individual artists are often guilty of this and you should review your proposal while asking yourself, "Do they need to know this?" Proposals are not about theory. They are about providing sufficient information so that a funder can see what your project will be and that you are the best one to carry it out. If you must supply a budget, try to lump like items together and don't break it down into such small categories as pencils. You may be trying to create trustworthiness, but instead may create doubts about your ability to plan and professionally carry out a large project on a budget.

In using the guidelines provided by the foundation, it is wise to try reading them as if you were the committee instead of the artist. By looking at them from another viewpoint, it may become clear that this project doesn't belong with this foundation. If this happens, go on to the next funding candidate on your list, choosing one where the connection is closer. Keep thinking about those circles and be sure they merge, at least somewhat.

A proposal should begin with a project summary. This should be one to two sentences long and include the amount of your request. Have someone else go over your whole proposal and be tough enough to take their criticism. If they ask you where such-and-such is and you've included it, you may need to give it more emphasis—after all, they didn't see it.

Don't be afraid to resubmit a declined proposal a second time. Before resubmitting it, try to find out why it wasn't funded. Perhaps there was a high-profile compelling need which won over your application but is not eligible again this year. Don't be afraid to send it back for another try. This is known in fund-raising as "Ask-ask."

The last part of the proposal process is recognition. You've been officially notified of your grant award and won't want to delay your thank-you's to both the president of the foundation and also to the staff person who was so helpful. Should the staff person ever leave, you will have connections at two funders and additional goodwill in the future for help on a new project. One way you can thank funders is by including their names on press materials or on a plaque at the site of your completed project. This benefits you, too, by giving you credibility and linking you with the funder in the future.

Funders like to fund artists with whom they've worked in the past. Believe it or not, they feel they have a stake in your success. For this reason, maybe you should go back to a past funder and ask again. While they may skip funding you for a year or two, they are still more likely to fund you—if they like your project—if they've funded you before.

PH: Dr. Levine, thank you for your insights into what makes a proposal's chances better, and into a way of thinking about grants that might not have occurred to our audience before.

If readers have specific questions, they may be sent with a SASE to Dr. Judy Levine, Cause Effective, 39 W. 14th St., Suite 408, New York, NY 10011.

PART 7

Planning and Measuring Results

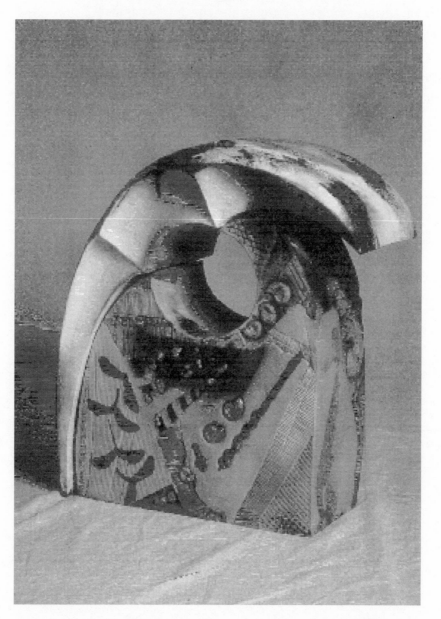

Quarter Moon, 1995, 20" x 15" x 13", Cheryl Herr-Rains, Alma, Michigan

CHAPTER 23

Art Plans

To Plan or Not to Plan: The Why's and How-to's of Creating a Market Plan

Ilise Benun

How many times have you wanted to write a marketing plan but thought you couldn't, or started the process and didn't finish it?

The truth is you don't have to have a marketing plan. It is possible to grow your business without one—many people do. However, it can only help you. The ongoing process of working a marketing plan provides the opportunity to continually learn about your business and your market while helping you achieve your business goals.

Designing a marketing plan doesn't have to be an overwhelming task. It doesn't have to be a 100-page manuscript that you slave over and then put on a shelf to gather dust. Anyone, with or without business experience, can create a marketing plan. It can be simple to write, easy to use, and can fit on one page.

What Is a Marketing Plan?

Your marketing plan is your map to more business. It includes a market you have carefully chosen, a series of steps that will lead you toward the goal(s) you have set for yourself, and a timetable of when and how you will follow the steps.

Since you design your own plan, you are free to do only those things you want to do and to change the steps according to the evolution of your priorities. Your marketing plan is not a weapon. It is a tool designed to help you, not hurt or burden you. It is as unique and individual as you are, and as flexible as you need it to be. It can save you time, energy, and money—if you let it.

Why Use a Marketing Plan?

The goal of any marketing effort is to create and develop long-term relationships with prospective clients.

Here are two types of plans to achieve this. The Specific Marketing Plan has a narrow focus and a finite timetable, with goals such as "I want to earn $60,000 this year," "I want three new retail outlets to carry my work," or "I want my work profiled in the local newspaper." The second type, the Ongoing Plan, is actually a set of tools that becomes an integral part of the running of your business on a daily basis—it is a vehicle that supports the ongoing development of your business relationships.

The Specific Marketing Plan

If you have a clear-cut goal, this plan is for you. Begin by following these five simple steps. To illustrate, we'll use potter Alice F. and her marketing plan.

1. Set a Marketing Goal

Alice wanted to market her small ceramic vessels to upscale floral shops and trendy housewares stores in the SoHo area of Manhattan. Her goal was to find three retail stores that would sell her work.

The key is to set a realistic goal by taking into consideration the money and time available to you. Don't be afraid to start very small or to break down a far-reaching goal into several smaller, more manageable goals. The smaller the goal, the easier it will be to accomplish it and to move on to the next.

2. Choose Your Market

Alice literally roamed the dozen or so small streets of SoHo collecting the names and telephone numbers of the shops she liked. This informal process of gathering information also served as a pressure-free way to begin to develop relationships with the store owners or buyers.

Focus your efforts in identifying your market by asking questions such as: With whom do I want to work, where do I have contacts, what is the ideal environment for my work?

Then, create a small list of prospects. Nobody said you had to market to 1,000 prospects all at once. Pick a number you think you can handle, like 100 or 20 or 5.

3. Select Your Promotional Tools

Alice decided to send a brief introductory letter with a few slides of her work and then to follow up with phone calls and a color copy of a photo of one of her vessels.

Tools for reaching your market can include letters, calls, postcards, trade shows, advertising, personal visits. Remember, more isn't necessarily better. You don't have to use every tool available. Choose the ones you feel comfortable with and use them to their fullest. For example, if you receive press coverage of your work, don't assume everyone has seen it. Maximize its impact by photocopying the piece and sending it to everyone on your mailing list, and include it as part of your standard promotional packet.

4. Determine Time and Money Budget

Marketing does not have to cost a lot of money. Alice chose to have a few color photocopies made rather than getting expensive four-color postcards printed (the standard minimum print run would have been 500 pieces). This allowed her the flexibility to create only as many pieces as she needed. Some tools—such as her use of a personal letter in place of a brochure—allowed her to spend time instead of money.

Keeping in mind that the marketing tasks needed to be integrated into her already busy schedule, Alice determined that she could devote four hours per week and a nominal budget for postage, letterhead, photocopies, and phone calls.

However, when creating your plan, you may not be able to finalize the time and money budget until after you have completed the next step.

5. Determine the Specific Actions to be Taken

To avoid becoming overwhelmed and unable to complete her plan, Alice assigned herself manageable tasks that realistically fit into the day-to-day management of her business. She broke the steps down to the smallest tasks possible and determined the order in which she would accomplish them. Here is Alice's plan.

Week and Task

1   Gather names and create a mailing list of ten potential clients, either on computer or mailing labels
2   Write introductory letter
3   Generate and send five letters
4   Send five follow-up color photocopies
5   Make five follow-up phone calls
6   Review and evaluate plan
7   Send five more letters
8   Send five more color photocopies
9   Make five more follow-up calls
10 Review and evaluate plan

Learning from Your Marketing Plan

Putting your plan on paper leaves you free to think about other things—like your art—so that when it's time to do your marketing you don't have to spend valuable time trying to remember where you were in the process, which market you were targeting, where your promo packets were, or how many people you had called. All that information is safely written down.

Carol K., a mask maker from Brooklyn, New York, says her marketing plan gives her structure. "I've always hated marketing. I thought it would be draining, but instead it has been energizing. My plan gives me steps to follow and that motivates me to do it."

Carol set out to find a gallery in London to represent her work. She planned to research and put together a list of ten prospective galleries, send them introductory letters and slides, then follow up with phone calls, spending two hours a week over the course of three to four weeks.

Contrary to her expectations, Carol found that between looking through international directories at the library and writing letters to verify contact names, putting the list together required six weeks instead of the two weeks she had originally budgeted. Through her research, she also learned which galleries were appropriate for her work and which were not. "Besides saving money which would have been wasted if I hadn't done the preliminary investigation, the most valuable thing I learned was how to make a realistic plan, one which breaks the tasks down into every little step."

The Ongoing Plan

New Jersey–based jewelry artist Lynne G. will be using the Ongoing Plan, the goal of which is to provide a way to continually nurture her relationships with prospective and current clients. Her tool: regular postcard mailings. She will be sending out color copies of photos of her recycled glass jewelry every six weeks to her list of fifty carefully chosen prospective retailers on the East Coast.

This simple strategy allows Lynne to get quality samples of her work in front of her clients and prospects on a regular basis, building familiarity so that when they are ready to order or reorder, they will have her number handy and can call.

Building her mailing list from scratch, Lynne is constantly on the lookout for potential clients. If she sees an article about or an advertisement for a store where her work might be appropriate, she calls for their address and puts them on her list. She also plans to call everyone on the list annually to see if they are receiving her materials.

Because there isn't the pressure of a sales call, mailing list maintenance calls often generate interest and can result in a sale.

Conclusion

Your marketing plan, whether you select the Specific or the Ongoing Plan, can be tailored to fit into the creation of your art and the running of your business. Easy to execute on any budget, both plans will assist you in building long-term client relationships and provide opportunities for you to be visible to your market in unique and creative ways.

Making a Business Plan

Barbara Dougherty

I've heard artists describe success as being in the right place at the right time. I have also heard that it just takes the right gallery, agent, or publisher. My experience is that it takes a more deliberate effort, and a business plan is essential. The main ingredients in a plan that can sustain an artist through good times and bad are:

- Focus on your vision and your art
- Define marketing directions that suit your personality
- Identify who can help you
- Build a patron list
- Build a reputation
- Look out for the alligators

Focus on your art and your vision

You are the only one who can do the art, thus the first ingredient is the most important. There is a right time to begin to execute a business plan—it is when your art is your style and your ideas. I remember when an artist friend, impressed with the style of art I had learned from Frank Hamilton, urged me to go out and seek gallery representation. I felt reluctant to follow his advice because all I was doing was copying a style; I had not evolved my own fashion, and I had not evolved my own idea. The history of modern art is a history of powerful ideas. If you have developed your own style and have a grasp on the idea that compels you to produce the art, then you have laid the foundation for a successful business plan. The execution of the art is of primary importance and laying hands on the idea is next. Verbalize it; even if you make the statement that "My art does not have a central idea," it is enough of a statement to support a sound plan. During the execution of a business plan an artist cannot lose sight of this personal and public identity.

Define marketing directions that suit your personality

The next step in the plan is to define marketing directions or projects. A fast paced art market has created options for success that never existed before the 1950s. There is room in that marketplace for experimentation. The only right choices are those in which you can sustain the energy required to bring about success. If you are a person who enjoys presenting your art to the public, you may choose differently than an individual who is exceptionally private. You must acknowledge your personality and be willing to identify the activities that make you uncomfortable—these make your own personal hell, and it is best to develop a strategy that keeps you in heaven. The following is a list of some basic marketing strategies.

- Enter competitions—you can win money, make sales, create credentials, and never show yourself in public.
- Attend outdoor art shows—unrelenting contact with the public, but the new agenda in major marketing even for big companies is direct public marketing.
- Attend indoor and juried art shows—almost as unrelenting as outdoor shows, but the public usually has a little more information about your reputation.
- Seek gallery representation—made for private individuals who can take a little bit of public contact.
- Seek agent representation—ultimate privacy.
- Market multiple images in galleries and art-related retail stores—a larger project of production and marketing and there are more items and more involvement.
- Pursue personal marketing—your own gallery, cocktail parties, studio showings, etc.
- Pursue corporate marketing—marketing in this environment takes a strategy of mail and phone contacts.
- Market in publications such as magazines and newspapers, and through direct

mail—like the previous choice, this involves commitment to a strategy of follow-up mail and phone calls.

- Do bidding for Art in Public Places commissions—the more contacts you make the easier it is to get commissions. This requires an ability to estimate materials, time, and cost.

The process of choosing the marketing strategy that fits your personality involves selecting which of these directions you can tolerate. Each one of these directions is like being on a golf course for the first time and trying to make par. It is not an easy achievement to be a success even if you have a superb style and a compelling vision.

You decide on projects and then you make a time management plan for making contacts and doing follow-up. In embracing the out-of-studio tasks, an artist either does too much or is unwilling to do enough. The remedy is resources. This is the third step in the business plan—identify who can help you.

Identify who can help you

Make a list of the team players who will help you with your marketing strategy. Rate their predictable performance and don't be afraid to replace a member of your team with someone more reliable. Here is a list of some of the resources you might need.

- A photographer
- A crating service
- A printer and designer for your brochures and mailings
- An accountant
- A legal advisor
- A public relations advisor
- A phone company
- A record keeper
- A secretary or organizer

If the only person on your team is you, my advice is to think over the project and have more respect for your time and the time necessary to create art.

Build a patron list

The fourth step for a business plan is to make a patron list. The concept is that no matter which strategy you go for in your business plan, success is finding people who will spend their money on your art—your patrons. Chart your patron list. It must grow so you can tell when marketing strategies are successful. Keep statistics on how many patrons you have per year and what the average sales price per year is of your work. This can be an impressive record in itself that indicates growth and seriousness. If you chart this you will be able to judge the advantage of opportunities as they are presented to you.

Build a reputation

When you achieve a point of predictable growth in your patron list, then you are ready for step five in the business plan. Each artist will reach this at a different time. An artist may only sell one piece a year but if that artist can comfortably predict that they will sell that one piece they are ready for this step. This is to do work to make your name a household word. My strategy to achieve this is to produce and publish my art in books that can be distributed in national bookstores and found in public libraries.

I remember when Andy Warhol was scheduled to talk on the campus of the University of California at Davis. I was a student then and it was in the sixties. Andy Warhol, it was later discovered, sent an impersonator, but at the time we thought it was really him. I remember the response that was given to the question "Why are you doing this speaking tour at college campuses?" The answer was "So they know who I am!" First you need a style and a concept, then you need to show it, then you need to continue to build a reputation.

Look out for the alligators

High rollers, sellers of junk bonds, and alligators are a few of the obstacles to being successful in any field. Step six is to avoid them.

Among the alligators I have found most treacherous are the time gobblers. These are a variety of friends and business contacts who have no respect for hours, minutes, and seconds. One of my worst encounters was a printer who delayed one of my projects for over two months. Remember, when you contract with people for goods or services you are negotiating three basic needs: price, quality, and time. My printer provided exceptional quality at a good price but ruined my marketing strategy by delay. Be bold enough to contract these necessities in writing. And don't fool yourself. If someone is not punctual or reliable about getting back to you or getting some commitment together the first time they probably won't be better the second time. They have a value system that they execute; your evidence is their performance. Do you need to see a movie twice before you know the ending?

Another of the alligators can be partners—especially if they are other artists or friends. It really is shame on you if you have a story to tell of a friend who worked with you on a business project and ended up taking advantage of your goodwill. The best way to lose a friend is to do business together. If you insist on the relationship of business with friends add something to keep it working. This can mean a legal agreement that defines what happens if things don't work out. Do this in the beginning, not when things start to go the wrong way.

Conclusion

This business plan is a perspective. The actual details of marketing differ from artist to artist, but you can clearly manage and describe the following elements: your artistic conception, your marketing arena, the resources to help you be a success, the patrons of your art, a strategy to gain a national reputation, and the relationships that hurt your project. Then you will have an advantage. You will have a direction and agenda that will help you outlast failures—and success.

The Business of Art: Being Your Own CEO

Barbara Dougherty

The collection of companies, agencies, galleries, and private patrons who commission, buy, and support art is the art marketplace. Being a skillful artist or having unique work is not sufficient preparation for success in today's marketplace. The activities that an artist can perform on an ongoing basis that can lead to successful marketing are:

1. Organizing your efforts
2. Defining the specific marketplace for your art or art skills
3. Packaging yourself and your art for that arena

The first step in defining the art marketplace is to get organized. If you are self-employed, whether you have an agent, intend to be represented by dealers, or sell your own work, you are essentially the chief executive officer (CEO) of your own company.

This is a particular position. No matter what tasks you perform, you are essentially the coordinator of the operation. You might help yourself by applying this definition to your activities.

The main responsibility you have as a CEO is to delegate responsibility. You may hire a secretary to track contacts and sales, an accountant to keep financial records, an agent for sales, a photographer to do documentation. Or you may delegate some or all of these tasks to yourself. Nevertheless you are a delegator, a coordinator, and the place where the buck stops. In other words, the success or failure of your project rests on your ability to do or delegate these tasks as well as to produce the art.

New ways of looking at certain situations can help stimulate new perspectives, attitudes, and procedures to deal with old problems. This is what I am suggesting by applying a management premise to the business of art.

As the CEO of your art business, your primary tasks of delegating and coordinating are management functions. Management must take into account six basic activities:

1. Definition of jobs
2. Describing the skills available or needed for the performance of these jobs
3. Prioritizing tasks
4. Forming a staff and hiring vendors for performing tasks
5. Creating systems that allow for accountability of performance
6. The formation of a style of management

If you take some time and comprehensively describe the current state of your organization, you will clearly see the strengths and weaknesses of your personal approach to managing your art business. For instance, you may find that in the listing of jobs and skills you have left out "channeling." Channeling is a certain amount of time spent each week making contacts with those who could potentially purchase your work. In addition to identifying overlooked tasks, the forming of a perspective as a manager or CEO of your own business might keep you from spending too much time on any one project to the detriment of other necessary tasks.

Identification of jobs, skills, and the resources to perform these is one part of being a good CEO. The other part is the formation of a management style or attitude. A clear statement of your attitude can go a long way toward the success of your negotiations.

As a CEO, part of your ever-changing, ongoing work includes making and reassessing goals. Your attitude is an important factor in whether you meet your goals. For instance, if you decide that your goal this year is to be represented by three galleries, the sharing of your attitude can help you and a gallery manager make decisions about the appropriateness of a particular opportunity.

In addition to goal setting and reassessing, a good management style includes a positive attitude toward others. Commitment to top performance is not the common ideal among employees who work for hourly wages. Their needs are rarely if ever met by the companies for which they work. When you interact with employees, whether yours or those that work for other companies, if you do not provide them with any incentive to do quality work then you should not be surprised at their poor performance. Incentives must take the form of personal recognition that includes a spirit of friendliness and understanding. The effort to relate to others in this way always has rewards. It has also been found by those studying quality management procedures that there are immense personal benefits to paying attention to others with whom you interact.

Setting goals, and defining and practicing attitudes, are critical tasks. However, for a CEO there is more.

That "more" involves mapping a strategy and charting your results. In order to map a strategy, once the goals are identified, the CEO has to identify the customer and get to know what it is like to be that customer. Many artists have embraced most of the tasks involved in being a CEO except for this one. This task means making yourself into a customer for the type of work or product that you intend to sell. You can do this without "going undercover." What you have to manifest is a need for the type of item or service you intend to sell. If you have difficulty manifesting the need or the ability to purchase, you might have discovered, head-on, the essential difficulty that you have as an art marketer. I paint and I like to purchase paintings. My budget is very limited so sometimes I try to trade my paintings for paintings of others I desire to own. A transaction takes two parties, the purchaser and the seller. If you are always being the seller, how can you ever expect to appreciate the position of the purchaser? As artists we have two basic gifts to offer our culture. The first is finding our creative springs and tapping them. The second is the attitude that the items created by our inspirations have value.

A friend of mine is a young art dealer. In the course of the current recession he has found that he is able to purchase and trade art at exceptionally low prices. My friend holds himself to the obligation of purchasing art for his own private collection on a monthly basis. He does this because he believes that his ability to be successful is dependent on a perception that if we want someone to purchase art from us then we must be willing to purchase art from others. As I considered his strategy it occurred to me that we as artists by becoming purchasers can stimulate the climate of our own success.

If you can identify a marketplace for your goods and services and you work to understand and identify with the needs of that marketplace, then you can map a strategy of interaction with that marketplace. However, before you can do this effectively you need packaging. Maybe you need to frame your work or make a portfolio. One way or the other, essentially it involves the packaging of yourself and your artwork.

Good packaging includes a brochure or a catalog. The basic brochure is on a letter- or legal-sized paper stock printed and three-folded to make six panels. It can be done in a costly fashion on slick paper with color printing or it can be done without color and by inserting some current photos of your work. The brochure is an incredible tool and the standard is to make the best brochure you can afford.

Here are some guidelines for making a good brochure.

- A picture is worth a thousand words—of course!
- Say it simply.
- Never make commitments you might not want to keep. This includes pricing.
- Be identifiable—have an attitude.
- Don't make claims you can't comfortably support—don't claim to be the best. Statements like that are better left to the judgment of others—clients and critics.
- Don't automatically make client lists in a brochure. Sometimes it is better to quote a collector—with his permission, of course—than to list one.

In addition to making a brochure an artist has to prepare a presentation. Once you have identified a contact and raised some interest with a brochure, then you will have to make a presentation. Different circumstances require different approaches. There are some principles, however, that will help you create effective presentations, no matter what the occasion. These include:

- Variety is not generally as impressive as the presentation of an identifiable style.
- If you use transparencies for a presentation then provide a light box.
- If you are presenting actual work rather than slides, if the works are large or heavy get someone to accompany you and help you with showing the work.
- A presentation that's set up ahead of time is better than one that requires setting up and showing simultaneously.
- Be selective about the work you show—don't show it all.

After a presentation there is a follow-up. Sometimes the follow-up is a contract proposal and sometimes the presentation of further materials and/or further negotiations. Your approaches to these tasks must be carefully considered and managed.

There is a lot of personal investment of time and money in an art business. If you can organize the tasks, you will find that the requirements of delegating, organizing, coordinating, identifying, experiencing, channeling, mapping, charting, packaging, and presenting are not really all that mundane. They are—in themselves—the challenging and creative part of being in the art business.

Your Art Desk

Peggy Hadden

For most of us, the studio is our prime work area—the center of our creative life. Even more than just physical space, we take it with us, inside our head, whenever we work on art elsewhere, or when we go to a life drawing session, or even just to a café, as I do, to work on an idea that isn't ready to be realized yet.

Although the studio might not actually be an entire room, it commands a great deal of our time as artists. But today's art world, with its many long-range projects, follow-ups and details to watch over, requires that we maintain another important area besides our studio. Rather than calling this your office, think of it as your Art Desk. Here you keep copies of resumés, reviews, price lists, proposals being prepared, calls for entry to exhibitions, slide packets, tax records. It might exist as only a desk, or you might have a more elaborate setup with files, a computer, and perhaps a light box—even better, a projector and screen—for viewing slides before sending them out.

In this article I'll propose some tools that you can buy or make that will improve the organization of your art business.

First of all, everything having to do with the business of being an artist should be kept together, by itself—not with art-making materials. Nothing is more self-defeating than happening upon a flyer for a show you had intended to enter buried under a pile of paint rags, three weeks after the deadline has passed. Conversely, nothing can make you appear and feel more professional as an artist than providing visitors to your studio with a price list, current resumé, and other relevant materials when they express interest in your work.

This kind of organization is not something that requires a great deal of space. One of the most efficient Art Desk workspaces I have seen was built into a closet. By making effective use of the overhead area and painting the whole space one color, the artist achieved an organizational oasis that was a pleasure to see and to work in.

Before arranging the space itself, you must spend some time being honest with yourself. Think about the art business you do that requires too much of your valuable time—simplify, simplify. If important letters don't get written, phone calls don't get made, or lost consignment lists cause you to lose work because you've forgotten who has it, I rest my case.

You will need certain supplies to keep your Art Desk functioning smoothly.

One of my favorite tools for faster communication is a yellow Post-It note. It's perfect for short messages when you're sending out other materials. Pads are available from your office supplier, but I prefer 3"x4" Post-It notes with my name and telephone number printed on them. They are inexpensive and I order them from Deluxe Business Forms, 1080 West County Road F, St. Paul, MN 55126, 800-328-0304.

Rubber stamps with messages like Do Not Bend, Return Postage Guaranteed, and Please Post will help your mailings go out and return safely.

At the beginning of each new year, order a new copyright stamp for your slides.

Mailing envelopes that can generously hold your slide packet, cover letter, and return envelope (with postage, please) are essential supplies. You may want to have some smaller mailers available, too, for times when you are only mailing one or two slides.

You need cardboard cut to envelope size for a firm backing to help protect your slides during mailing. Cut these from larger corrugated boxes or use those boards that have been put into shirts at the laundry.

If you hold a full-time job, the minutiae of art business can accumulate if you don't tackle a little bit each day. Sometimes, just assembling and mailing a slide packet can seem like climbing Mt. Everest; getting it done, though, will make your non-art day job more fulfilling. Don't forget that 86 percent of all artists have other employment while they make art—you're not alone.

Start a folder marked "Plan." Keep notes to yourself there on people with whom you want to communicate or places you'd like to show work.

Keep a daily desk-size calendar handy; mark it whenever you send things out so you can follow up promptly.

Make a list of newsletters you would like to get and do the necessary calling or writing to start receiving them. These newsletters will act as a catalyst for other events that will come to your attention as you receive them. They are one of my favorite sources for information and events that I don't want to miss.

Get a bound notebook (important, as it will get lots of use) and establish a method for tracking your slides. Make columns with these headings: date slides mailed, where they were sent, to whose attention, response to the work (e.g., "please resubmit in six months"), number of slides or name of series, and if and when slides were returned. By combing this record periodically, you will find those contacts with whom you haven't been in touch for some time, or that your slides haven't been returned and a reminder note is thus in order. You can also tell at a glance how much contacting you've been doing this year versus to-date last year. I sent out eighty-four slide packets last year, but only twenty-three the year before. This record book should also hold details of your dealings with art consultants and other dealers, including their consignment lists and your sales records. At tax time, you'll have all the information you need in one place.

Make a file folder for each piece of your mailing packet, such as resumé, reviews, statements, etc. It will shorten the collating time when you need to put materials together. I once saw a gadget in a P.R. office that I've decided could be very useful. It was really just a small series of shelves held together by an outside framework. Mounted on a wall, its purpose was to hold twelve stacks of material to be collated. The person doing the collating worked left-to-right and top-to-bottom, taking one sheet of paper from each pile. The same result can be achieved by using a 1'x10' plank mounted across the work area; by placing each stack of material to be mailed along the plank in the order in which you want them to be seen, collating them will be a breeze. Thus prepared, the only time required for a new packet will be for the creation of a friendly and current cover letter. The easier it is for you to send things out, the more you will send and the higher your percentage of possibilities will become.

I keep a series of 3"x5" index boxes, each marked for a different category: private dealers and consultants, university galleries and museums, nonprofit exhibition spaces, out-of-town commercial galleries. These hold file cards for every exhibition space where I'm interested in showing. On each card I note the name, address, phone number, and director or curator of the space. I also write everything I hear about the space, even gossip. For instance, they might be interested only in artists with established reputations.

All these bits of information can help you decide whether it is worthwhile to pursue this gallery or put your energies elsewhere. I mark the card whenever I send the space anything, whether slides or announcements. I also note exhibits at the space I've attended and whether I particularly enjoyed them. This information will help to refresh my memory at the time of making my next contact, and it will help to make my cover letter more personal and possibly open a dialogue. It also reflects genuine interest on my part.

Don't forget to put a bulletin board in your Art Desk area. Post the deadlines which will occur during the next year that are relevant to you as an artist. This should include the dates when nonprofit exhibition spaces will be reviewing slides and proposals for future shows. Likewise, your calendar should reflect these dates, with a reminder note posted a few weeks before the actual deadline. Then you won't find yourself at the last minute frantically trying to create a statement or harassing the color lab to get your slide dupes back to you before the deadline.

Stationery is an expensive, but necessary, item for your supply list. Here's an idea for cutting the cost. Cards from past exhibitions you've participated in will carry your name printed in various typefaces and sizes. You can cut one of these up, enlarge or shrink it on a copier, then play with placing it on a blank piece of copy paper. Make several different styles; when you get a placement you like, erase any dark-edged lines that may appear with correction fluid. Then insert a few sheets of high-quality bond paper into the machine, and presto—custom stationery that can also include drawings or graphics designed by you. Some copy shops will sell you time at the copy machine on an hourly basis or let you play during non-peak odd hours. You can buy envelopes separately; some copy shops sell small packets of paper and envelopes for a minimal investment.

Have a file for shipping, insurance, and storage information, forms, and labels. You might think it isn't a pressing concern now, but wait until you've promised someone that you'll get work to them overnight. You could end up paying much more for shipping than necessary. Get into the habit of getting, and keeping, postage stamps. Half the battle will be won if you can just get things off to their destinations in a timely manner.

Also maintain a folder marked "techniques" to hold art-making processes that are involved, archaic, or hard to find. Mine contains helpful suggestions for applying gold leaf, formulas for silkscreen preparation, and a note on using milk as a fixative for pastels. I'll bet you have similar obscure processes that would be difficult to replace if they went astray.

A couple of useful paperbacks should be within reach. I have three: the first is Carla Messman's *The Artist's Tax Guide and Financial Planner*. The second is a thesaurus—this is very handy when you're writing and have used the word "exhibition" three times in the same sentence. The last of these is my national Zip Code directory. Many a mailing has been delayed for lack of a Zip Code. Your phone directory or Yellow Pages has a map featuring Zip Codes in your area, so copy this and staple it to the inside of your Zip Code directory.

If all of this information for organizing your career is daunting, let me confess that this article is the product of having done everything the hard way for a long time. You might not even feel that your needs have reached the Art Desk stage yet, but on this I must disagree: the more you feel like the art professional you hope or intend to become, the more you will behave like one.

Large scale or small, organization is easier to handle if you've given it some thought. If you don't feel like thinking about it, you can hire an organizational expert or consultant, hand her this article, and return to your studio. You could also trade a friend artwork in exchange for getting you set up and organized. One thing is certain, though: once you see how much more you get accomplished, you'll wonder how you ever managed before.

An Artist's Down Time

Peggy Hadden

"Ha!" you say, "I don't have any!" The sensitivity haunts me year-round, and the push to create never goes on vacation. Plus there are the exhibition contacts and feelers for sales opportunities I send out all year.

But there are times when the artist takes a break—a week, maybe a month—and steps back from making art for a while. I used to feel guilty about this, feeling that my love of art should keep me working constantly. And what if I stopped and couldn't start working again?

Other artists convinced me, though, that some breathing room could be beneficial. Most of us, whether we know it consciously or not, work at art in large overall patterns. I always get a lot of work done in the summer, for example. Because lots of workshops and short classes are offered, I try to add to my technical know-how. On the other hand, the period from Thanksgiving to the New Year is filled with family and social obligations so it isn't a very productive time for me. Too much on my mind to hear my inner self.

If you can spot when you have a work streak coming, you can prepare to make the most of it on several levels.

First of all, get your supplies ready. Dried out brushes, paper with dings in it, or canvases that need to be tightened on the stretcher won't help your art be all that it can be.

Likewise, your studio or work area must be navigable or you won't want to be there. This is a good time to get your work tools off the table and hung on a wall or put neatly onto shelves. Clear a space where works in progress will have room to dry and rest between stages of being worked on.

Next, organize upcoming art projects so you'll be ready when requested artwork is due. If you're in a show that's coming up, think about framing now—for once, don't leave it until the last minute.

If you have unfinished or unstarted projects that you keep meaning to wrap up—a video about your work or a new brochure, for example—gather all the pertinent notes, invoices, estimates, and telephone numbers into one place and set some year-long priorities. More and more, the organized parts of the art world—galleries, museums, and other nonprofits—are planning months, even years ahead. Yet most artists are still mapping out their careers one day at a time.

Some of it can't be rushed. Artists don't usually have the funds available to plan projects that only vaguely seem to have the possibility of coming into being. But taking an overview every few months could save you time—on projects you haven't had time to think through carefully, for example—and money.

If this is the year you want to curate a group show, start by finding out which non-profit organizations sponsor such events and when application deadlines come. Then, work backward from those dates, planning each week before the deadline and mapping out what you must accomplish. I've seen application forms that include a chart set up in calendar fashion, so you can plot when you'll get things done. These organizations want to feel secure that you know what you'll be taking on if they give you space or a budget to curate a show. I'm convinced that appearing organized is at least as important as the work that you plan to show, in getting a show. You'll need a title or theme for the show, something more intriguing than just "Paintings" or "New Work." A catchy, imaginative theme can prompt a critic to come to the show, or help gain necessary funds if you're proposing to an organization. One-person shows often don't stand as good a chance as groups, so if you know of artists you'd like to show with, you may have the beginnings of your exhibitions already set. If you don't know who you want to show with, call and arrange a visit to an open slide registry. Allow yourself plenty of time to choose artists—maybe even several return visits—before you definitely decide and make phone calls. Also send calls for entry to *Art Calendar*. Allow plenty of lead time, give lots of info on what you're looking for, and give good contact information.

Another long-range project you might want to undertake is traveling and making or showing art as you go. The artists I know who have done this successfully have started planning months in advance. It takes a plan to find travel funds, get the names of people and places where you want to connect, and do the necessary letter-writing to make things start happening. If you want to sublet your residence while you're away, this project-within-a-project will require time and effort, too.

Maybe next year you'd like to go away and work at an art colony. For that to happen, you'll need to start now with application forms, letters of recommendation, and good slides of your work—all of this is pretty boring, but necessary. Where colonies are concerned, it has been my experience that one might have to apply several times before being accepted. Again, it pays to think long-range. One exception I know of: an artist who had only two weeks to spend at a colony. She was accepted to thirteen colonies for the same two-week period—an embarrassment of riches!

In doing these preparatory tasks, I prefer to have several going at one time. That way, if one project doesn't pan out, I have several other plans in the works and rejection time is minimized. I always hedge my bets with an alternative plan.

How should you start all this long-term planning? Get a couple of file folders and label them—it's that simple. Now your inquiries, maps, notes, and sketches have a place to exist. Your daydreams have a concreteness that you can hold in your hands. Those folders will fill up and be bulging very quickly, and you will have turned an idea into a reality, just as you turn an idea into a painting.

Planning is contagious.

CHAPTER 24

Tracking Your Results

Charting Your Transactions

Barbara Dougherty

Transactions—art transactions—these are the core ingredient of successful art marketing. Charting the transactions you attempt and consummate—in a day, a week, a month, a year—is an activity that can turn you from a financial failure into a marketing genius.

Charting is a term that means keeping track of the number of transactions that you have attempted. The record distinguishes the ones that were successful, the ones that failed, and the ones that are incomplete with a potential for later success.

The information revealed by charting can be the catalyst that converts you into a financially successful person. It provides a technique for analyzing your efforts.

If, for instance, you find that you attempt at least one art transaction a day for an extended period of time, you may find yourself unable to produce quality art. That is, the transactions may take too much time. However, if you only attempt one transaction a month this might in itself reveal a slowness in your marketing—a downturn.

In the late 1980s the word "diversity" began to be used to describe financial portfolios, manufacturing activities, and industry investments. This word is also an important one for artists. Art marketing seems to have to embrace a number of activities. For instance, in the 1980s an artist might have decided to market by seeking gallery representation alone. Now, that strategy can be enhanced or substituted with a variety of private showings, publishing activities, free-lance teaching or writing, and more.

Transactions are the building blocks of diverse marketing activities, and it is important to chart these and to consider the elements of quality transactions. The following are items to consider:

- IDENTITY. Where in the transaction will there be a place for you to identify yourself? Do you have literature available that supplements this information? Do you make follow-up communication possible?
- RECEPTION. Do you know very much about the other person/people? Do you give them a chance to identify themselves? Do you listen carefully to their needs? Do you treat them with the same respect you desire from them?

- OPPORTUNITY. Do you spend time carefully describing the situation and the potential contract, or carefully listening to it being described to you? Do you take the time to understand all the parameters?
- TERMS. Have you prepared beforehand an idea of the extent of the negotiations? Are you prepared to consider all the contingencies like insurance, commissions, copyrights, layaways?
- NEGOTIATIONS. Are you prepared? Do you have resources or procedures available, like sample contracts?
- DESIRES. Do you enter a transaction knowing what you want and what you have to give? Do you know the extent of your willingness to compromise?

Preparation of your emotions, literature, and contract proposals are some tools that help in achieving successful transactions.

Armed with knowledge and preparation, you can analyze which transactions are succeeding and which are not, and you can determine why.

Journals Mean Business: An Old Friend and a New Tool

Bonni Goldberg

Thinking about journals and diaries may conjure up lovelorn teenage girls or juicy tidbits about the rich and famous. Or, like me, you may already keep an artist's or writer's journal to record and stimulate ideas for your work. If so, you already know the value of a journal for your creative side.

But journals or logs are a resource for the business of art as well. Ships' captains of bygone days understood their usefulness, and so do modern-day entrepreneurs.

Business journals can track a variety of activities connected to the art business including potential clients, marketing activities, new markets, promotional materials, and productivity. The best news about using a business journal is that it can be extremely effective while taking only about five minutes a day.

There are several ways to set up a business journal. The easiest method is a biweekly structure using the following steps.

1. Select up to nine areas of your business you want to track. Some examples: current marketing activities, potential clients, accounts payable, accounts receivable, mar-

keting ideas, new markets, comments about your work. Your categories should reflect significant areas of your business that you want to monitor.

2. Use a notebook, weekly planner, daily planner, small memo pad, or computer. Block out two-week segments assigning each topic to one day during the two-week period. Assign the tenth day as a "Review Day."

3. Each day, take five minutes to enter information into the journal about the designated topic. Your entries can take the form of bulleted phrases, lists, or a paragraph. Some days your entry might be in the form of clippings, or even a cartoon.

4. On the tenth business day of each two-week period, spend a few minutes reviewing the two weeks of entries you've made and use the last minute or two to make notes to yourself either on what you have observed about the last two weeks, or about what you plan to accomplish in the two weeks ahead.

5. At the end of three months, it helps to review all the entries from that time period. A review like this takes one to two hours. This is the time to gather the information that will generate marketing plans, spending plans, time logs, potential client lists, etc., according to your current priorities and goals. For instance, you might use the comments you've recorded about your work to write new promotional material or revise an artist's statement. Those comments might even suggest a market you hadn't considered before.

This process not only provides you with a record of what is happening on the business end, it will also remind you to focus on the outcome of your business efforts. After a couple of months, being aware of the business will become a habit instead of an effort.

The information in your journal is a resource for maximizing returns for the next quarter, as well as being a useful document for preparing income taxes and doing general accounting. In addition, at the end of the year, you have an essential tool for developing next year's business and marketing plan.

It's remarkable what we forget to remember. A business journal is the best assistant an artist can hire.

PART 8

Emotional Matters

Still Life, 1997, oil on paper, 9" x 11", Elvi Jo Dougherty, Upper Fairmount, Maryland

CHAPTER 25

Knowing When to Become, Not Become, or Stop Being a Full-Time Artist

The Transition to Being a Full-Time Artist

Tony Saladino

Doing what you enjoy for a living is everyone's ambition. But quitting another field to become a full-time artist can be a drastic move. It is fraught with unexpected roadblocks; the chances of success are slim without solid preparation, especially during a recession. It can be done—but you must remain flexible and learn to operate intelligently.

As I do my monthly bookkeeping the figures remind me of how fortunate I am to have started with a business background. Most artists have no such background, and they start their careers not anticipating the demands and pressures of having to sell their work.

As artists, we don't always think of our work as having utility. Our society has a market-based economy that acknowledges performance, sometimes over excellence. No matter how academically or aesthetically enticing our work may be, if it doesn't have enough market appeal we'd better not count on commercial success. This doesn't mean it has to have universal appeal, only that there has to be a niche for it.

My transition was very gradual and began about seventeen years ago. I had a degree in marketing and had worked in retailing for around eight years before opening my own business. Although I now worked for myself, something was still missing. Luckily, after a few years I discovered the joy of making art. It was gratifying like nothing else I had ever done, so I set out to make this my life's work. I was able to make a gradual transition to painting full time.

After doing it for years, I know how precarious a rope we walk as artists. We grapple daily with the need to make non-aesthetic decisions that will either weaken or enhance our position in the art world. We don't have the structure that is in place in most other jobs or careers. So we as artists have to be more than talented: If you're willing to acknowledge that clear thinking and organization are prerequisites to any worth-while pursuit, then you have already completed step one in the transition.

If you have not yet made the leap of deciding to go full-time, talk with others who are now working exclusively at their art. Go to the library and check the statistics for typical yearly incomes for people in this profession—and don't delude yourself into thinking that you'll be an exception. Look at the broad range of what you can do, decide where in that range you'll be comfortable, and—if possible—ease into it gradu-ally. Working at your art in your spare time is considerably different from having to pro-duce all day every day.

Identify what you want from your art. Find out what is selling. Is there a niche for what you're comfortable doing?

There are many ways to make it as an artist, but finding the one that works for you is important. Consider establishing gallery relationships or entering commercial shows to test the waters. If you've just come from an academic setting, then entering juried shows might be a natural way to begin. If your training is less formal or you're interested in sell-ing immediately, then entering some commercial shows is a good start. Whatever you do, don't let your ego get in the way of making intelligent decisions. Choosing galleries or shows takes analysis. Don't accept a gallery's offer to show your work if you're uncomfort-able with the arrangement.

Respect for you as an artist begins with your own confidence that what you're doing is valid. If a gallery doesn't appreciate you or your work, keep looking until you find one that does. An old Chinese proverb says, "Everything has beauty but not every-one sees it."

To increase your chances of impressing potential galleries or clients, develop a portfolio based on shows, collections, and commissioned work with professionally pho-tographed slides, a laser-printed biography, and well-presented original work.

When I worked as a non-artist businessperson, I had to do much left-brain think-ing that culminated in reports, projections, and decisions based on quantitative data. Within the infrastructures of most large businesses, there is a practice of regularly reviewing expense and sales figures. What I developed was a habit of recognizing trends, and the ability to act accordingly, aware that a sense of urgency is necessary to accomplish most goals.

Today, as an artist, it's much more difficult for me to be objective about my income and expenses. Since creative work takes so much focus, it's easy to be lulled into neglecting to look at what's happening on the financial front or in your gallery relationships. I usually know on a subconscious level that things are economically OK or not, but sometimes I have to push these thoughts away when I'm making art.

This, by the way, is a dilemma of art. Art focuses our energies such that everything else seems unimportant. Psychologically this might be very therapeutic, but economically it can be disastrous!

Setting up goals and priorities and making lists is important. I get organized by setting up priorities that help me cut through the unimportant to do what is necessary. "Things to do" lists help me get the most important things done first. The practice of checking goals for progress is also helpful. Short-term goals are easier to achieve—and added up, they make you reach your long-term goals.

There doesn't have to be a conflict between your right-brain creative work and the left-brain work done to help you survive financially. Examine a typical workday: you probably will notice a time that you're more comfortable working creatively. I'm a morning person and usually come into the studio around 7:30. I paint or pull prints or whatever. But around 1:00 or 2:00, creatively things go downhill—so I plan to do the books, make telephone calls, or run errands then.

The self-discipline involved in running your own business (maybe you haven't thought of yourself as an independent businessperson but there is no denying that fact) is a challenge, to be sure, but being creative and practicing self-discipline are not mutually exclusive. They are necessary ingredients to a successful art career. You are free of the imposed structure of rules, time limits, and deadlines found in other businesses. Developing a sense of urgency and the skills and discipline to do your financial homework is as important as figure drawing or color theory.

Some thinking about the efficacy of art will help point out how the market works. I think that the viability of work relates to the effect it has on others. The more people a work stimulates, the more successful I think it is. I am not talking now about commercial success, but the success that comes from recognition of the merit of a piece of art. The people I refer to are not necessarily the masses but the ones who I think count—those people whose opinions I value. It could be argued that art done for the masses is viable because it gives so much pleasure, like Norman Rockwell's art. This is acceptable but so is the notion that a work that affects just one person is viable. You have to decide where you are comfortable, at what position you can feel good about your work.

I work on different levels. I don't have a conflict with this, but others might. I happen to enjoy making "pretty pictures" and I enjoy pleasing others, so much of what I do is commercially viable. However, this is not enough to stimulate me for long periods of time, so I do the more personal and intellectual work along with the other. Some would call this lack of focus, but I think change of style and content can be refreshing and I choose to work this way. I have to endure the consequences—this approach, I think, keeps me out of academic circles. But if I limited myself to a certain style or focus to please the world of academia then I would be guilty of pleasing not the masses but the elite. Anyway, when you're tired, don't quit work, change work.

The change of focus applies not just to art itself but also to other jobs around the studio. After going full time, I was surprised to find that creating forty or fifty hours a week was impossible. So now I shift from printmaking to sculpture to painting to avoid burnout in one area. I also intersperse long creative periods with travel or writing or odd jobs around the studio. There is no rule that says artists have to be creating art all the time. Change of work is stimulating. I have found that writing helps me synthesize my thoughts, and that putting thoughts on paper is conducive to painting on canvas.

Left-brain people run the world. Learn to work within that system. For example, if you're making a presentation to a company to sell them a piece of your work (or to a gallery), don't be surprised to find that their criteria for choosing work are different from yours. Explaining and selling aesthetic considerations is not an easy job. They will often be reluctant to buy work on aesthetic merit alone—besides, they will want the theme and color scheme to fit in. You'll have to remember that there are many other talented artists doing work that might fit the company's needs better. This is not an affront to your artistic freedom. You cannot be all things to all people. Find the niche you're comfortable in and pursue that area.

Don't be discouraged by rejections of your work, especially if your appeal is not universal. Art is very personal—the more personal, the less universal the appeal.

Some works have universal interest but not broad appeal. For example, I did a painting based on the war in the Middle East. The topic is universal in its interest, but this painting has little appeal to the masses. The same, of course, applies to entries to juried shows. I enter shows every month; I get into only a few of those and I get awards on even fewer pieces. I've learned from business that it takes many tries to reach just a few accepting eyes or pocketbooks. Learn not to view a rejection as a personal failure, and you will be miles ahead of the rest of the pack. Direct mail marketers consider a tiny return (2 percent) on their mailings to be successful. Take a tip from them: Play the numbers!

Money is not the only barometer of success. Does anyone think less of Van Gogh because he was a financial failure? Does anyone think less of Picasso because he was so financially successful? A purchase award or recognition of work is as important to me now as the profit on a profit-and-loss statement.

I am lucky to be doing what I enjoy, but to be able to continue takes more than just creative energy. In order for me to continue doing art I must work intelligently. It is difficult to get used to the notion that artists aren't appreciated enough in this society— but we can, and must, use the disciplines of other areas of expertise such as business to enhance our chances as artists. We cannot afford to believe that we are "just" creative beings and that these other areas are beneath our dignity or not worthy of our study.

Moving to the Country

Alan Bamberger

An artist wrote to me asking, "How do I know when it's time to quit my day job and pursue my art career full-time? I'm thinking about moving from the city to a country setting where the cost of living is lower and making it as an artist will be easier. If my current sales remain the same or improve, it will work. I figure I'll be able to sell locally as well as long distance."

This artist should seriously consider several points before making this change. First of all, you'd better have a good, solid, established, and trustworthy gallery or sales network in operation at your current location before you move. Trying to maintain sales over long distances can mean problems especially regarding collecting money, expanding your customer base, and maintaining your present one. For example, collectors generally prefer to buy local or regional names, which means that you may lose some business when you move, unless you are very well known.

Regarding your move, keep in mind that you'll most likely have to reduce prices on all art that you sell at this new location. The cost of living being less means that everything will be less expensive, including art. Furthermore, the local art market may be weak or nonexistent. Research it thoroughly before you leave so that you know what your sales prospects are. Don't assume that you'll have no trouble building a new collector base similar to the one you already have.

Another point to keep in mind: you'll be experiencing a level of cultural as well as general isolation that you don't experience in the city. Once again, know what to expect before doing anything permanent. Imagining what your new life will be like is nothing like actually living it. If you haven't already done so, spend at least a month or two in this new country setting and get an idea of what your daily routine will be. Note what you enjoy and what you miss. Hopefully, the positives will outweigh the negatives.

Most important is the issue of quitting your job and getting into art full-time. You're the only one who can decide when that moment arrives. When it does, facilitate the transition by having at least six months of living expenses saved up and having some skill or moneymaking ability available to temporarily fall back on or supplement your art income should the initial going be a little rough. Making a major life change is never easy, but it can be extremely rewarding when it's well thought out ahead of time.

This Magic Moment

Barbara Dougherty

As a student at UC Davis in the 1960s, I encountered a ceramics department headed by Robert Arneson. The emphasis on creative modern expression kept most of the students using hand-building techniques. The multitude of potters' wheels sat idle, like monsters of a traditional and past art. My best friend, however, loved to work at the wheel and soon the two of us were spending an inordinate amount of time after class hours at these wheels.

Arneson was not a quiet or unimposing presence at the ceramics lab there; out of our fear of incurring his wrath, we explained our activities as "experiencing the material." Thus for literally six months we worked entirely on centering the clay. The second six months was on raising the walls. And so went the years. I don't think I ever completed a piece that was "thrown from the wheel."

I loved working at the wheel, having my pants covered in clay, and being involved in the symphony of movement of my hands, the wheel, and the clay.

I left Davis in 1969 and embarked on a journey that involved traveling the United States, teaching, reacting to the political climate, getting married, and having children.

In 1972 I was living in western New York. A friend had left a potter's wheel at my house for safekeeping while she went for a few years to nursing school. I sat down at the wheel and suddenly I was overwhelmed by the flood of feelings produced by my hands once again on the clay. What I was producing was exactly that: a flood of feelings, not a flood of items.

At that time I was waitressing for extra income for our family. It was not a project I enjoyed. In my imagination was the notion that I should be able to produce income by doing work that I did enjoy.

Thus I purchased a small kiln and paid the entry fee to the local annual art show. The items I produced for that show were not the quality of the fine items that were generally for sale at that show; in fact, none of my pieces sold.

My imagination, however, was on fire—I knew that I had begun a great new adventure and that all I had to do was make more refined ware and I knew it would be purchased. Thus I embraced the "marketing of my art." From that time on I was producing items. I had been producing feelings.

Marketing my art was a solution to the challenge of controlling the quality of my life and determining how I spent my time. I wanted to spend time working on projects that were consistent with my interests. These were projects that I found valuable, rather than projects I embraced because they simply made money.

The problem I faced by producing pottery for monetary gain was that I might lose the ability to produce good feelings and good art.

That moment in time when I added the production of items to the production of feelings I call the Magic Moment. If you stand facing a genie who has suddenly emerged from a bottle to offer you three wishes, that very moment might be the beginning of a terrible or a wonderful future. Like any other magic moment, the nature of the future depends almost entirely on you. Even though a genie might offer you fabulous wealth, an inordinate amount of greed might make you a prisoner of your own making. In the same way, the embracing of the marketing of your art can lead to a wonderful or a terrible future.

It is now more than 20 years after the Magic Moment for me. I have constantly struggled with the vision of losing myself to the genie in the bottle. In order not to do so, I have challenged myself to embrace the next task, the next technology, the next idea, and the central passion of making in art the images that resemble my feelings. I have, therefore, at times made immense leaps even though I knew that there would be a negative effect in marketing. For instance, even though in the 1970s I became a fairly successful potter I knew the quality of my work was limited by my inability to draw. So I reordered my time and began to work on drawing and painting.

Marketing opportunities also sometimes had to be overlooked so that the genie would not make me a prisoner. Once, an agent told me my technique was great but my subject matter was not commercial. I pursued the subject matter rather than the agent. The real acid test has been whether or not the sense of excitement is still there as I do the work of making visual art.

During those 20-plus years, I created a good income almost exclusively from selling my art. I have also never written a resumé to speak of, never really created a good portfolio, never correctly labeled my slides, and never joined an art organization. What I have done instead is to share with the public that I am really dedicated to being the best artist I can be.

Now I am facing another great moment in my life as an artist. A few months ago, I had immersed myself in the life's work of a great artist. Having been asked to do the photographic documentation of the work of Edward Hagedorn, I handled 750 of the 3,500 pieces of this artist's life's work. As I worked, the fact of his separation from the world of marketing weighed heavily upon my thoughts. He had been able to sustain himself with a trust fund. He had never embraced the marketing project, and his art was overwhelming in its power and profundity. The marathon affair of the work separated me from my normal routines and made me face the reality that my own work had become, within the last year, too easy. It had become too easy to do a painting that the public would buy.

I could no longer trust myself with the notion that each new painting was my best, that I was taking on the next challenge—maybe I was just doing my art for the sake of the next dollar. This was because I know that deep in my art is something even more—something that can emerge only after years and years of handling paint—practicing technique—something deeper and more profound and probably less acceptable to the general public.

Thus I have, after more than 20 years of making a living as an artist, accepted a job. I will look to that job to provide my basic monthly monetary needs so that when I spend my time painting I can trust that I will not be painting for a dollar.

It took a certain naiveté to jump into the art marketplace. The result of this was being able to spend a huge amount of time doing art. In the time I was able to dedicate,

I could embrace complete skills and techniques and I could challenge myself to the next idea. I know that I have been able to spend more hours in the last 20 years making visual images than most people spend in a lifetime.

Now it takes a certain amount of courage and probably also naiveté to reorder the dedication of my time. Yet I feel that these are the seasons of my life. I also feel that as artists there are times to be in the marketplace and times to withdraw. Our greatest challenge is the freedom we maintain in our creative expression.

The new job I have taken on is working on the staff of *Art Calendar* magazine. I hope to bring my energy and my creativity to the task of communicating and embracing the needs and opportunities of professional artists: that we might find money and recognition for our work because it is a free expression of our passions.

CHAPTER 26

Attitudes and Ethics

Artists and Attitude: Something Is Wrong in Mudville

Barbara Dougherty

In April, I visited galleries in the Washington, D.C. area. One of the highlights of the trip was "Old Town" Alexandria, Virginia, a quaint and up-and-coming gallery haven just outside the city.

I also attended a weekday evening show opening at an official government building in Washington. The usual wine was served, and some edibles. The works were mounted on unfinished and unkempt display boards. The light cords hanging from brass lamp fixtures were obtrusive and haphazard. An artist's statement was posted at the entrance. A nicely printed description of intent, place, and price was posted next to each piece—about twelve pieces were hung. Eight paintings were priced around $900, and the remaining four were priced between $2,000 and $4,000. By the time I got to the show, all of the $900 pieces and one of the higher-priced pieces had sold.

But I was informed that the show was sponsored by the family of a U.S. senator. I couldn't help wondering whether attendance and purchasing at the show was more a matter of political constituency than love of art.

Maybe I'm just getting old. On the other hand, maybe I'm getting more idealistic rather than less. But somehow or other, I'm feeling that something is wrong in Mudville.

I am an artist. I don't consider this an occupation—I consider this an identity. I am proud of this identity in the same way I am proud to be an American. Though I prefer to ignore what is shameful, lately I have found myself apologizing about certain attitudes and practices adopted by artists. And right here and now I'm going to rant and rave about these.

First, artists should stop fooling themselves. If you want to make a lot of money, give up your anonymity, and have all the good things in life, you probably should not be an artist. If you are an artist, your commitment is to the next piece—fulfilling the next inspiration.

That inspiration is not the same as a commission. It is an urge toward an idea that is fulfilled by the work of bringing to life a visual image. If you separate urge, inspiration, and the patience to work with the medium, essentially you're sponsoring cultural disintegration. In other words, the artist sometimes needs to accept commissions to survive—but to restrict your work to commissions alone probably won't give you the sense of magic that the practice of art generates, generating in turn more real, heartfelt art.

All of us are influenced. When I paint I know I have heroes. For example, looking at the work of Winslow Homer taught me to bend over the figures in a landscape for better perspective. Working with Frank Hamilton taught me patience for detail and color theory. Studying the Impressionists inspired me to use soft colors rather than aggressive ones. My love of modern art creeps into my work all the time.

I acknowledge these influences every time I show my work. Furthermore, when I was apprenticing with Frank Hamilton and was painting in his style, I disclosed in my displays and in a form I gave every client that this work was done deliberately in a style that was Frank's, not my own.

In case you haven't guessed yet, this is my second beef: disclosure. Disclosure handles many problems. It allows us to do the work we want and still be conscientious about the truth.

At Artexpo New York, a huge annual booth-format, fine art show held at the Jacob Javits Center, there was a lot of work done in the style of other artists this year. For instance, much work was executed to look as if it had been done by Tarkay, whose work has sold big-time at past Expos. There were also lots of Chagall and Modigliani knockoffs. Personally, I think that by the time an artist is ready to show in an arena like Artexpo they shouldn't be working in the style of someone else. But if they do, it should be clearly disclosed and explained.

Other disclosures, too, should now be standard.

For example, reproductions should come with a statement of the quantity produced, the edition, and the technique used to produce them. Even if only the book publishing industry standard is used, it would be an improvement—in books the copyright page discloses which print edition the book came from and the date of production. The book industry does this because they are willing to acknowledge that the public does care about this kind of detail. Why is this not done in art publishing?

When it comes to original prints, what is this new leniency in artist proofs? Artist proofs are the first pieces printed that are done to check the quality of the print. They do not have as high a value in the auction marketplace as a numbered piece. It is not acceptable to print many of these—some appraisers say that more than five is too many. Suddenly, for convenience, an artist's proof is supposedly more valuable—but the standards on when and how many are printed is no longer clear.

Do we mean to wash away the standards of value that have been created over time? The result will certainly be that an artist's proof will have no value whatsoever.

Exhibition disclosures, too, are needed. Sponsorship is valuable to the artist and meaningful to the public. However, there are times in most artists' lives when despite a lack of sponsorship the art must be shared. Art is free speech and it needs a forum. Artists' co-ops should clearly indicate to the public that they are co-ops. Rental exhibitions should clearly indicate they are rented spaces.

In this way we can inform the public that there truly is not enough sponsorship for art. We also indicate that artists are collaborative and vivacious—that they seek to communicate and are willing to bear the costs if necessary. If we don't inform, we don't teach the public the nature of our needs and our commitments.

And what has become of pricing? I hate to hear the phrase, "Price for what the market will bear." I find naive the formula that takes into account time and materials without considering technique, experience, and a body of finished works.

Our industry cries out for better pricing standards. Again, we are teaching the public not to believe us. Every time a person buys a piece of art and later finds that he cannot possibly resell it for even half the purchase price, that is a defeat to our standard of value. I am not impressed by the story depicting the innocence of the buyer and the suave sell.

Trained and experienced appraisers are listed in the Yellow Pages and in a catalog published by the American Society of Appraisers in New York City. Take your work to one of them, bear the cost, and hear the truth about your work from an expert.

If you find that what you thought your work was worth is not reflected in the appraisal, embrace the problem and find the solutions.

If a registered appraiser gives your work a value and you share this with the public, then you are helping to rebuild the confidence that has been shattered. The shattering of confidence in the price of artwork is the major reason for the difficulties we have today in our marketplace.

Sometimes I think that being an artist means to some of us that the public owes us a living. We see ourselves as sacrificing our lives to the work we create. We think opportunities should be handed to us and the costs borne by others.

True, we are bold enough to try to live by our dreams—we want to create, and we have the courage to undertake the effort. We think of our cost and our risk and our determination. But somehow we blind ourselves to the time it takes to review our work, display it, and invite others to see it. Certainly some galleries and exhibitions have exercised greed in dealing with artists, but this does not mean we should be blind to the very real costs of giving us exposure.

It is our responsibility to know about these costs and to harbor a responsible attitude toward others who will assume them.

If we fail to do this, again, we teach a detrimental truth. We teach that artists have no respect for someone else's commitment to market our art. When we encounter a problem of greed on the part of a promoter, then we need to dialogue and explain and sometimes take action. But the time has passed for enemies—we need new strength in our industry and a spirit of working together. Being too passive or too aggressive is not the solution.

Now is the time for a new language and a new experience in art. If we do not undertake this, then, like the great batter in Mudville, we will strike out. To the artist who says "I won't sell my work," I say, nobody should have to sell his work. Instead you should share it, exhibit it, have it sponsored, have it purchased. It should also be hung so the comments, dialogue, and intrigue are brought to bear on our culture. Art is meant to be a commitment to culture, and selling it is not selling soul. It simply is not a prostitution to offer your work to others at a fair cost.

When I think of artist's identity I see Georgia O'Keeffe in my mind. I see an artist who dressed like herself, lived as herself, and acted as herself. I don't think we need to wear tuxedos or cowboy boots or spiked hair to our shows—we need to wear an expression of ourselves, because as artists we are those who are in the practice of expression.

When we write a resumé, why must we pack it full of words and lists that really have little consequence to the reader? I am often tempted to refuse to even have a resumé, for I have seen so many that are full of meaningless information. In the story *Les Miserables* by Victor Hugo, the hero is an ugly, criminal man who deals with the human condition as anyone might. Like Hugo's tragic hero, we are sometimes tempted to steal and cheat and lie. In our effort to redeem our souls we, too, encounter the greatest grief and the greatest joy. Let us grieve over our inability to be significant without the meaningless lists. Let us have joy as truth and sincerity become the hallmarks of our value.

Our attitudes bespeak our practices. As artists, we are honorable people who have somehow lost, in a few places, the thread of integrity that brought us to the art we make. Unless we examine these issues and reach agreement, our future is foretold, and there can be no joy in Mudville if mighty Casey strikes out.

Create for Your Inner Voice

Barbara Dougherty

One of the greatest challenges in art today is "What should I paint, photograph, or sculpt?"

Sometimes, we know, certain subjects have a commercial appeal. These subjects are dear to the American public and include dolphins and whales, horses and cowboys and Indians and wolves, flowers, and young children.

Sometimes it is almost demanded that art have no objective appeal, as in those exhibitions calling for "contemporary art." In this case the word "contemporary" is supposed to mean abstract.

Also in many instances an artist is asked to define his approach. Do you make your images in a traditional, realistic, impressionistic, or nonobjective fashion?

Embedded in all of these distinctions and descriptions is the issue that is bringing artists to their knees in this country. For whom do you create?

I propose that you create for only one voice: your inner voice. If you like to paint or sculpt in a style, then do it. Face the fact that it has already been done before you. Face the fact that very little in this world is completely original.

Find inspiration where you find it! The task of an artist is not first to make original work—the task is to find that magic energy that keeps you bringing into reality your inspirations.

The task of the artist, more closely defined, is to search for inspiration, identify that inspiration when it is experienced, and to create an image to share that inspiration. We are not essentially making art, we are essentially caretakers of inspiration.

One artist might be inspired by a black line crossing a host of other lines. Another artist might be inspired by the light as it leaves the day. This is what we ought to be sharing with the public. The distortion has been our own fault—images are not of subjects, they are of inspirations.

And inspirations have no limits. The products of our inspiration, and what we do with these, is another story.

I think the best approach to marketing is to share. Share the extent of your inspiration and your willingness to undertake to handle the materials. If an artist is skillful in the use of certain media, this is information for marketing and resumés. If an artist uses found objects or nontraditional materials, then the intention is the information needed by the marketer and the potential customer.

The point I'm making is that the business of art and making a living as an artist must be rethought. We as artists are not selling works, images, products. We are selling creations—the images created from our inspirations. Therefore our first effort must be to share the experience of searching for and resolving inspiration.

Thus, I believe an artist's statement is a critical item in the sharing of our work. That statement is not a psychological unveiling of our innermost being. It is a carefully articulated rendition of our experience as artists—a mission statement, if you will. I do not believe that the statement should be longer than two sentences. My statement is, "My artwork is dedicated to the vanishing agricultural lands." This doesn't say anything about my media or my journey to this point. It does, however, state clearly and in a powerful way exactly the experience that is my inspiration. And I believe it is all that is necessary.

It is up to us artists to rebuild our economic foundations; galleries are changing and failing, and many nonprofit institutions lack appropriate and sufficient funding. I believe the key to a successful restructuring is to look at the presentations we make and to have more clarity and force. We artists feel things in mostly overwhelming ways. This cannot be easily described, especially if our resumés and statements look the same as those in other professions.

We can reidentify our lives and our efforts. By doing this, once again we discover why the world loves its artists.

CHAPTER 27

Are You Happy?

Taking Stock

Constance Hallinan Lagan

No, this article is not about investing in the stock market. Nor is it about stock photography. It isn't even about inventory control. It is about you!

It is a good idea to take stock occasionally—of ourselves. Are we doing what makes us happy? After all, that is why we chose to pursue a career in the creative arena of art and in the autonomous world of self-employment, right?

As a career counselor I have often found that people who chose to tread "the path least traveled" years ago assume they are doing what they really want today. What has vanished from their lives as they live them today, however, is the singular spark, the unbridled energy, the unquenchable thirst that characterized their lives when they first chose their creative careers and independent lifestyles many years ago.

If you often ponder one or more of the following questions, it may be time for you to take stock:

- Why do I put off getting started on my work every day?
- Why do I find reasons for frequent breaks from my daily routine?
- Why do I turn "quickie" phone calls into in-depth discussions so often?
- Why do I find myself tired and irritable these days?
- Why do I constantly insist upon tallying up the negatives of being self-employed when I used to see only the positives?
- Why am I browsing the classified employment ads every Sunday?
- Why do I turn away business because the account is "too much trouble" or "not challenging enough"?

Reassessment is a necessary part of every life and of every business plan. Looking at what is going on today does not necessarily mean you will reject your current lifestyle tomorrow. Many times a reassessment leads to renewed effort, to revitalized determination, to restored belief, to rejuvenated energy—to a reborn entrepreneurial artist.

Happiness guru Barbara Sher advises us to ask ourselves four questions to determine what life's work will best fulfill us. I suggest we ask ourselves these same four questions when taking stock and reassessing our current life's work.

1. Who do you think you are?
2. What do you love—what would you do if you knew in advance that you could not possibly fail?
3. What did you enjoy doing when you were a child?
4. What is stopping you from pursuing your dreams?

I would ask you a fifth question to get a complete understanding of your aspirations: What would you love to do if you were not dependent on it for income—in other words, what would you do if you were independently wealthy?

You may find you are doing exactly what's right for you. If that is the case, wake tomorrow giving thanks to your Higher Power for allowing you to be in exactly the right place at exactly the right time doing exactly what fulfills you. Having done my own reassessment recently, an old French proverb comes to mind: "It is by believing in roses that one brings them to bloom."

If you find you are no longer fulfilling your inner desires, set about changing. Years ago you set out on the path you most desired. You can do it again. After all, "Life is always at some turning point," advises philosopher Irwin Edman in *The Uses of Philosophy*.

Keep in mind that The Answer is not always the answer. Sounds paradoxical, you say? Well, it is—the answer is often the question. Nineteenth-century Scottish philosopher James McCosh wrote, "The book to read is not the one which thinks for you, but the one which makes you think." If McCosh were pondering the nature of questions today, he might say, "The question to ask is not the one which gives you an answer, but the one which makes you question."

Recommended Reading

- Brown, H. Jackson, *Life's Little Instruction Book*, Rutledge Hill Press.
- Brown, Melanie, *Attaining Personal Greatness: One Book for Life*, William Morrow & Company.
- Dyer, Wayne W., *Real Magic: Creating Miracles in Everyday Life*, HarperCollins Publishers.

- Jampolsky, Gerald G. and Diane V. Cirincione, *Change Your Mind, Change Your Life*, Bantam Books.
- Kaufman, Barry Neil, *Happiness Is a Choice*, Fawcett Columbine.
- Robbins, Anthony, *Awaken the Gift Within: How to Take Immediate Control of Your Mental, Emotional and Physical Destiny*, Summit.
- Sher, Barbara, *I Could Do Anything If I Only Knew What It Was: How to Discover What You Really Want and How to Get It*, Delacorte Press.
- Sher, Barbara, *Wishcraft: How to Get What You Really Want*, The Viking Press.

The Artist's Backpack

Barbara Dougherty

An artist lives on the freeway of society. As with a hitchhiker, somehow the normal traveling mechanisms are not provided. It sometimes seems as though everyone else is riding around in cars and trucks. On the road the backpack for an artist's survival requires four things in it:

1. A dream and a technique to create images
2. A business plan
3. Personal files and information notebooks
4. A first aid kit

The subject of this article is the personal files and first aid kit, and it is a "more" article. It is about more to do and more to try. Many of the suggestions you read here will be things you have seen, thought about doing, or even tried. However, in this article there is something more embedded in each of these proposals.

Personal files and information notebooks are like having fishing gear. You need different outfits for different occasions, and you find yourself doing a lot of untangling line and baiting of hooks. But these notebooks and files make information available. Also, by creating these resources an artist develops the knowledge that there are possibilities. These are the notebooks and files to keep:

1. A project notebook, or freshwater gear
2. A professional résumé file, or saltwater gear
3. A career opportunity notebook with an accompanying financial résumé file, or deep-sea fishing gear

The notebook of projects (your freshwater outfit) includes ideas for your artistic production and a list of activities to pursue when sales are slow. The extra projects are designed to allow you to use your art skills for income. These projects might include hand painting clothing, making signs, designing gardens, illustrating family trees, repairing damaged artwork, researching the history of art objects for others, painting street numbers in neighborhoods, creating designs for certificates or other printed materials, designing and creating public murals and sculptural installations, running seminars, etc. It is hard to think of these things when you need them most, so a notebook of ideas and contacts for materials and potential customers is an essential diary.

The resumé files include a resumé, a statement of your art intention, and the photography that clearly documents your work. Having them allows you to take advantage of situations that present themselves unexpectedly. Wallace Stegner says it this way: "Accident, they say, favors the prepared mind. Opportunity knocks only for those who are ready at the door."

Your resumé is a one-page document that summarizes the depth of your learning and experience, and includes some specific documentation. It is not a list of your shows, awards, and collectors. Those are supporting lists that can be included in a presentation when such information is appropriate. A resumé does not have to be an objective statement of facts; after all, you are advocating yourself. The goal of a resumé is to open a door and keep that door open. It should be a "crowd stopper." I keep a file of my experiences and successes and I like to create a resumé that is appropriate for the situation at hand. A resumé that includes some failures as well as successes may be surprising in the attention it generates.

Like your resumé, the statement of your intention as an artist may change over time. This statement is not an easy one to make. It needs to be brief and articulate. It shares the depth of your commitment to your work, and it adds your voice to the experience of viewing your work. To send a package of slides and a resumé in hopes of gaining some opportunity without including such a statement is like sending a letter without your signature. The artistic intention does not have to be a declaration, it may very well be a question.

Photographic documentation is a necessary evil. Thirty-five millimeter slides do not ever have the impact of the original work and there are too many times when they are only viewed on a light table rather than projected. I have photos of my work on file that are 4"x6", 8"x10", and 11"x14". I send at least one of these in every circumstance from which they are not specifically excluded. In addition, my technique for making 35mm slides is different (and expensive) but has been very effective. I have all my 35mm slides made directly from my 4"x5" transparencies. In sending photographic documentation more is better. It is better to send six to ten images rather than one to five.

There is considerable effort involved in creating this package of resumé, statement, and photography. However, once you have it together, you can experiment with the effect that it creates and gain some good publicity by taking the package to your local town newspaper. Show it to a reporter or editor there. Reporters and editors are trained to see the impact in the printed word and visual image. Their response to your package may give you the necessary insight you need to make improvements. The effort might also generate some local publicity. Newspaper people like to use information that is readily available, and readers like stories about artists. Help yourself and at the same time tempt a reporter.

For your deep-sea fishing gear you need another notebook. This one is for lifestyle and career alternatives. This is for when you need to make a change. For instance, if you're an artist looking for ways to arrange your life so that you can pursue the experimentation and the creation you are compelled towards, then an alternative worth exploring is art at college. This is an alternative for adults as well as recent high school graduates. Grant money is available but the techniques for finding it cannot always be found in the "getting grants" literature. When our youngest daughter started college at the California College of the Arts and Crafts in Oakland, she obtained enough grant and loan money to pay for all her tuition and housing. From her work to obtain these funds, I learned the following:

1. A financial resumé is an important file and document to create. The information in this resumé should be the same as the information requested by a bank on loan applications.

2. Local newspapers will publish stories on artists seeking specific opportunities who need money—this is the best way to seek philanthropic contribution. Let the reporter know that you hope to find through the article some private sources of funding.

3. Seek acceptance to the institution first and then the grants. The institution can help you obtain grant money you cannot get on your own.

4. Seek help from grant writers. These are professionals who get paid a commission for finding you grant money. This is a business in which there are impres-

sive professionals. It is better to hire a grant writer who works on commission than a writer who wants to be paid a fee for writing the proposal. A good way to find grant writers is to place an ad in the "services wanted" section of the classified ads.

5. Send photocopies of one or two art awards with applications even if it is not asked for. A mere list of awards might not have the same impact.

In addition to art at college, there are art residencies and art institutions that provide art environments for times when a lifestyle change is the best alternative. Again, keeping a separate notebook like a diary of the places and opportunities you come across is a valuable effort and preparation.

An artist's life of dreaming, creating, selling, and fishing can sometimes be stifled. For these times, have a first aid kit on hand. An artist's life is taped together with possibility and opportunity, and undertakings can help—but then there just are those times you can lose faith in your creative ability or at least become so depressed (or obsessed) that it becomes impossible to do any work. Sometimes this is an interior psychological problem that needs to be addressed, sometimes it is just a need for a change of pace. When you need a change of pace then you reach for your first aid kit. The fix-its in my first aid kit include:

1. Visiting museums
2. Going to galleries and outdoor art shows in which I am not a participant
3. Going to a lot of movies
4. Auditing lectures on art
5. Getting on the road and having the wind blow my hair

There is much to love about the independent and unregimented life of an artist. But sometimes as we revel in our independence and freedom we abandon the ordinary implements our peers use to survive the hardships of everyday life. Everything I have mentioned in this article requires an extra effort on the part of the artist who is probably too busy doing art and keeping house and parenting to perform the tasks or undertake all the activities suggested here. If nothing else, keeping the knowledge before us that there are some alternative undertakings and procedures to prepare for hard times can make the difference between problem and crisis.

Self Portrait in Reds, 1997, oil on canvas, 18"x26",
Elvi Jo Dougherty, Upper Fairmount, Maryland

About the Authors

Alan Bamberger is a nationally syndicated columnist and the author of two books on collecting art affordably. He answers *Art Calendar* readers' questions on art business practices and can be reached at 2510 Bush St., San Francisco, CA 94115.

Ilise Benun designs marketing strategies for the creatively self-employed. To order her marketing workbook ($7.95) or a sample ($1.00) of her newsletter "The Art of Self-Promotion," contact Benun at Creative Marketing & Management, P.O. Box 23, Hoboken, NJ 07030, 201-653-0783.

Carolyn Blakeslee was the founding editor of *Art Calendar* magazine. A realist oil painter, she studied at the Corcoran School of Art. She is active in the pro-life movement and is also a pianist.

Barbara Dougherty is an accomplished agricultural watercolorist and oil painter. She also enjoys working with cameras, computers, and filmmaking equipment. The author of the book *Harvest California*, she is the publisher/owner of *Art Calendar* magazine.

Karen Gamow and her husband own Whispers from Nature Photography. They offer a mailing list of 800 gift shops and 300 nautical theme gift shops, all in tourist areas in the U.S. For details, send a SASE to Whispers from Nature, 14618 Tyler Foote Rd., Nevada City, CA 95959, 916-292-9415.

Bonni Goldberg creates artwork in which text is the focus. Available for consultation, she gives workshops and lectures on creativity, communication, and other aspects of creative career management.

Peggy Hadden, a graduate of the Parsons School of Design, is a painter and mixed media artist whose home and studio are in New York's West Village. She also regularly organizes panel discussions addressing the concerns of professional artists.

Constance Hallinan Lagan is an award-winning quilt designer who lectures nationally on art and craft marketing. She can be reached at the Entrepreneurial Center for Small Business Development, 35 Claremont Ave., North Babylon, NY 11703, 516-661-5181.

Kay McCrohan, an artist, is on the board of Maryland Printmakers. She gives artists permission to photocopy her article and provide it to arts organizations and show sponsors.

Debora Meltz is an artist and free-lance writer who divides her time between Newton, NJ and Manhattan. A painter and pastelist, she has frequent solo shows in university museums and other prestigious spaces. Her writing has been published in *The Artist's Magazine* and other publications.

Steve Meltzer, author of the book *Photographing Your Craftwork*, is a professional photographer who has been shooting two- and three-dimensional artwork for 20 years. He gives workshops for artists nationwide.

Caroll Michels, a career coach for artists, is the author of *How to Survive and Prosper As an Artist.* She gives private consultations, public lectures and seminars, and she regularly schedules workshops in Manhattan. She can be reached at 491 Broadway, New York, NY 10012, 212-966-0713.

Roberta Morgan is an artist and critic living in Laurel, MD. An award-winning oil painter and pastelist, she earned her degree at the Maryland Institute, College of Art. She writes for the *Gazette* newspapers, a chain of local papers serving Montgomery County, MD.

Tony Saladino, a resident of Hurst, TX, earned his degree in marketing and worked in retailing for several years. He is a former gallery director who turned to full-time art 10 years ago. To avoid artist burnout, he works in a variety of media: painting, printmaking, and sculpture.

Drew Steis is the editor-at-large of *Art Calendar* magazine. He worked for UPI for 18 years in a variety of capacities including being Washington, D.C. bureau chief for the *Boston Herald Traveler.* He also served as a consultant to the National Endowment for the Arts. He was the founding publisher of *Art Calendar* magazine.

Beth Surdut has moved to Hawaii to live among year-round flowers and has opened her own gallery/boutique where she sells silk paintings and painted silk wearables, and is working with textiles and fashion designers, including Mary McFadden. Her current address is 12A Mill Road, Harvard, Massachusetts 01451.

About the Artists

Bonnie Auten, an artist living in Tecumseh, Michigan, works in colored pencil. Her work is in numerous corporate and private collections, and her work was included in the 1994 Rockport Publishing book, *The Best of Colored Pencil II*.

Elvi Jo Dougherty, an artist who works in a variety of media including oil paints, clay, charcoal, and paper-mache, now lives in Upper Fairmount, Maryland. She attends the University of Maryland Eastern Shore. Other schooling includes: University of California at Santa Barbara, College of Creative Studies, Parsons School of Design, and the California School of Arts & Crafts.

Cheryl Herr-Rains is a ceramic artist living in Alma, Michigan. She teaches ceramics at Delta College, University Center, Michigan, and has taught at other institutions on the college and high school levels. She earned her M.F.A. at Michigan State University.

Vincent Koloski, an artist who works with neon, lives in San Francisco, California. His work has been exhibited at Cheney Cowles Museum, Zenith Gallery, and other spaces nationwide. One of his works was produced in an edition of 200 as *Artist Lamp #3* for the Sharper Image company.

Doris Miller, a ceramic artist living in San Antonio, teaches raku. Her work has been exhibited at the San Francisco Craft and Folk Art Museum and other spaces, and her work is in numerous corporate and private collections. She has been featured in print and on television.

Peter T. Quidley is a painter living in South Chatham, Massachusetts. He worked as a combat photographer in Vietnam, then worked for ten years as a filmmaker. For the last fifteen years he has been working exclusively as a painter, doing commissioned portraits.